THE
DEAFENING
SILENCE

A Shapolsky Book
Published by Shapolsky Publishers

Copyright © 1987 by Rafael Medoff

For any additional information, contact:
Shapolsky Publishers, Inc., 56 East 11th Street, New York, NY 10003

10 9 8 7 6 5 4 3 2 1

Library of Congress Cataloging-in-Publication Data:
Medoff, Rafael, 1957-
The Deafening Silence

Bibliography.   Includes index.
1. Jews—United States—Politics and government.
2. Holocaust, Jewish (1939-1945)
3. United States—Ethnic relations.
I. Title.
E184.J5M42   940.53'15'03924073   87-9538

ISBN 0-933503-63-6

THE DEAFENING SILENCE

Rafael Medoff

Shapolsky Publishers
56 East 11th Street
New York, NY 10003

RAFAEL MEDOFF received his graduate training in Jewish history at Yeshiva University and Hebrew University. Medoff is a respected researcher and investigative journalist whose essays have appeared in *Global Affairs, Midstream, Middle East Review* and elsewhere. He is editor-in-chief of the *Israel News Bulletin*, an independent news service.

Medoff lives in Jerusalem with his wife, Carin, and their daughter, Avital.

Acknowledgments

The following institutions graciously permitted me to examine their collections: the American Jewish Historical Society, the American Jewish Archives, the American Jewish Committee Library, Metzudat Ze'ev (the Jabotinsky Institute), the Manuscripts and Archives Division of the Yale University Library, the YIVO Institute for Jewish Research, the Manuscript Division of the Library of Congress, the Jewish Division of the New York Public Library, the Princeton University Archives, the Herbert Lehman Archives of Columbia University, the Jewish Theological Seminary Library and Archives, the Hebrew Union College Library and Archives, the Franklin Delano Roosevelt Library, the National Archives, and the Records Management Division of the Federal Bureau of Investigation.

Acknowledgment is due: Mordechai Haller, who assisted in the arduous and often thankless task of research; Peter Goldman, who offered valuable advice; Dr. Jeffrey Gurock, whose suggestions concerning an earlier version of this manuscript were important to the final composition of chapters five, seven, nine and eleven; and Malcolm Jordan-Robinson, Seymour Borovsky and Jeffrey Appner, who contributed their editing expertise.

Above all, I am grateful to my wife, Carin, who has been a source of unlimited patience and encouragement. As our sages have written, "He who has an understanding wife has everything." (*Zohar,* Vayikra 52)

Contents

STEPHEN WISE

"IF YOU KEEP SILENT NOW, IF YOU REFRAIN FROM PROTESTING ON BEHALF OF YOUR BRETHREN, THEN WOE TO YOU ON THE DAY OF JUDGEMENT—FOR YOU HAD THE OPPORTUNITY TO ACT, BUT DID NOT."

Midrash, on *Esther* 4:14

Death
In London,
Silence
In New York

Prologue

Jewish leaders abroad won't be interested. At eleven in the morning you will begin telling them about the anguish of the Jews in Poland, but at one o'clock they will ask you to halt the narrative so they can have lunch. This is a difference which cannot be bridged. They will go on lunching at the regular hour at their favorite restaurant, so they cannot understand what is happening in Poland.[1]

Such was the bitter scenario that leaders of the Polish Jewish underground sketched for their courier, Jan Karski (Kozielewski), as he prepared to travel to England and the United States in October 1942.

The world of European Jewry was in flames. As many as 2 million Jews had already been massacred by the Nazis in the forests of the Ukraine, in the newly constructed gas chambers of Treblinka and Auschwitz, in the typhoid-infested ghettoes of Poland. On that cold October evening in 1942, Karski met several Jewish underground leaders in the ruins of a house near Warsaw and asked them what message they wanted him to transmit to the free world. The Jewish representatives presented several specific proposals. First, they demanded that the Allies bomb German civilian centers and enact punitive

11

measures against German prisoners of war, as retaliation for the German murder of Jews. They warned that the Allied nations would bear "historical responsibility" if they stood idly by. The Jewish underground men had little hope that Jewish leaders in the free world would press for Allied action. They doubted that their brethren abroad would be moved to set aside their regular lunch hour and take meaningful steps on behalf of the Jews in Nazi-occupied Europe. "Tell the Jewish leaders that this is no case for politics or tactics," the Warsaw Jewish representatives implored Karski. "Tell them that the earth must be shaken to its foundation, the world must be aroused. The Jewish leaders should go to all important English and American government offices and not leave, not eat and drink, until a way has been decided to save the Jews."[2]

In November, Karski delivered the message to Shmuel Zygielbojm, one of two Jewish representatives with the Polish government-in-exile in London. Zygielbojm had already received numerous detailed reports on the slaughter of Polish Jewry, which had been under way since late 1941. Now, from Karski, he heard firsthand the anguished plea of Warsaw's remnants as they prepared for a desperate, hopeless revolt against their Nazi tormentors. Zygielbojm promised Karski he would do everything in his power to fulfill the Jewish underground's request. But British Jewish leaders and government officials alike ignored his appeals.[3] The Warsaw plea likewise made little impression upon the political figures and Jewish leaders whom Karski met in the United States several weeks later.

On April 19, 1943, the Jewish fighters of the Warsaw ghetto launched an armed rebellion against the Nazis. As the news of the ragtag revolt and its brutal suppression trickled in during the spring of 1943, Zygielbojm was haunted by the plight of his brethren and his own helplessness in the face of the tragedy. On May 12, in his London apartment, Shmuel Zygielbojm protested the indifference of the Allied nations in the most dramatic manner imaginable: he took his own life. Within days, the text of Zygielbojm's suicide note had reached the news media. The note lambasted "the inactivity with which the world is looking on and permitting the extermination of the Jewish people." Zygielbojm warned that "the responsibility for the crime of murdering all the Jewish population in Poland falls in the first instance on the perpetrators, but indirectly also it weighs on the whole of humanity, the people and governments of the Allied States, which so far have made no effort toward a concrete action for the purpose of curtailing this crime."[4]

The suicide note was not the only information on the subject to find its way into the newspapers. On May 19, the New York daily *P.M.* and the Jewish Telegraphic Agency's *Daily Bulletin* published stinging excerpts from the October 1942 message from the Warsaw underground about "Jewish leaders abroad" who would "go on lunching at the regular hour at their favorite restaurant" despite the raging Holocaust. The *Bulletin* strongly implied that the failure of Jewish leaders to heed the Warsaw underground's plea had contributed to Zygielbojm's decision to kill himself.

The news of the Zygielbojm suicide and the publication of the bitter Warsaw message provoked soul-searching among some American Jews. An editorial in *The Recontructionist,* a prominent Jewish monthly, noted that while Zygielbojm's suicide note did not specifically criticize American Jews, "he might with propriety have levelled his accusation against them also." The essay concluded: "We salute the martyred Zygielbojm. May his sacrifice not be in vain. May it move the Jews of the world and the governments of the united nations to a heightened awareness of the plight of Israel in its exile."[5] A columnist for *Opinion,* another leading Jewish monthly, was similarly critical of what he regarded as American Jewish indifference to the Holocaust:

> Only to a lesser degree than our Gentile neighbors have we grown callous to the mass murder of our brethren and go about our daily tasks and pleasures with the consolation that nothing can be done to rescue the remnants of European Jewry. That such a comforting fallacy has taken hold of us, constitutes a lamentable commentary either upon the influence of American Israel, or its will, or both.[6]

But the publications of the major American Jewish organizations treated the news of the Zygielbojm suicide in a strikingly different manner. *Congress Weekly,* the journal of the American Jewish Congress, published a one-paragraph news brief asserting that Zygielbojm had "died suddenly at the age of 49," which it attributed to the fact that he was "depressed and heartbroken generally." No reference was made to his protest against Allied apathy or Warsaw Jewry's protest against the apathy of the Jews in the free world. Zygielbojm's death was relegated to

Congress Weekly's "Chronicles of the Week" section, while the death of composer Joseph Achron was accorded the entire lead article of the issue.[7] The American Jewish Committee's *Contemporary Jewish Record* similarly trivialized the Zygielbojm suicide, allotting it a single paragraph on an inside page.[8] Dr. Stephen Wise, who was president of the American Jewish Congress as well as editor of *Opinion,* did not deem the death of Shmuel Zygielbojm significant enough to merit editorial mention.

Many weeks later, after the *New York Times* published the entire text of Zygielbojm's suicide note, *Congress Weekly* finally saw fit to print an excerpt from the note. But the editor diluted its impact by tacking on a disclaimer which asserted that American Jewry was powerless to "obtain a release of the Jews, or to see that they are fed."[9]

The only mention of the message from the Polish Jewish underground to appear in a publication of a major American Jewish organization was this veiled reference in the August 20, 1943, issue of *Congress Weekly*:

> At the height of Nazi butcheries in the Warsaw ghetto the Jewish leaders in Poland probably envisioned the idea that delegations of British and American Jews would besiege their respective governments and refuse to leave the premises until drastic actions were taken to stop the wholesale murders. Fantastic as this idea may seem to us it must have appeared most realistic to the Polish Jews who were being led to slaughter by the thousands.[10]

Was the proposal for dramatic protests at Allied government offices indeed "fantastic," as the journal of the American Jewish Congress asserted? Was it merely the desperate fantasy of those facing torture and death? Or was it precisely the sort of tactic necessary to shock the Allies into rescuing Jews from Hitler?

Were American Jewish leaders losing sleep over the persecution of their brethren in Europe? Or were they in fact "going about their daily tasks and pleasures" when they should have been trying to shake the world, as critics charged?

Why was the news of the Zygielbojm suicide distorted, trivialized, or ignored by major Jewish organizations? Was it merely that the death of one more European Jew could not compare with the deaths of millions? Or did the circumstances of the suicide constitute an embarrassing indictment of those who stood idly by in the West while the Nazis slaughtered their co-religionists?

The message brought from Warsaw by Jan Karski, the suicide of Shmuel Zygielbojm, and the response of American Jewish organizations to both of them raise compelling questions about the behavior of American Jewish leaders during the Holocaust.

REFUGEE SHIP IDLES OFF FLORIDA COAST

Liner St. Louis Is Watched by Coast Guard—Efforts to Find Haven Continue

Special to THE NEW YORK TIMES.

MIAMI, Fla., June 4.—The Hamburg-American liner St. Louis, carrying some 900 Jewish refugees from Germany to whom Cuba has denied admission, cruised leisurely through Caribbean waters tonight after twenty-four hours spent idling along the lower Florida East Coast. She had previously anchored twelve miles offshore.

The Coast Guard patrol boat CG244, out of Fort Lauderdale, stood by the ship as she moved down the coast, barely making way, to prevent possible attempts by refugees to jump off and swim ashore.

[A large steamship, possibly the St. Louis, dropped anchor off Miami Beach at 1 A. M. today, The Associated Press reported.]

No overtures were made by Captain Wilhelm Schroeder to dock in this country, but it was known that a series of conferences both here and elsewhere were being held during this afternoon by representatives of American Jewish organizations to try to work out some plan whereby the ship might land her passengers in the Dominican Republic.

The refugees appeared more hopeful than when they left Havana, the Coast Guardsmen said, some even smiling a greeting as the patrol boat passed.

A Coast Guard plane that flew over the ship late today on its regular patrol trip reported the St. Louis still was proceeding south-eastward.

New Plea to Cuba

HAVANA, June 4 (AP).—Lawrence Berenson, New York attorney, conferred today with President Federico Laredo Bru and other government officials in an effort to gain entry for 907 German Jewish refugees forced to leave Cuban waters last Friday aboard the German liner St. Louis.

Mr. Berenson secluded himself in his hotel room at the end of the day long conferences and declined to say whether he had met with any success. His secretary said there was "nothing yet to give out."

Luis Clasing, Cuban representative of the Hamburg-American Line, characterized as "absurd" and "false" a report that the St. Louis was sighted off the Florida coast.

He also denied that the ship might be headed back to Cuba. A United States Coast Guard vessel sent out from Miami to trail the ship reported it headed southeast, in the direction of Cuba.

Señor Clasing asserted firmly that the St. Louis followed her course toward Hamburg during the day.

300 Jews Turned Back

HAMBURG, Germany, June 4 (AP).—After turning back to Cuxhaven and landing approximately 300 Jews who had started to emigrate to Cuba, the Hamburg-American liner Orinoco tonight again was en route to Havana.

i

"All the News That's Fit to Print."

The New York Times.

LATE CITY EDITION

VOL. LXXXVIII..No. 29,717.

NEW YORK, MONDAY, JUNE 5, 1939.

P P P

THREE CENTS

AS GERMAN REFUGEES WERE BARRED AT HAVANA BY CUBAN GOVERNMENT

PHOTO: NEW YORK TIMES

Some of the 907 Jews from the Reich waving from the decks of the German liner St. Louis as the ship sailed out of the harbor

PHOTO: NEW YORK TIMES

One of the women aboard the St. Louis is waving hysterically to relatives as she was forced back on the ship by Cuban soldiers.

PHOTO: NEW YORK TIMES

Relatives and friends of some of the passengers on the liner are trying to communicate with them from a launch near the ship.

SLAYING OF JEWS IN GALICIA DEPICTED

Thousands Living There and Others Sent From Hungary Reported Massacred

DEATHS ARE PUT AT 15,000

Many Are Said to Have Been Machine-Gunned—Poverty and Hunger Widespread

Massacres of thousands of Jews deported from Hungary to Galicia and the machine-gunning of more thousands of Galician Jews by German soldiers and Ukrainian bandits are reported in letters reaching Hungary from Galicia and eye-witness accounts of Hungarian officers who have returned since the deportations ended on Aug. 10, according to information received by reliable sources here.

One account by a Hungarian officer told of massacres in the Kamenec-Podolsk region of 2,500 deportees from Hungary, many of whom were originally refugees from other countries, and 8,000 Galician Jews. Other reports place the number of deaths as high as 15,000.

The deportation of Jews from Hungary to Galicia during July and the first part of August is said to have involved 18,000 persons. They are reported to be living in villages scattered along the Dniester River. It is among them and the native populations of the villages that the massacres are said to have taken place.

Reports tell of the victims being machine-gunned as they prayed in their synagogues and of being shot as they fled from their assailants. The deaths are reported to have been so numerous that bodies floated down the Dniester with little attempt made to retrieve and bury them.

These accounts say that Aug. 27 and 28 were declared days of mourning by the deportees.

It is further reported that the Galician Jews are destitute and unable to provide food or medical-supplies for the deportees. The plight of the Galician Jews themselves is said to be so serious that they face hunger and other hardships.

Meanwhile, other reports received by cable from Hungary say the deportation of Jews has been resumed. The present Jewish population of Hungary is put at 800,000, including the territory acquired by Hungary in this war.

Nazis Ban Writings of Maurois

BERLIN, Oct. 25 (P)—A ban on all writings of André Maurois, prominent French author, was announced today in the official gazette. His books had been popular in Germany.

Reich and Norway at War, German Tribunal Decides

By Reuter

STOCKHOLM, Sweden, Oct. 25—According to a Berlin report to the newspaper Dagens Nyheter, the prize court at Hamburg has confirmed the seizure by Germany of a Norwegian whaling fleet of seven vessels on the ground that "a state of war still exists between Germany and Norway."

No compensation will be paid.

OSLO, German-Occupied Norway, Oct. 25 (P)—A Norwegian court-martial sentenced a former high police official to 100 days' arrest today on the charge that he had indulged in propaganda for the Norwegian royal house in a private lecture before law students at Oslo University.

ALLIES ARE URGED TO EXECUTE NAZIS

Report on Slaughter of Jews in Poland Asks Like Treatment for Germans

CURB ON REICH IS SOUGHT

'Only Way to Save Millions From Certain Destruction,' Says the Appeal

Wireless to THE NEW YORK TIMES.

LONDON, July 1—The Polish Government in London has been urged in a report on the slaughter of 700,000 Jews in German-occupied territories to call on the Allied governments to adopt a policy of retaliation that will force the Germans to cease their killings.

"We believe," the report says, "that Hitler's Germany in time will be punished for all its horrors, crimes and brutality but this is no comfort for the millions menaced with death. We implore the Polish Government, the guardian representative of all the peoples of Poland, to protect them against complete annihilation, to influence the Allied governments to apply similar treatment against Germans and fifth columnists living at present in Allied countries.

"Let all Germans know this, know that punishment will be meted out to Germans in the United States and other countries.

"We realize we ask the Polish Government to do something most difficult and unusual but this is the only way to save millions of Jews from certain destruction."

The report, describing the Jews' ordeal in occupied Poland and German attempts to exterminate the Jewish population, reached London through underground channels. Szmul Zygelbojm, Jewish Socialist leader and member of the Polish National Council in London, received it and vouched for its trustworthiness. He said the sources were absolutely reliable, although the story seemed too terrible and the atrocities too inhuman to be true.

700,000 Victims Listed

The report is supported by information received by other Jewish circles here and also by the Polish Government. Its figure of 700,000 Jews slain by the Germans since the occupation—one-fifth of the entire Jewish population of Poland—probably includes many who died of maltreatment in concentration camps, of starvation in ghettos or of unbearable conditions of forced labor.

Here are the main items in the report:

From the first day of the German-Soviet occupation of East Poland the Germans began the extermination of Jews. They started in East Galicia last Summer. Males between 14 and 60 were herded into public squares and cemeteries, forced to dig their own graves and then were machine-gunned and hand-grenaded.

Children in orphanages, old persons in almshouses, the sick in hospitals and women were slain in the streets. In many places Jews were rounded up and deported to unrevealed destinations or massacred in near-by woods.

At Lwow 35,000 were slain, at Stanislawow, 15,000; at Tarnopol, 5,000; at Zloctrow, 2,000; at Brzezany only 1,700 were left of 18,000. The massacre still continues in Lwow.

Last Fall the slaughter of Jews was extended to the Vilna and Kovno districts. By November 50,000 had been murdered in Vilna and only 12,000 were left. In the two districts the victims of the German slaughter numbered 300,000.

Simultaneously a massacre started in the Slonim district in Eastern Poland. Nine thousand were killed in the town of Slonim, 6,000 in Baranowicze. In Volhynia the killing began in November and in three days 15,000 had been massacred in Rovny County.

Gas Chambers Are Used

In the early Winter the Germans were methodically proceeding with their campaign to exterminate all Jews. They sent special gas chambers on wheels to Western Poland, territories incorporated in the Reich. In the village of Chelmno near Kolo ninety persons at a time were put in the gas chambers. The victims were buried in graves dug by them in near-by Lubarski forest.

About 1,000 gassed daily from the townships of Kolo, Dabie, Izbica and others between November, 1941, and March, 1942, as well as 35,000 Jews in Lodz between Jan. 2 and Jan. 9. Two thousand "gypsies" were gassed. They probably were Yugoslav prisoners and terrorists.

In February the murder wave reached the Gouvernement General area in Central Poland, Tarnow, Radom and Lublin. Twenty-five thousand were taken to an unrevealed destination from Lublin. Nothing has been heard of them since. A few were detained in the suburb of Majdanek; the others disappeared. No Jews were left in Lublin.

In Warsaw a "blood bath" was arranged in the ghetto on the night of April 17. Homes were visited by the Gestapo and Jews of all classes were dragged out and killed.

"This shows," the report concludes, "that the criminal German Government is fulfilling Hitler's threat that, whoever wins, all Jews will be murdered."

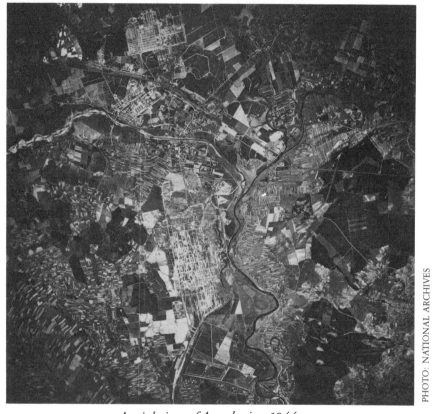

Aerial view of Auschwitz, 1944

HOW WELL ARE YOU SLEEPING?

Is There Something You Could Have Done to Save Millions of Innocent People—Men, Women, and Children—from Torture and Death?

With the irresistible advance of the heroic Russian armies, regaining their native soil, the monstrous treatment the Germans mete out to Jews receives new confirmation. Stories of horror which must shake the conscience of humanity—if civilization is to survive—are being published by eyewitnesses. One of these horror stories is reproduced on this page. Have courage and read it!

Perhaps you will recoil. It may disturb your sleep at night. But it may also fill you with anger, with zeal to do something to stop such atrocities, to rescue the Jews who survive.

Not because they were Poles or Dutchmen, not because they were peasants or officers—just because, and only because, they were Jews, more than two million men, women and children have been deliberately murdered by the Germans.

The Jews of Europe have suffered more fatalities from atrocities than all the European Nations combined. In the face of such a tragedy it is folly, indeed it is sinful, to debate whether Jews are a religion, a nation, or a race—to insist on calling them "refugees"—and thus to remain passive to their disastrous plight, ignoring it and surrounding it with silence.

They are a specific group of human beings whom our common enemy has publicly threatened to exterminate entirely. This Committee believes it is an inescapable duty of all Americans to actively oppose Hitler in this respect also, and to do all that is humanly possible to save the four million Jews who are still alive in Europe.

These Four Million Can Be Saved!

Experts agree on that. Sweden and Denmark have just proved it by saving six thousand Jews in a few days.

They are safe for only one reason: the doors of a neighboring country were unlocked.

And because of that fact, the escaping Jews found the resources and energy to reach these doors of safety. What Sweden did so simply, so humanely, other nations are being urged to do, must do if their consciences are to be clear for the peace to come!

Read what this committee has already accomplished, what its further plans are.

Our Program of Action!

AT THE EMERGENCY CONFERENCE HELD IN NEW YORK, ON JULY 20-25, 1943, EXPERTS FROM ALL PARTS OF THE UNITED STATES FORMULATED A PROGRAM OF EFFECTIVE ACTION THAT CAN AND MUST BE TAKEN NOW TO SAVE THE JEWISH PEOPLE OF EUROPE. THEY URGED THE GOVERNMENTS OF THE UNITED STATES AND THE UNITED NATIONS TO ADOPT A PLAN EMBRACING THE FOLLOWING OUTSTANDING MEASURES:

1. To create a Governmental Agency specifically charged with the task of saving the Jewish people of Europe.

2. To seek guarantees from the Axis-satellite countries, through the International Red Cross, neutral countries, or the Vatican, to insure Jews the same treatment given to other nationals.

3. To relieve the starvation and disease which are decimating the Jewish people in Axis-held territory.

4. To insist that the Axis-satellite countries, which now seek to gain the goodwill of the victorious Allies, withhold their Jews from Hitler's slaughter houses and permit them to leave their borders.

5. To urge neutral countries Sweden, Ireland, Portugal, Spain, Switzerland, and Turkey—to grant the Jewish people temporary asylum.

6. To request neutral countries to grant transit facilities to all Jewish people passing from Axis-controlled lands to any United Nations territory, regardless of whether the persons involved be refugees, immigrants, or expatriates.

7. To obtain from the Governments of the United Nations temporary asylum with the understanding that after the war these refugees will be removed from their territories if they are not wanted.

8. To insist that Great Britain, pending this tragic emergency, open the doors of Palestine, where 600,000 Jews have expressed their desire to share their homes and land with their suffering brothers, thus putting an end to the discriminatory immigration laws that exclude only Jews from their own country.

THIS COMMITTEE CAME INTO EXISTENCE TO ACHIEVE THE RESCUE OF THE JEWS OF EUROPE

Here is Part of Its Record:

Our offices and representatives in Washington and in London, in Palestine and in Turkey, are urging the respective governments to undertake large-scale action to save the four million Jews in Europe's death trap.

We brought the problem of the Jewish disaster to the masses of American people by nation-wide advertising in the leading newspapers in this country and through national radio-broadcasts, as well as through books, periodicals, and leaflets.

We organized mass expressions of public opinion demanding immediate action, through a mass petition movement, mass rallies and dramatic pageants.

We organized the pilgrimage of five hundred Rabbis to Washington.

We requested and obtained the week of compassion and prayer by six thousand Christian Churches.

We initiated the movement to pay tribute to Sweden and Denmark.

We organized the protest against the omission of the Jewish disasters from the Moscow statement on atrocities.

Now, we are able to state with satisfaction that the President, at his press conference on November 6, and Secretary Hull, in his historic appearance before the joint session of Congress, specifically mentioned their concern with the Jewish tragedy. The ring of silence around the catastrophe of the Jewish people was broken.

More than that. In all our activities, we put forward as the first and most immediate demand, the creation of a specific Governmental Agency with the task to effectuate the rescue of the millions of Jewish people still alive in Europe.

Now a Bipartisan Resolution Has Been Introduced in the Senate and House Demanding the Creation of Such an Agency

This resolution recommends to the President:

"...The creation by the President of a commission of diplomatic, economic and military experts to formulate and effectuate a plan of immediate action designed to save the surviving Jewish people of Europe from extinction at the hands of Nazi Germany."

This resolution was introduced by leaders of both Parties: in the Senate by Senator Guy M. Gillette and eleven of his colleagues; in the House by Congressman Will Rogers, Jr. (D) of California, and Joseph Clark Baldwin (R) of New York.

The hearings of the Foreign Affairs Committee of the House have just opened. Prominent men from all walks of American life are testifying, urging this resolution's passage. Wendell Willkie declared this resolution of *"paramount importance. The urgency of the situation demands immediate action. The bill deserves the wholehearted support of every American."*

You Can Do Your Part, Too!

Wire or write to your Senator and Congressman. Write also to the members of the Foreign Affairs Committee of the House. Demand their co-operation!

You can do your part, too, to carry out our tremendous plan of activities. You can help us mobilize public opinion from coast to coast. You can help us keep alive our headquarters in Washington, London, Palestine, and Turkey to continue our work for a people in deepest agony and despair. For each day dooms thousands that can be saved. *This is strictly a race against death!*

This Committee is asking the American people for substantial financial support with which it will be enabled to carry on its work for the rescue of the Four Million martyred Jews in Europe.

We need your financial help *immediately*— NOW! You can sign your name below and enclose your contribution to speed the effectiveness of our work to save the Jewish people of Europe. Whatever you give is evidence of your conviction that human life is worth saving!

Nazi Massacre Of Kiev's Jews Told by Witness

Victims Stripped, Lined Up at a Gulley, Shot; Babies Merely Thrown In Alive

German troops massacred Kiev's Jews during the first days of the Nazi occupation of the now-liberated Ukraine capital, robbing them of their clothes and jewelry and lining them up naked at the edge of a gulley, where they were shot, the Russian Tass News Agency reported yesterday.

Tass quoted an eyewitness story written for the Moscow newspaper "Izvestia" by Dmitri Orlov, a resident of Kiev:

"Several days after the Germans entered Kiev (on Sept. 20, 1941) I went to Lvovskaya Street. An incessant procession of people was streaming through it, and both sidewalks were lined with German patrols . . . The Germans were driving the Jews to Babyi Yar gulley, beyond the city.

"I also stealthily made my way to that place. I was able to stand the sight of what I saw there only for ten minutes, and after that everything went black before my eyes.

"The Germans forced the people to undress, and then methodically gathered their clothes and loaded them on trucks. In separate trucks they put underwear.

"Then they tore from the naked people—there were men and women among them—rings and watches, if they had any, and ranged them up, shivering from the cold or from mortal terror, at the edge of the gulley and shot them.

"The Germans did not waste any bullets on little children, but simply hurled them alive into the gulley.

"Those who were naked they turn round silently. Some sang or even laughed. I could see that those who laughed were already insane.

"And this thing lasted three days. All these whom the Germans had not, as yet, driven to their death knew what was in store for them. The old men put on mourning clothes and gathered in their homes for prayer. Then they went to Lvovskaya Street. The invalids were supported by others, and some were even carried. And all of them were killed."

EMERGENCY COMMITTEE TO SAVE THE JEWISH PEOPLE OF EUROPE

One East Forty-fourth Street, New York 17, N. Y.   MUrray Hill 2-7237

EXECUTIVE BOARD

CO-CHAIRMEN:
Peter H. Bergson   Louis Bromfield   Ben Hecht   Stella Adler
Rep. Will Rogers, Jr.   Mme. Sigrid Undset

VICE-CHAIRMEN:
Dean Alfange   William Helis   A. Hadani Rafaeli
William S. Bengel   Prof. Francis E. McMahon   Lisa Sergio
Kasand Burasriel   Dean George W. Matheson   Rep. Andrew L. Somers
Jo Davidson   Herbert S. Moore   Dr. Maurice Williams
Oscar W. Ehrhorn   Fletcher Pratt

TREASURER: Mrs. John Gunther

MEMBERS:
Stella Adler   Nathan George Horwitz   Michael Potter
J. J. Amiel   E. Jabotinsky   Victor M. Ratner
Al Bauer   Rose Keane   Curt Riess
Y. Ben-Ami   Emil Lengyel   Arthur Rosenberg
A. Ben-Eliezer   I. Lipshutz   K. Shtridbareni
M. Berchin   Lawrence Lipton   Johan J. Smertenko
Rabbi Philip D. Bookstaber   Sadi Ludwig   Angad Sayk
Bishop James A. Cannon, Jr.   Gov. Edward Martin   Irvin Taitel
Lester Cohen   Gov. J. Edward McGrath   Thomas J. Watson
Babette Deutsch   S. Merlin   Gabriel Wechsler
Rep. Samuel Dickstein   Alex Wilf

V

A
Dignified
Silence

1

Germany emerged from World War I with its economy devastated, its military might crushed, and its national pride deeply wounded. The Treaty of Versailles, which the victorious Allies compelled the vanquished Germans to accept, mandated exorbitant reparations payments as well as substantial territorial concessions. The one imposed an impossibly heavy burden on the shattered Germany economy; the other imposed an emotional burden of defeat and humiliation on the German national psyche. The civil, political, and economic chaos of postwar Germany intensified the bitterness of defeat. It brought to the surface the fears, fantasies, and chauvinism that comprised German nationalism: xenophobia, pan-German militarism, a mystic belief in Aryan racial superiority. When inflation spiraled out of control in the 1920s, followed by worldwide depression in 1930, desperate Germans turned to the man who promised them salvation through dictatorship, conquest, and Holocaust.

The United States emerged from World War I with its economy relatively unscathed. The fighting took place far from its shores, resulting in little domestic economic dislocation. Other aspects of American society were significantly affected, however. Isolationism became a major force in American politics; the Treaty of Versailles was repeatedly amended and then finally rejected altogether as Congress succumbed to suspicions that the terms of the treaty would obligate the United States to intervene in future overseas conflicts. Racial tensions exploded when blacks migrated north to fill jobs vacated by departing soldiers; in Chicago, Tulsa, and elsewhere race riots over employment and housing conflicts resulted in scores of deaths and injuries. Cross burnings and lynchings became commonplace during the 1920s, as membership in the Ku Klux Klan reached an all-time high. Fear of Communism became a national obsession in postwar America due to the recent triumph of the Bolsheviks in Russia, the rise of militant labor unions and a subsequent wave of paralyzing strikes in numerous industries, and a series of bombings by left-wing radicals directed at anti-Communist politicians. There was widespread public support for the Government raids of 1920 in which thousands of suspected Communists were rounded up and jailed without charge; likewise when six socialists elected to the New York State Assembly were expelled from the Assembly by a majority vote on the grounds that they were "perpetual traitors."

The Jewish immigrants who populated New York's Lower East Side embodied everything that the average American feared and despised. They were foreigners; they were active in unions; their voting patterns revealed them to be partisans of the left. Precisely in order to reduce to a bare minimum the number of such people who would be allowed to enter the United States, the nativist forces introduced the restrictionist Johnson Immigration Act of 1924, legislation which would ultimately insure that America would offer no haven to those perishing in the Holocaust.

The Johnson Act replaced the American tradition of hospitality to refugees with annual immigration quotas based on national origin. The combined yearly total from all countries was set at 154,000. More than half that total was allotted to Great Britain and Ireland, due to the influence of racial theorists like Madison Grant and Lothard Stoddard, whose writings persuaded many Americans of the racial and cultural superiority of Anglo-Saxon immigrants. Those nations from which large numbers of Jews would soon be fleeing were deliberately confined to the low end of the immigration spectrum: Germany —27,370; Poland—6,542; France—3,085. After the stock market crash of 1929 and the Great Depression that followed, opposition to immigration became even more widespread. President Herbert Hoover quickly responded to the restrictionist mood. On September 8, 1930, he instructed American consuls abroad to strictly enforce the requirement that each prospective immigrant demonstrate that he or she was not "likely to become a public charge" upon settling in the United States. This policy was maintained by Franklin Roosevelt when he became President in 1932, and continued throughout his four terms as chief executive. As a result, most of the quotas would remain unfilled throughout the Holocaust years.

In pre–World War II America, anti-immigration sentiment, nativist pride, and paranoia about "creeping Bolshevism" were often accompanied by thinly veiled anti-Semitism. The rhetoric of Father Charles E. Coughlin exemplified this tendency. Coughlin spearheaded the rise of the reactionaries in the 1930s with fiery radio speeches which reached and influenced millions of Americans each week. Anti-Semitism was not a major component of Father Coughlin's verbal arsenal during his first years in the public limelight, but there were unmistakably anti-Jewish references in his rhetoric. In one March 1935 broadcast, for example, Coughlin singled out Jewish-surnamed banking houses as "internationalists whose god is gold and whose emblem is the red shield of exploitation"; he went so far as to label presidential adviser Bernard Baruch "the acting President of the United States, the uncrowned king of Wall Street".[1]

Coughlin made frightening political advances during the Depression years. In 1935, Coughlin led the fight against United States participation in the World Court project. His lobbying efforts succeeded in dealing the Roosevelt administration a major foreign policy rebuff, as the Senate vote fell seven votes short of the two-thirds majority needed to ratify the proposal.[2] During the spring 1936 congressional primaries in Ohio and Michigan, Coughlin scored major new political successes. Several Democratic representatives targeted for defeat by the Coughlinite forces were indeed beaten due to a torrent of votes "directed to their opponents by Father Coughlin," according to the *New York Times*. Fifteen of the thirty-two congressional candidates endorsed by Coughlin's National Union for Social Justice swept to victory, prompting the *Times* to observe that the NUSJ's strength "was one of the biggest surprises of the [Ohio] Statewide primary. Democratic and Republican leaders had an inkling that the organization's influence would be felt in the primary, but never suspected its actual strength.''[3] In a Michigan Democratic senatorial primary, a Coughlinite lobbyist with no previous political experience won over 115,000 votes, falling just 8,000 votes short of triumph. Six other Coughlin endorsees were victorious in other Michigan congressional contests. In September 1936 the Coughlin forces flexed their political muscles in Massachusetts. Coughlinite candidate Thomas C. O'Brien, competing in the Democratic senatorial primary, captured more than 9 percent of the vote—despite the fact that his name was not even on the ballot. All of O'Brien's 37,186 votes were write-ins.

Within the halls of the United States Congress itself, the forces of the extreme right made their presence felt. Numerous senators and representatives displayed a fierce xenophobia that was often indistinguishable from outright anti-Semitism. One anti-Jewish outburst by Rep. John Rankin (D-Miss.) in 1941 actually caused a Jewish congressman to suffer a heart attack and die on the floor of the House of Representatives.[4]

Although leading American Jews were loath to concede that the land that had granted them unprecedented freedom and opportunity was in fact riddled with anti-Jewish bigotry, by the 1930s the evidence could no longer be denied. A report issued in 1935 by one of the largest American Jewish organizations concluded that the United States was ''infected'' with anti-Semitism. ''The press, the radio, the church, the lecture platform, the schools are being used for the propagation of men like Father Coughlin,'' the report asserted.[5] In 1936, the group's president bluntly wrote, ''There is the possibility of building up a strong anti-Jewish movement today in America.''[6]

The leaders of the organized American Jewish community were divided over how to react to the perils of Nazism in Germany and nativist anti-Semitism in the United States. The American Jewish Committee advocated the use of backstairs diplomacy. The Committee had been founded in 1906 by a handful of well-to-do German Jewish immigrants who wanted to insure that American Jewry would have a ''respectable'' representative in its dealings with the Gentile world. Quiet intercession with political figures and the distribution of dignified memoranda were their cherished methods of operation. Although the Committee presumed to speak for American Jewry, its leaders were chosen by virtue of their wealth, sophistication, and political connections rather than by the votes of American Jews. This disdain for the sentiments of grass-roots American Jewry was nowhere more sharply illustrated than in the AJCommittee's opposition to Zionism, which persisted despite the remarkable spread of sympathy for Zionism among American Jews during the 1930s and 1940s. The Committee's anti-Zionist stand stemmed from the fear that American Jewish support for the establishment of a Jewish state in Palestine would compromise American Jewry's exclusive loyalty to the United States.

The attitude of the other major American Jewish defense organization was considerably more complex. The American Jewish Congress first appeared in 1916 largely as a protest against the elitist, undemocratic, and anti-Zionist nature of the AJCommittee. In contrast to the restricted membership of the AJCommittee, the new AJCongress sought to attract support among Eastern European immigrants who were less self-conscious about their ethnicity. The rhetoricians of the AJCongress scored the "hush-hush" policy of their AJCommittee rivals and verbally championed the idea of forcefully pursuing Jewish interests in the public arena. While such sentiments certainly reflected the views of the AJCongress rank and file, the AJCongress leadership in fact mirrored that of the rival AJCommittee in more ways than the Congress would have cared to admit. On the issue of Zionism, to be sure, the Congress and the Committee could not have been further apart. But on matters pertaining to American Jewish defense, the differences that separated those who ran the AJCongress from those who ran the AJCommittee were more of style than of substance. Ultimately, the struggle between the two organizations revolved less around a quarrel over ideology than around a fight of the "ins" versus the "outs."

The two organizations competed for different social and ethnic constituencies, but both sought to be recognized as the leading representative of American Jewry. The leaders of the AJCommittee deeply resented the AJCongress's drive to usurp the throne. The American Jewish Congress "was created with the intention of destroying the American Jewish Committee," the president of the latter believed.[7]

While it is unlikely that the Congress leaders actually intended to destroy the Committee, they were unquestionably bent on achieving at least some sort of parity. The Congress used the secular and Jewish media as a means of staying in the Jewish public's eye; it conducted persistent grass-roots membership campaigns; above all, it never ceased hammering away at the theme of democracy versus elitism in

American Jewish life. By the early 1930s, the AJCongress had made major strides toward establishing itself as a legitimate spokesman for Jewish interests.

These two Jewish defense organizations, with their respective approaches to the art of Jewish diplomacy, were put to the test when anti-Jewish violence erupted in Germany during the first week of March 1933. Chancellor Adolf Hitler had set new elections for March 5 in an effort to solidify his power base, and his stormtroopers spent the days prior to the poll beating and killing Jews at random.

The orgy of government-sponsored anti-Jewish violence in Germany was featured prominently and in considerable detail by the major American daily newspapers. The reports stirred some sympathy in the United States Congress, and within weeks there were congressional moves afoot to alleviate the plight of those German Jews interested in emigrating. At the House Immigration Committee's first meeting of the spring 1933 session, on March 22, committee chairman Rep. Samuel Dickstein (D-New York) announced that he would introduce a resolution recommending the admission to the United States, "free of the quota restrictions," of all German Jews who were "related to American citizens" and were "fleeing from persecution in Germany."[8]

Dickstein knew he would run into opposition from the restrictionist camp. What he was not prepared for was the discovery that there was opposition from American Jewish leaders as well.

Dr. Stephen Wise was the first American Jewish spokesman to testify with regard to the Dickstein bill. Wise was by far the most dynamic Jewish leader of his era. His oratorical talents brought him to prominence as a young Reform rabbi in turn-of-the-century New York City, where he grew up and was educated. It was as a social activist that Wise first made his mark. He had studied with Thomas Davidson, a leading intellectual in the Social Gospel movement, and was influenced by other progressive reformers, including Josiah Strong, Washington Gladden, and Walter Rauschenbusch. These men believed that the injustices that existed in American society could be ameliorated through sociopolitical reforms, and that ultimately no problem was insoluble so long as reason and goodwill prevailed. In Portland, Oregon, where Wise had a pulpit from 1900 through 1905, he spoke out forcefully against child labor; eventually he was appointed by the governor to the Board of Child Labor Commissioners there. Upon his return to

New York in 1906, Wise founded his own Free Synagogue in midtown Manhattan, using its pulpit as a platform for activism on a wide range of social concerns: Negro civil rights, the grievances of striking workers, women's suffrage, and the like. Wise's political activity extended across a wide range of Jewish concerns as well. He was one of the founders of the seminal Federation of American Zionists, later serving as longtime president of its successor, the Zionist Organization of America. He established the American Jewish Congress to put an end to the monopoly that the elitist, anti-Zionist American Jewish Committee held on the ways and means of Jewish defense. He established the World Jewish Congress to defend Jewish rights worldwide.

Wise was highly principled, frequently clinging to controversial positions regardless of the consequences. He served as a leader of American Zionism even though the overwhelming majority of his colleagues in the Reform rabbinate were anti-Zionist. He spoke his mind from his pulpit, even though it sometimes distressed the most important contributors to the synagogue. He demanded equality for Negroes, although it generated a torrent of hate mail from bigots. He defended the rights of the unions, although it gave the Red-baiters ammunition to accuse him of being a Communist sympathizer. The immigration question, however, was unusually problematic. Wise may have stirred up the antagonism of the reactionaries when he spoke out on behalf of minority groups, but at least he did so with numerous liberal Gentiles at his side; clergymen, civic reformers, liberal intellectuals, and the like were his allies when he lobbied for what they perceived as a return to the true progressive heritage of America. Not so on the issue of immigration. Most liberals' voices were muted by the fear that new immigrants would take away jobs from American workingmen, a concern intensified by the severe unemployment crisis of the Depression years. Relatively few liberals mustered the courage to demand that asylum be granted to the persecuted regardless of the economic consequences. Equality for minorities, rights for women, a fair wage for laborers—these could be demanded in the name of the Bill of Rights, the Declaration of Independence, the American way. But it was hard to argue that increased refugee immigration, in the very midst of the Great Depression, was somehow good for America. A fine humanitarian gesture, certainly—but hardly of any practical benefit to the host country. If Stephen Wise was to plead for the liberalization of the immigration restrictions, he would be asking for special treatment for the Jews.

Wise's testimony before the House Immigration Committee on the morning of March 22, 1933, evinced a discrepancy between his dire assessment of the crisis in Germany and his hesitancy about urging U.S. intervention. He began by stressing his conviction that the behavior of Hitler and the Nazis represented "an attempt, if not physically, to destroy, at least economically, and morally to exterminate the Jewish people."[9] On the other hand, Wise explained, he was opposed to any action on behalf of German Jewry which would involve "special amendments to American immigration laws" or "new legislation with respect to the victims of persecution." Wise asserted that he and his colleagues in the American Jewish leadership "have accepted without demur the philosophy of immigration which now seems to obtain in the halls of Congress."[10] Wise said that his support for the revocation of Hoover's 1930 edict was conditional on such a move being taken "without reference to the German situation, but purely with respect to the general immigration restrictions." Rep. Dickstein promptly "adopted Dr. Wise's suggestion and later introduced a bill in conformity therewith."[11] The Dickstein resolution, as reformulated in the wake of Wise's testimony, urged that in the case of "children and aged and infirm relatives of naturalized United States citizens," consuls abroad would be directed "to disregard the presidential order of September 8, 1930, and revert to the provisions of the law in force prior to that date in examining applicants for immigration visas."[12] Dickstein scheduled the first hearing on the measure for March 29. A wide range of religious and political figures were invited to testify, including Dr. Wise and the vice-president of his AJCongress, Bernard Deutsch, and Cyrus Adler, the elderly president of the American Jewish Committee.

Adler's professional training had prepared him for a career as a scholar, a librarian, and an administrator, not a political activist. When he became president of the American Jewish Committee in 1929, Adler had no inkling that thousands of German Jews would soon be counting on him to help rescue them from the clutches of a mad dictator. Fate had unexpectedly thrust Cyrus Adler, age seventy, into a role for which he was hardly suited. Adler, like Wise, recognized that German Jews were imperiled, but would not urge the Roosevelt administration to act on their behalf. In his private correspondence, Adler labeled the situation in Germany "indescribably bad" and "absolutely unparalleled in modern times."[13] Nevertheless, his AJCommittee was unwilling to lobby against the immigration laws. In a letter dated March 31, 1933, AJComittee spokesman Max J. Kohler complained to Rep. Dickstein, "You create a situation where it will be charged with force that American Jews want to sacrifice America's obvious and essential interests on behalf of their German Jewish co-religionists!" Kohler concluded by urging Dickstein to "let your resolution die a natural, quiet death."[14]

A third major American Jewish organization, the B'nai B'rith, joined the AJCongress and AJCommittee in refusing to campaign against the quota regulations. Although primarily a fraternal society rather than a political group, the B'nai B'rith boasted the largest membership of any American Jewish organization, which gave it some political weight despite its nonpolitical orientation. An editorial in the April 1933 issue of the official B'nai B'rith journal expressed the hope that the new administration of President Franklin Roosevelt would adopt "a more humane attitude toward the stranger," but added: "Not that there is to be expected any loosening of immigration restrictions, particularly in times like these. The new administration, like the old, will continue strictly to enforce the quotas for the purpose of protecting American labor."[15]

Neither Dr. Wise nor his aide, Bernard Deutsch, were anxious to appear before the House Immigration Committee to tangle with the thorny question of whether or not a Jewish organization should be lobbying to bring in more foreigners during a period of severe unemployment. Both Wise and Deutsch therefore declined to testify, although Wise was in fact in Washington, D.C., on the morning of the hearings.[16] A junior AJCongress deputy, Elias A. Cohen, was dispatched instead. In his testimony, Cohen took a step back from Wise's qualified support for revocation of the Hoover edict. Cohen stressed that the AJCongress "did not ask for a change in the laws" regarding immigration. Cohen sought to deflect the focus from altering the immigration regulations; he urged that "before making any attempt to revoke the Executive Order of September, 1930, those committed to helping the victims of Nazism should try to persuade [the Roosevelt administration] to interpret the 'public charge' clause as leniently as possible."[17]

Within some Jewish groups, opinion was divided on the wisdom of pressing for liberalization of the quota system. Such division was evident at the annual convention of Conservative Judaism's United

Synagogue of America in New York that May. Convention chair Hyman J. Reit, in his address to the gathering, urged the delegates to pressure Congress "to show some interest in saving humanity"; USyA president Louis Moss seconded Reit's call and went even further, calling for a Jewish lobbying effort with the Congress and the President "to open the doors of immigration to those in Germany who have endured oppression." Reit and Moss were sharply admonished by Elias Margolis, president of the Conservative movement's Rabbinical Assembly; Margolis warned the delegates that they were obliged to "look into their own ranks and wipe out injustices before demanding justice from the world."[18]

Rep. Dickstein was not intimidated by the lack of Jewish support for his bill. At his insistence, hearings on the measure were resumed in May. Max Kohler testified on behalf of the AJCommittee and B'nai B'rith:

> I am not here, neither is any of us, to challenge the propriety of the so-called "Executive Order of 1930," which has practically checked the immigration of people who are laborers, as they are likely to compete with laborers of this country. I think that is a salutary and desirable thing, in view of the situation we have confronting us.

Kohler emphasized that he would support only very limited action, and even then only with regard to "nonlaborers and some exceptional persons, whose admission ought to be passed on by somebody else than by the haphazard action of the consuls abroad."

> I am chiefly interested in the situation as it exists in Germany, though I would not recommend special legislation for them. I do not favor opening the doors to people who are laborers to come here and be in competition with our citizens here. I think the Executive Order of 1930 was wise, and we do not attack it. We do think, however, that these few cases of injustice ought to be carefully considered.

Therefore, Kohler explained, he would support the Dickstein bill if it would "simply allow in a few particular cases review of the refusal of visas by the head of the State Department with the advice of such persons as he may call in." But, he stressed, "if it is likely that the person is to become a public charge . . . or if his admission is going to be harmful in competing with the laboring class in this country, it is different."[19] Nathan Perlman, appearing on behalf of the AJCongress, seconded Kohler's testimony. "In view of the economic conditions now existing," he testified, "this organization does not oppose such a ground of exclusion" (the "public charge" clause).[20]

In their desire to appear patriotic, the spokesmen for the major American Jewish organizations had inadvertently pulled the rug out from under Dickstein's feet. Restrictionist opponents of the Dickstein bill had based their opposition on the presumed competition new immigrants would pose to American workers. By agreeing that immigration should be restricted if it might result in such competition, Kohler of the AJCommittee and Perlman of the AJCongress had in effect sided with Dickstein's foes. Dickstein ultmately had little choice but to comply with Kohler's request to let the bill "die a natural, quiet death."

The Roosevelt administration publicly opposed any efforts to loosen the immigration restrictions. Yet the administration was not entirely immune to pressure for increased immigration. FDR's advisers were sensitive to the currents of public opinion. Polls indicated that while widespread opposition to increased immigration persisted, there was substantial public sympathy for Hitler's Jewish victims. The administration was wary lest an alliance of aroused Jewish groups and congressional liberals exploit that sympathy to campaign for increased immigration. In an attempt to preempt such a campaign, the administration moved in late 1933 to quietly institute two changes in the application of the immigration regulations. According to standing policy, persons seeking entry to the United States were required to possess sufficient funds to demonstrate that they would not become "public charges." Now, under the changed rules, American friends or relatives of the refugees would be permitted to post the required bond. The second modification was to allow applications for visas to be filed by German Jews residing outside of Germany; previously they had been accepted by an American consul only if the applicant was a citizen or permanent resident of the country in which the consul was stationed. These administrative changes resulted in a slight increase in German Jewish immigration to the United States—from 2,732 Jewish refugees in 1933 to 4,134 in 1934 and 4,837 in 1935. Still, these figures were a far cry from America's total annual immigration quota for Germans, which remained unfilled. And they were minuscule compared to the number of German Jews who would have fled to the United States if immigration was unrestricted.

Why were American Jewish leaders reluctant to demand that the German quota be filled or to challenge the immigration restrictions themselves? For one thing, conditions in Germany had not yet deteriorated to the point where it seemed necessary for substantial numbers of Jews to emigrate. Certainly the state of affairs in the Rhineland was deplorable, even heart rending; but it still seemed possible that the entire Hitler episode might prove to be a brief and ultimately insignificant chapter in German Jewish history. Hence the remark by a spokesman for the American Jewish Congress, in April 1933, that his organization's aim was to help ''re-establish the position which the Jews have occupied in Germany'' rather than foster the emigration of the German Jewish community.[21]

Equally important in shaping the attitude of American Jewish leaders was the fear that Jewish demands for increased immigration would arouse anti-Semitism in the United States. On more than one occasion, prominent non-Jews explicitly warned American Jews of this danger. Daniel W. MacCormack, the U.S. Commissioner General of Immigration and Naturalization, reminded a Jewish gathering that ''there is in this, as in all countries of mixed population, latent racial and religious antagonism, smoldering always and at times bursting into flames. One of the best ways to promote such antagonism is to advocate increased immigration, particularly during a period of depression and unemployment.''[22] Henry Pratt Fairchild likewise wrote in the pages of the liberal *New Republic* about the ''powerful undercurrent of anti-foreignism and anti-Semitism in particular running close to the surface of the American public mind,'' which, he suggested, was ''ready to burst out into violent eruption'' should large numbers of ''alien Jews'' be granted admission to the United States.[23] For the American Jewish leadership, a frightening conflict was beginning to emerge between the instinctive desire to aid oppressed Jews abroad and the fear of jeopardizing the comfort of Jews at home.

The issue that absorbed the attention of active American Jews during the months following the rise of Hitler was not the possibility of increased immigration but rather the emotionally charged debate over whether or not to boycott German products. The Dickstein resolution

Even with the hindsight that the perspective of more than half a century affords, it is difficult to assess the impact of the eight-year-long world Jewish boycott of Germany. The statistics remain open to considerable interpretation. What can be said with a reasonable degree of certainty is that if the boycott ever had a meaningful chance of inflicting harm upon the economy of the Third Reich, that chance was during the first months of Hitler's reign. The ability of the Führer to retain power was closely tied to the still-unstable German economy, which urgently required Western markets for its produce.

What were the attitudes of American Jewish leaders in early 1933 to the idea of the anti-Nazi boycott?

An informal boycott arose as a spontaneous reaction by concerned American Jews to Hitler's assumption of power on January 30. During its infancy, the boycott was loosely coordinated by the tiny Jewish War Veterans of America. Later, in May, it would come under the more formal sponsorship of an ad hoc organization calling itself the American League for the Defense of Jewish Rights. The major Jewish organizations, on the other hand, opposed the boycott. "The boycott is likely to stimulate anti-Semitic activity," warned an internal position paper of the American Jewish Committee; "boycotting will strengthen the hands of the anti-Semites, who make use of the myth that the Jews exert a so-called 'world economic influence.'"[24] Morris Waldman, the executive secretary (later, vice-president) of the AJCommittee, noted in a letter to a colleague that the "noise" of Jewish boycotting would "generate" more anti-Semitism in this and other countries."[25] Joseph Proskauer of the AJCommittee called the boycott "a doctrine of destruction for American Jewry." Proskauer declared, "I oppose an organized boycott which imperils the foreign relations of my country—which is America —with a government with whom we are at peace."[26] AJC president Cyrus Adler went so far as to telegram Oscar Wasserman, president of Hitler's Deutsch Bank, to assure him that the AJCommittee had "taken no part" in anti-Nazi activities. "No responsible body in America has suggested boycott," the message declared. "We have been and are doing all in our power to allay agitation."[27]

The leadership of the B'nai B'rith felt similarly. A feature article in the B'nai B'rith journal denounced the boycott as "undignified" and "little short of madness." It condemned the boycott leaders as "emotionalists" and asserted:

At all times there was but one solution. There was but one salvation and that was our fortitude, our patience, yes, call it submission. Our ancestors have gone through many stages of persecution, always with a fortitude and humility that has disarmed their enemies. Emotionalism, upon which Hitler rose to power and by which he still holds the German nation in his grasp, is destined to spend itself. The world will learn, however, that a dignified silence, silence with suffering, may become more potent than emotion. It may become thunderously loud in the attainment of justice.[28]

An essay published in the rabbinical journal of Conservative Judaism likewise complained that non-Jews would view an organized boycott as "uncivilized."[29]

Within the American Jewish Congress, matters were more complicated. During the spring and summer of 1933, a vociferous tug of war broke out between rank and file AJCongress activists, who enthusiastically supported boycott, and the leadership, which resisted the grassroots pressure. AJCongress chief Stephen Wise was well aware of the growing pro-boycott sentiment which he referred to as "the pressure under which we have been to give opportunity for the expression of the deep indignation of American Jewry, a great part of which is included within the American Jewish Congress. I cannot remember Jewry being so wrought up against anything happening to American Jews."[30] In his private correspondence, Wise repeatedly expressed anguish over the grass-roots demands for boycott action. "You cannot imagine the feeling that rages throughout the country," Wise wrote in March. "There are all sorts of things being spoken of, such as boycotts of goods."[31] To another colleague, he confided, "You cannot imagine what I am doing to resist the masses. They want organized boycotts. They want tremendous street scenes."[32]

Fate presented Stephen Wise with an unusual opportunity to glimpse the serious potential of the boycott weapon. Hitler announced a national boycott of German Jewish stores to begin on April 1. Wise responded by announcing his intention to sponsor an anti-Nazi rally at Madison Square Garden on March 27. The extent to which Hitler was dependent on Western markets for German produce can be gauged by the fact that his government made several private overtures to Wise, both directly and indirectly, to cancel the planned protest rally in exchange for a modification of Nazi policy on the Jewish question. When Wise refused, the Nazis went ahead with their April 1 action, but

Hitler took the advice of his Cabinet and suspended the boycott after barely forty-eight hours in order to avoid international repercussions.

Nevertheless, Wise continued to hope that the Roosevelt administration would take some action against Hitler which would preempt the necessity of lending his endorsement to the mushrooming anti-Nazi boycott movement. Wise honestly believed that FDR would be moved by the plight of German Jewry; the AJCongress chief also feared that a Jewish boycott campaign against Hitler without the endorsement of the U.S. administration would be perceived by non-Jews as Jewish disregard of the desires and interests of the United States government. In a letter to a colleague on April 17, Wise said that he had refrained from joining the boycott because it still did not have "the sanction of our government."[33] Three days later, Wise repeated this theme when he spoke to delegates from some six hundred Jewish organizations invited by the AJCongress to a meeting at the Hotel Pennsylvania in New York: "We can't expect our government to act towards Germany as if we were in a state of war. We do not want to go to war with any people in the world. The fact that no American ambassador has been sent to Berlin is sufficient in itself."[34]

Yet Wise and his American Jewish Congress could not indefinitely withstand the pro-boycott pressure and hope to retain the support of their constituency. The administrative committee of the AJCongress, conceding that there was "enormous public pressure in America" in favor of the boycott, met in urgent session in August 1933 to consider the issue. One faction of the AJCongress leadership continued to oppose the boycott. Horace Kallen, spokesman for this faction, openly expressed his fears that a boycott would provoke anti-Semitism; he warned his colleagues of "the possible injury that the publicly declared boycott might have on Jewish interests in America."[35] Dr. Wise, who was away in Europe at the time, cabled his view that action on the matter should be postponed. But a majority on the administrative committee voted to endorse the boycott nonetheless.

For more than six months, Wise and his colleagues had hesitated. It was enough time for Hitler to consolidate his political power and make strides toward staving off the economic chaos that might have toppled his new Reich. A crucial moment of historical opportunity for the American Jewish leadership had passed unexploited.

31

The years 1933 and 1934 were a period of consolidation for the new Nazi regime. Although some anti-Jewish laws were enacted and occasional outbursts of violence made life for German Jewry increasingly uncomfortable, the German Jewish community as a whole was not yet under consistently intensive attack. In 1935, however, two major blows left German Jewry reeling. In mid-July, a series of violent anti-Jewish outbreaks rocked Berlin. Jews were pummeled in the streets, Jewish women were seized and ravaged by gangs of roaming storm troopers, Jewish property was vandalized or torched.

Then, in September, the Nazis enacted the Nuremberg laws in order to effect the legal disenfranchisement of Jewry from German society. The laws barred Jews from German citizenship, stripped them of all political rights, and provided for the dismissal of thousands from a wide range of professions.

American Jewish leaders observing these ominous developments could not help but suspect that emigration might be the only real solution to the German Jewish problem. "There is only one thing that can be done about the Jews in Germany, and that is to *get them out,*" a feature story in Stephen Wise's monthly journal, *Opinion,* declared. "They must be rescued, as the residents of a burning house, trapped by devouring flames, are rescued by Firemen."[36] But once they were rescued, where were they to go? Immigration to Palestine was limited by the British, countries in Europe and South America were unwilling to accept more than a token number of refugees, and American Jewish leaders feared to challenge the policies of their government. Wise's *Opinion* even published a lengthy defense of American restrictionism:

> To allow aliens, Jew or non-Jew, to enter this country without funds, seeking employment where no employment is to be found, or coming to families already destitute, would be economic folly and unfair to the alien, his family and to us as Americans. Restriction is necessary where ten or more millions are out of work.

The author then spelled out the dilemma facing American Jewish leaders:

> [I]f too many of the Jews in foreign lands were admitted here in any one year, it would arouse the bitter and positive resistance of the restrictionists as well as cause a rise in the anti-Semitic movement in this country. In essence, the question put to a number of prominent Jews was this: is

it desirable to insist upon the admission of possibly 25,000 more Jews from Germany (and later from Poland, Austria, etc.) and thus give fuel to the claims of the anti-Semites here that we, the Jews, were seeking to bring all the unfortunates to this country in these unfortunate times, or is the wiser policy to safeguard the mental, physical, and social happiness of the four million Jews now in the United States by refraining from bringing too many more Jews here?[37]

Phrased in these terms, American Jewish opposition to increased immigration seemed reasonable and prudent. No objective assessment could equate the threat of American Jewish discomfort with the reality of German Jewish misery. But in the climate of fear that enveloped American Jewry during the 1930s, objectivity easily gave way to emotionalism.

During 1936 and 1937, spokesmen for the major Jewish organizations appeared at hearings on immigration bills in order to declare their opposition to any campaign against the quotas. The Kerr-Coolidge bill, providing for the deportation of criminal aliens from the United States while permitting some noncriminal resident aliens to legalize their status, was considered by the Senate Committee on Immigration in March 1936. Maurice Rosenberg, the Washington, D.C., representative of B'nai B'rith, testified that the measure was "meritorious" because "those who are permitted to remain are subtracted from the quota, and therefore there is no enlargement of the quota numbers under the appropriate section of the immigration laws."[38] Subtraction from the quota meant, of course, that fewer refugees would be granted entry. That was precisely the point, for Rosenberg's testimony was intended as a demonstration of American Jewish sympathy for restrictionism.

The Starnes-Reynolds bill, a measure similar to Kerr-Coolidge, was debated by a subcommittee of the Senate Immigration Committee in April 1937. Celia Davidson, testifying on behalf of the AJCommittee and the National Council of Jewish Women, declared, "I think there are very few of us who want to open the doors to new immigrants at this time. We realize that the consuls have been very careful about giving visas to persons, to make sure they will not become public charges."[39] That same month, Rep. Donald O'Toole (D-New York) announced his intention to introduce a measure to provide asylum for those fleeing Nazi persecution. Stephen Wise successfully pressured O'Toole to abandon his effort. In a letter to O'Toole, Wise bluntly outlined the position of the American Jewish leadership on the immigration controversy:

33

I wish I thought that it were possible for this measure to be passed without repercussions upon the Jewish community in this country. I have every reason to believe, unfortunately, that any effort that is made at this time to waive the immigration laws will result in a serious accentuation of what we know to be a rising wave of anti-Semitic feeling in this country.

Wise noted that at a recent meeting of "the representatives of all the leading Jewish organizations,"

It was the consensus of opinion that such bills at this moment in the light of the inspired propaganda directed against the Jewish people, and circulated throughout the country would be injurious to the purposes which all of us would like to serve. For that reason it was decided that no Jewish organization would at this time sponsor a bill which would in any way alter the present immigration laws.[40]

Although the immigration question was of crucial importance to German Jewry, it was not a prominent issue on the agenda of the American Jewish leadership during the mid-1930s. Of far greater concern was a proposal by the American Jewish Congress to convene a "World Jewish Congress" to defend Jewish rights abroad. The controversy over the WJC did not reflect directly upon the responses of the American Jewish leadership to the German crisis, but it helps illustrate the similarities and differences between the two major Jewish organizations in determining public policy.

The AJCommittee bitterly opposed the World Jewish Congress proposal. "We are already regarded in many quarters as a sort of international people," Joseph Proskauer complained. "If we let the notion back of the World Congress idea go without protest, we will be giving our enemies the best alibi for anti-Semitism they have ever had. We must fight. We cannot afford to let it pass by in silence. Our objective should be so to undermine the movement as, if possible, to smash it entirely."[41] While Proskauer and his colleagues in the AJCommittee feared that the World Congress would arouse anti-Semitism, the AJCongress's rejoinder was that an open, public gathering would dispel the anti-Semites' suspicions about secret Jewish conspiracies. "[T]he false charge that Jews maintain an international organization with divided allegiance is due perhaps to the policy of silence and secrecy of some Jewish leaders," AJCongress vice-president Bernard Deutsch wrote to the AJCommittee leadership in December 1934. "The nonsense of the Protocol of the Elders of Zion can be dissipated only in the degree that the mystery and mystifications about Jews are abolished; and the only method in which these may be certainly abolished is the open and full discussion of Jewish problems by freely chosen representatives of world Jewry."[42] Thus, as the debate over the World Jewish Congress sharpened during the spring of 1935, the major Jewish organizations staked out diametrically opposed positions based on the same consideration: how non-Jews would react.

The debate became public when Proskauer wrote in the *New York World-Telegram* on February 5, 1935, that "when it comes to international action, American Jews must act through the American State Department and through the Congress of the United States, and not through any other congress." He emphasized: "We know no divided allegiance. We are not hyphenated Americans, but Americans."[43] In reply, Stephen Wise charged that Proskauer's accusations would inflame anti-Semitic feelings against World Congress proponents: "[T]he inference is inescapable, the charge is clear. *Not we but you!... you* who participate in the World Jewish Congress, *you* who recognize the national and racial unity of Israel—*you* are hyphenated Americans! Could incitement to anti-Semitism be more direct? Could provocation against the Jew go further?"[44]

The controversy was given a full airing in the February issue of *Opinion*. James Marshall, a member of the AJCommittee's executive committee, denounced the WJC plan because "it would undoubtedly raise doubts in many minds as to the legal and political status of the Jews" and would therefore "be the basis of propaganda by anti-Semites."[45] Jerome Michael of the AJCongress responded. Noting the prevalence of "accusations that the Jews are disloyal as citizens and are organized internationally for world domination," Michael argued that "the substitution of the methods of free and open discussion for secret and indirect means will, instead of increasing anti-Semitism, prove to be its best antidote."[46]

The vocal opposition of the AJCommittee to the World Congress idea put the AJCongress on the defensive. At a special conference in Philadelphia in March 1935, the AJCongress voted to postpone the WJC "until after division and disunion had lifted their paralyzing touch from American Israel," as Dr. Wise later described it.[47] As the

WJC proposal was repeatedly delayed, the World Congress proponents began retreating from their original proposals. Whereas previously the AJCongress weekly, *Congress Bulletin,* had referred to the World Congress as "the parliament of the dispersed Jewish people,"[48] by the summer of 1936 it was asserting that "[t]here is no suggestion of a Parliament, or a Super-state, or any action that might affect the status of Jewish citizens in any country; it does not propose to deal with all Jewish questions; it does not assert Jewish solidarity."[49] Successive issues of *Congress Bulletin* hammered away at the AJCommittee's criticism, stressing the theory that Jewish openness would dampen anti-Semitic accusations. "[I]s there not the possibility that the sinister motives which anti-Semites ascribe to Jewish internationalism may be exposed as fictitious if a Congress should convene and deliberate in the open?"[50] asked one editorial. Another declared:

> Secret Jewish international diplomacy is far more dangerous than open international gatherings on which anybody is invited to throw a strong searchlight if he so desires, and to which the whole world is permitted to listen in. The World Jewish Congress is an international Jewish gathering. It proclaims it to the entire world. The international diplomacy of the American Jewish Committee is a secret action. It shrouds in dark mystery its perfectly legitimate work of cooperation with Jewries of other countries. It is dangerous not for what it does but for the way it does it.[51]

The World Jewish Congress was at last convened in Europe in the autumn of 1936, but the dispute between proponents and opponents continued to simmer long afterward. During 1937 and 1938, American Jewish leaders were again preoccupied with a controversial electoral proposal by the AJCongress. This time it was a plan for internal American Jewish elections. At a conference in Washington, D.C., on November 28, 1937, the AJCongress voted to hold, by the following June, an American Jewish plebiscite on the creation of what it called a "united democratic front against anti-Semitism." The ballot was to contain four questions:

> First: shall the American Jewish Congress, established on a democratic basis in accordance with American ideals, be the representative agency of the Jews of America in the defense of the equal rights of Jews?

Second: Do you favor the reorganization of American Jewish communities on a democratic, representative basis; and the management of all community activities (including welfare and federation funds) on the same democratic, representative principle?

Third: Do you favor the establishment of a free Jewish State in Palestine?

Fourth: Do you favor the continuance of the boycott against Nazi Germany, including within the boycott the recently annexed province of Austria?[52]

The other major Jewish organizations were unhappy with the AJCongress proposal for two reasons. First, they feared that the establishment of a single representative Jewish agency "would be seized upon by anti-Semites as proof of an exaggerated ethnic solidarity."[53] Second, they were suspicious that the entire election plan was a scheme by the AJCongress to crown itself the undisputed spokesman of Jewish America.

The AJCommittee issued a public denunciation of the elections plan:

The Committee...takes a firm and uncompromising stand against any undemocratic attempt to make of Americans who are Jews a distinct political unit. Americans who are Jews, like all other Americans, are, above all else, individuals. They fall, naturally, into every line of interest and activity—social, philanthropic, educational, economic and political. Any contrary impression is false.[54]

AJCongress officials responded by asserting that the elections would be a test of American Jewish loyalty to democracy. "We cannot accept democracy as American citizens and reject democracy as members of American Jewish communities," asserted Horace Kallen of the AJCongress. "By electing democratically the men and women who are to be responsible for the conduct of Jewish affairs, Jews show that for them democracy begins at home."[55] Stephen Wise declared, "The loyalty of American Jews to the democratic process may well be tested in the elections at the close of June."[56] Likewise, an editorial in *Congress Bulletin* called the elections "an expression of the will of Jews in America to do their duty as Americans, to accept the American way of life."[57] But Dr. Wise bowed to the pressure of his critics and, in May, agreed to a dramatic revision of the plebiscite ballot. According to Wise's reformulation, the ballot would now feature just a single question: "Do you favor a union of all American Jewish groups engaged in safeguarding the equal rights of Jews, which shall undertake to create, for the defense of such rights, a single all-inclusive agency organized on a democratic, representative basis, in accordance with American ideals?"[58]

Wise began to have serious second thoughts about the referendum when he learned that President Roosevelt was unhappy about the election plan. In a confidential memorandum to his assistants Louis Lipsky and Lillie Shultz, Wise revealed some of the details of a conversation in early June between the President and Samuel Rosenman, who was both adviser to FDR and an official of the AJCommittee:

> [Rosenman] said the Chief used this term: "the whole thing is loaded with dynamite." First the four questions were read to him. He claimed that the Chief was filled with horror when he read the second question, which, I believe, although I am not sure, dealt with Palestine. He stated the Chief suddenly said to him: "Won't this enable Americans to say that the fellows who wrote the Protocols of the Elders of Zion had some justification?"

Wise conceded his fear that even if the *New York Times* provided accurate coverage of the elections, "the Des Moines Register will not and the people in Des Moines and Texas will read of a Jewish election for Congress." According to Wise, FDR complained that "one of the days of the election is a Sunday, something which will give special offense to good Orthodox Christians"; Wise suggested that the election therefore be shifted from Sunday to Tuesday.

"The important thing," Wise concluded, "is that the Chief is terribly exercised." He made clear his reluctance to go against "the judgment and the wishes" of FDR, whom he referred to as "the All Highest."

Wise noted that he had warned Rosenman against any attempt by opponents of the plebiscite to publicize Roosevelt's opposition. "[I]f it came to be known that the Chief was against the Congress and against the elections," Wise cautioned, it could get "the Jewish people into a great deal of trouble"; there might even be militant elements in the AJCongress "whom we could not control, who would say that it was none of the Chief's business and they would publicly say so, and very unpleasant things would result."[59]

Wise's extreme, almost obsessive concern with the attitude of President Roosevelt functioned on three interrelated levels. First, Wise recognized the importance of maintaining good relations with the President, since traditionally the friendship of the highest secular authority in the land was the most important factor making for the security of the Jewish community. Second, Wise was constantly monitoring the barometer of American public opinion and feared that Jewish criticism of a popular President, or Jewish disregard of the President's desires, could provoke an anti-Semitic backlash. Third, and perhaps most significant, was Wise's fierce personal loyalty to FDR. Wise was enthusiastic over the social justice themes of Roosevelt's New Deal, and he was moved by the President's occasional denunciations of Nazi anti-Semitism, however tempered those criticisms were. In the years to follow, Wise's fondness for FDR would evolve into an adoration that was often as one-sided as it was zealous—with dire consequences for oppressed Jews abroad who were counting on Wise's ability to influence the American administration on their behalf.

Even
If
Some Hardship
Results

2

While the major Jewish organizations were embroiled in the controversy over the American Jewish Congress election plan, events overseas suddenly seized world Jewish attention. On March 12, 1938, German troops marched into Austria to fulfill one of Hitler's fondest dreams. On the very first page of his terrifying autobiography, *Mein Kampf*, Hitler had written of the urgent need to "return" Austria to "the great German Motherland." Now his wish would be realized. Hitler's victory parade through the streets of Vienna and his declaration annexing Austria as "a province of the German Reich" were cheered wildly by huge crowds of Austrian well-wishers.

For the 185,000 Jews of Austria, the German occupation was a nightmare. A prosperous, cultured, and highly integrated Jewish community suddenly found itself the target of mob attacks. Local Nazis engineered a campaign of brutal violence and economic despoilation that rivaled and perhaps even exceeded the viciousness of the pogroms that had accompanied Hitler's rise to power in Germany five years earlier. Jewish businesses were plundered. Jewish property was confiscated. Jews were beaten, maimed, arrested on the slightest pretext and shipped off to concentration camps. Men and women, old and young alike, were forced

41

to scrub the gutters on their hands and knees while jeering crowds gathered to taunt and spit upon them.

The Jews of Austria, many of them wealthy and thoroughly accultu-rated, had never seriously considered the idea of emigrating from their beloved homeland; now, almost overnight, emigration became a viable and even highly desirable option. Austria's neighbors, however, were in no mood to absorb large numbers of fleeing Jews. Italy, Switzer-land, and Czechoslovakia successively sealed off their borders to refugee immigration.

With the Austrian crisis in the world's headlines, Roosevelt administration officials feared that liberal pressure for U.S. inter-vention would ensue. A State Department memorandum cited liberal journalists and "certain Congressmen with metropolitan constituen-cies" as "the principal sources of this pressure" for American action. Secretary of State Cordell Hull and Under-Secretary of State Sumner Welles decided that the administration would have to "get out in front and attempt to guide the pressure, primarily with a view toward forestalling attempts to have the immigration laws liberalized."[1] Welles conceived the idea of an American-sponsored international refugee conference to accomplish this aim.

On March 24, President Roosevelt announced that the United States was inviting thirty-three Western nations to send representatives to Evian, France, in July to discuss the refugee crisis. Yet Roosevelt cou-pled his announcement with a specific warning that "no nation would be expected or asked to receive a greater number of emigrants than is permitted by its existing legislation."[2] Despite the fact that the Presi-dent omitted any mention of the Jewish refugee problem or the need for Western countries to be more generous in granting entry to the per-secuted, Stephen Wise hailed FDR's announcement as "a great act of faith and generosity." Exulted Wise, "Without special designation for the victims of German and Austrian Nazis, it yet was an in-vigorating summons for the nations which had not foresworn civiliza-tion nor repudiated humaneness to gather on behalf of earth's exiled and homeless."[3]

Wise hoped that the West would agree to absorb large numbers of Jewish refugees. When congressional action was initiated to achieve precisely that aim, however, Wise and his colleagues lobbied against it. On the very day of the White House refugee declaration, the chairman of the House Judiciary Committee, Rep. Emanuel Celler (D-New

York) announced his intention to introduce a resolution urging unrestricted immigration for victims of religious or political persecution; Rep. Samuel Dickstein declared that he would propose a similar bill, recommending that unused quotas be allocated for refugees seeking entry to the United States. Dickstein scheduled hearings on the bills for April 20. On April 4, leaders of the AJCongress, AJCommittee, National Council of Jewish Women, and several Protestant, Catholic, and nonsectarian groups met in New York to consider the pending legislation. The AJCommittee representative, Harry Schneiderman, suggested that the bills should be opposed lest they "evoke editorial comment which might damage the government's plans" for Evian. Schneiderman noted with approval that some of the restrictionists' criticism had been "disarmed by the clear statement of Secretary Hull that the relief measures to be taken [at Evian] will not involve the modification of existing immigration laws." Schneiderman pressed his colleagues to back the Roosevelt administration by fighting Dickstein and Celler. He succeeded. The conferees agreed unanimously "that such of the organizations as have any personal contact with Dickstein or Celler, should endeavor to persuade them against going ahead with the hearing." It was also agreed to issue a threat to Dickstein "that if the hearing is held, the organizations represented at the conference, if they do appear, will take the position that the proposed legislation is inadvisable because it may interfere with the government's plans in connection with the international conference."[4]

It is clear from the internal memoranda of AJCommittee officials that they were greatly influenced by fears that a Jewish fight against restrictionism would arouse anti-Semitic sentiment in the United States. AJCommittee vice-president Morris Waldman, in a memo to his colleague Sol Stroock, warned that any statement on the immigration question by AJCommittee representatives at Evian "might have an undesirable effect here by creating the impression that these Jewish organizations were trying to promote a larger immigration of refugees into the United States."[5] In another private letter, an AJCommittee official said that it was "very inexpedient to propose a change in the immigration laws because this may lead to unpleasant repercussions and many people consider that the best thing to do is to leave the law as it is, even if some hardship results from it."[6]

Meanwhile, Celia Razovsky of the National Council of Jewish Women contacted "a person connected with the State Department" to express her "misgivings regarding the proposed hearing" (the Dickstein hearing scheduled for April 20). Razovsky excitedly reported back to her friends in the AJCommittee that she had been assured "that the Department would take steps to prevent the hearing."[7] As a result of the combined opposition of the American Jewish leaders and the Roosevelt administration, Rep. Dickstein finally agreed to cancel the scheduled hearing and withdraw his proposal.[8]

Just when they thought that they had succeeded in squelching any plans to tamper with the immigration laws, however, the AJCommittee staff was horrified to discover that the editor of a small Brooklyn Jewish weekly newspaper had been engaged in a one-man campaign against the immigration laws. Rabbi Louis Gross, editor of the *Brooklyn Jewish Examiner*, "has been carrying on this agitation not only in his weekly publication but also by sending private letters to prominent personalities, conducting a census of who is in favor and who is against" liberalizing the quota laws, an internal AJCommittee memo complained. An AJCommittee representative was promptly sent to visit Rabbi Gross, "with the purpose of persuading him to discontinue his agitation to increase the United States immigration quota to enable more refugees to come in." Gross was warned that "not only the American Jewish Committee but other Jewish organizations are opposed to such tactics." The rabbi was told that his activities were "injuring the welfare of our people." Gross evidently succumbed to the pressure and ceased his lobbying efforts.[9]

The preparatory work for the United States delegation to Evian was handled by a specially appointed President's Advisory Committee on Political Refugees, which met twice weekly during the months prior to the conference. Stephen Wise agreed to serve on the eight-man committee. The Roosevelt administration apparently expected Wise to serve as a shield against liberal and Jewish criticism of American restrictionism. At the group's first session, on May 15, 1938, Assistant Secretary of State George Messersmith bluntly set forth the administration's terms for the position that the United States delegation was to articulate at Evian. "[I]n view of the generally disturbed economic conditions in so many countries which usually have and which would like to continue to welcome immigrants in large numbers," Messersmith asserted, "the problem is a difficult one which must from the practical point of view be considered within the framework of existing immigration laws and practice of the States participating in the [Evian conference]."[10]

"So far as the United States is concerned," Messersmith concluded, "the American representative [at Evian] could say that conditions in this country do not permit any change in the immigration laws at this time or any major change in our immigration practice." Messersmith instructed the PACPR members to depict U.S. policy as being "as liberal an immigration policy as any country today"; to insist that "our treatment of aliens within our borders is perhaps more liberal than that of any other"; and to emphasize that "the former German quota of 25,957 and Austrian of 1,413 have been consolidated into one quota for Germany which permits a total of 27,370 to enter this country from Germany in one year." That total was, however, a pittance, since the Jewish populations of Germany and Austria totaled over 700,000. Stephen Wise was the first to speak when Messersmith concluded his presentation. Wise did not question U.S. immigration policy. Instead, he asked if the State Department would permit the U.S. delegates to Evian to "discuss informally with the British representative the possibility of an upward revision of the schedule for immigration to Palestine." Messersmith rejected the suggestion; the Roosevelt administration had no desire to meddle in Britain's colonial affairs, "even informally."[11]

The Evian conference, which lasted from July 6 to July 15, was a dismal failure. The assembly's participants reaffirmed their standing policies of refusing to permit increased refugee immigration. The chief U.S. delegate, Myron Taylor, not only held fast to the hard-line American position on immigration, but even suggested that large-scale Jewish refugee immigration to the West would cause anti-Semitism in the countries of refuge: "How much more disturbing is the forced and chaotic dumping of unfortunate peoples in large numbers. Racial and religious problems are, in consequence, rendered more acute in all parts of the world."[12]

Rather than criticize the Evian failure, Stephen Wise chose to defend American restrictionism. "American generosity and British caution" was the phrase which best described Evian, Wise wrote in *Opinion*. He criticized "the supercaution of many nations which have much more to gain from refugees than to give them," but cited as "the appalling disappointment of Evian" the "failure of the British Government to rise to a great occasion."[13] He was, however, unable to satisfactorily explain how the position of the American government had differed from that of the British government.

The AJCommittee, in its response to the Evian outcome, likewise carefully omitted any criticism of U.S. policy. "No nation seemed fully willing to open its doors," declared the AJCommittee organ, *Contemporary Jewish Record*. It noted that the debates at Evian "were devoted to a defense by each delegate of the existing immigration policies of his respective country"; France, Britain, Australia, Canada, and the Latin American countries were cited by the *Record* for their failure to help. Yet the American delegation was praised for "indicating that the United States might admit immigrants up to the limit of the 27,370 quota for Germany and Austria."[14] During the ensuing year, *Contemporary Jewish Record* published only one major article on the refugee problem; that article likewise criticized the restrictionist policies of the European nations, Canada, Australia, and eleven individually cited South American states, but offered not a single critical comment on U.S. policy.[15]

There were those who seemed to search high and low for something positive to say about Evian. Jonah B. Wise of the American Jewish Joint Distribution Committee—U.S. Jewry's premier philanthropic agency for overseas matters—found it "heartening" that the Conference "did not deteriorate—as it might have—into a public discussion of the undesirability of Jews as immigrants or settlers."[16] Criticism of the Evian outcome would have put the U.S. Jewish leadership squarely at odds with the policies of a popular President. It would have meant challenging the restrictionist mood of the American public, possibly engendering anti-Jewish sentiment. And that was something no American Jewish leader was prepared to risk.

The first half of 1938 was a period of anguish for world Jewry. The German annexation of Austria intensified the European Jewish refugee crisis, while the meager results of the Evian conference demonstrated that the nations of the free world were unwilling to participate in the alleviation of that crisis. The only source of hope during those anxious months was the sudden and unexpected establishment of a working alliance between the four largest American Jewish organizations.

Unity among Jewish defense groups was generally hard to come by and harder to maintain. Tensions between American Jewish organizations arose over deep-seated ideological differences as often as over petty power struggles, personality clashes, and competition for the attention and recognition of the non-Jewish world. The American Jewish Congress supported Zionism; the American Jewish Committee opposed it; B'nai B'rith was neutral. The Congress and the Committee battled each other for the right to be considered American Jewry's sole legitimate representative; B'nai B'rith, less politically involved than the others, made no such pretensions. The small but vociferous Jewish Labor Committee was also making inroads in the Jewish community during the 1930s. While the JLC's anti-Zionism won it sympathy among American Jewish Committee types, its stridently socialist orientation horrified Jewish leaders who were always denying Gentile suspicions about Jewish radicalism.

External crises on occasion compelled these fiercely rivalrous organizations to forge temporary alliances. Invariably, however, such alliances came apart as soon as the interests or prestige of an individual organization came into conflict with the interests of the umbrella group. One of the earliest attempts at unity had been the establishment in June 1933 of a Joint Consultative Council consisting of two representatives each from the AJCongress, AJCommittee, and B'nai B'rith. In theory, the JCC was meant to serve as the instrument for unified action on issues of Jewish concern. In practice, however, the individual groups were inclined to "consult" each other and then go their own way. Early in its brief existence, the JCC was wracked by a dispute over whether or not to include in its ranks other, smaller Jewish organizations. The leaders of the AJCommittee and B'nai B'rith were suspicious of what they perceived as attempts by the AJCongress to dominate the organized Jewish community, and thus were happy to have in the JCC other groups that would help rein in the Congress. Naturally the leadership of the Congress grew apprehensive at the prospect of the smaller Jewish organizations having an equal say. At a March 13, 1934, meeting of the administrative committee of the AJCongress, sentiment was clearly in favor of pulling out of the JCC before it got too crowded. Complained Samuel Margoshes, a vice-president, "[I]f organizations such as the Workers Committee and the Synagogue Council, who are clamoring for representation, are granted such rights, the Congress will become merely a member of a number of other groups." Therefore, Margoshes recommended, "a way must be found of either withdrawing from the Council or closing the doors to other groups." Others on the administrative board supported the Margoshes proposal and recommended that the AJCongress delegation to the JCC "be entrusted with working out a method of withdrawal from the Council."[17]

47

The Council remained shakily intact but largely ineffective until it finally collapsed in 1936. The straw that broke the camel's back was the insistence of the AJCongress that a petition to the League of Nations concerning Jewish rights be dispatched under the auspices of the World Jewish Congress rather than that of the Council. The AJCommittee had of course fought against the idea of even creating the World Jewish Congress in the first place and it naturally balked at the idea of affiliating with it in any manner, preferring to break up the Council instead.

One of the few useful functions the Joint Consultative Council had managed to perform was to help avoid duplication of effort among the major Jewish organizations. This was a benefit the groups could enjoy without having to sacrifice their independence or prestige. Hence, in early 1938, a Committee on Cooperation was briefly maintained for that exclusive purpose. Although the CoC was by no means an instrument for unified action, it no doubt helped serve as a needed psychological bridge between the bitter feelings surrounding the dissolution of the Joint Consultative Council and the mood of cooperation that was necessary to foster the events of later that spring. The initiative for the unity moves in the spring of 1938 can be credited to Edgar Kaufman, a wealthy businessman prominent in the Pittsburgh Jewish community. In late May, Kaufman arranged a meeting of representatives of the AJCongress, AJCommittee, B'nai B'rith, and Jewish Labor Committee to propose an alternative to the divisive plan for American Jewish elections for which the AJCongress had been lobbying. Kaufman's idea was to establish a "General Jewish Council," consisting of five representatives from each of the four groups, to formulate joint action on matters of Jewish concern. The crucial difference between the proposed council and previous umbrella groups was that a two-thirds vote in the council would make a decision binding on all its members.

Negotiations over the Kaufman proposal continued with a meeting of senior officials of the four organizations in Pittsburgh during the first week of June. Ultimately, each of the four agreed to the establishment of the General Jewish Council, for its own reasons. The AJCongress assumed that by playing a leading role in a body that had the endorsement of all major Jewish groups, its claim to be the true representative of U.S. Jewry would be enhanced. The Jewish Labor Committee leaped at the chance to attain a level of prominence comparable to that of the larger Jewish organizations. The B'nai B'rith and especially the AJCommittee were not particularly enthusiastic about the union idea itself but were prepared to go along with it because it appeared to be the only plan that "would lead to the abandonment of [the] proposed [American Jewish Congress] election and referendum and avoid public controversy," as one AJCommittee official put it.[18] Unity in Jewish organizational life, however dangerous to the prestige of the AJCommittee, was preferable to the wave of anti-Semitism that AJCommittee leaders feared would erupt if the American Jewish Congress went ahead with its election plan. Much to their delight, the AJCommittee and B'nai B'rith would soon find that the General Jewish Council could be used effectively to muzzle the more militant voices within the AJCongress and veto activities which they feared might provoke the ire of non-Jews.

As
Heartless
As
It May Seem

3

In the autumn of 1938, events took a dramatic turn for the worse for European Jewry. Hitler annexed the Sudetenland region of Czechoslovakia in September and expelled its 20,000 Jews. A month later, they were joined by 17,000 German Jews of Polish origin whom the Nazis summarily pushed across the German-Polish border. On November 8, the anguished son of one of those desperate refugees assassinated a Nazi diplomat in Paris. Here was the pretext the Germans needed for "Kristallnacht," the Night of Glass, so named because the amount of plate glass shattered in Jewish houses and shops was so enormous. But much more than glass was devastated in the savage pogroms that swept Germany on the night of November 9-10. Dozens of Jews were murdered, hundreds more maimed; more than 7,000 Jewish businesses were destroyed; nearly two hundred Jewish homes were burned down; some two hundred synagogues were torched, of which seventy-six were totally decimated. At least 30,000 Jews were arrested and shipped off to the Dachau, Buchenwald, and Sachenhausen concentration camps.

The immediate result of the Kristallnacht terror was a new wave of Jewish emigration from Germany. Demand for visas quickly exceeded the number available from countries willing to issue them; the American consulate general in Berlin reported that 160,000 Germans had already applied for visas, with the total increasing by over five hundred daily.[1] Mass emigration was, in fact, Hitler's initial "solution" to the Jewish problem. Until 1941, his aim was to effect the expulsion of all Jews from Greater Germany. "We will carry on the struggle until the last Jew is removed from the German Reich" is how Hitler phrased it.[2] As early as November 1938, Hitler was seriously considering a proposal to ship all of Germany's Jews to the African island of Madagascar.[3] In a memorandum to Hitler, S.S. Chief Heinrich Himmler referred to "a large emigration of all Jews to Africa or some other colony" as the answer to the Jewish question; Hitler wrote "very good and correct" on the paper and distributed copies of it to his aides.[4] Also under active consideration was the idea of deporting the Jews to a huge autonomous reservation in the Lublin district of eastern Poland.[5] The decision to annihilate the Jews, rather than merely expel or resettle them, would not be made until early 1941.

The Kristallnacht pogrom forced many in the American Jewish leadership to reconsider the notion that they could "re-establish the position which the Jews have occupied in Germany," as one AJCongress spokesman had framed his organization's position some years before.[6]

Cyrus Adler of the AJCommittee was especially agitated over the developments in Europe. When the Nazis announced their intention to deport the 17,000 German Jews of Polish origin, Adler had telegrammed Secretary of State Cordell Hull, demanding U.S. intervention. Hull responded that the administration "must confine its representations to foreign governments to matters which directly affect American citizens or American interests."[7] But Hull's cold refusal did not discourage Adler entirely. In the wake of the Kristallnacht horrors, Adler suggested to his colleague Morris Waldman that Jewish groups press the Roosevelt administration "to admit freely children from Germany and not charge them against the quota"; or, alternatively, "to admit freely old persons who have children or relatives in this country and are willing to support them"; a third possibility, he added, would be "to take three years' immigration quotas and put them into one."[8] Adler's recommendations were ignored. The overwhelming majority of AJCommittee leaders favored a continuation of the group's established policy. A post-Kristallnacht AJCommittee position paper explicitly declared:

While humanitarian accomplishments in bringing...victims of persecution to the United States and finding work for them cannot be
highly enough praised, this is helping to intensify the Jewish problem
here. Giving work to Jewish refugees while so many Americans are out
of work, has naturally made bad feelings. As heartless as it may seem,
future efforts should be directed toward sending Jewish refugees to
other countries instead of bringing them here.[9]

Likewise, Samuel Rosenman told President Roosevelt on December 5 that
he opposed any attempt to allow more refugees into the United States
because such a move would "create a Jewish problem in the U.S."[10]

The immigration question and other means of alleviating the plight of
German Jewry were debated at two successive meetings of the General
Jewish Council, on November 13 and again on December 13, in New
York. The representatives of the AJCongress, AJCommittee, B'nai B'rith,
and Jewish Labor Committee found themselves face to face with the
unpleasant question of immigration. They agreed that "on humanitarian
grounds mass immigration of German Jews could not be opposed," but
were equally concerned "that other countries, with far more semblance of
right than Germany (overcrowded Poland?) might demand a similar solution for very genuine population problems."[11] Some Jewish leaders,
Stephen Wise among them, feared that a forced emigration of German
Jews might jeopardize Jews in other Western countries—perhaps including those in the United States. In a 1936 essay, Wise decried talk of
mass Jewish emigration from Poland; such an undertaking, he said,
"might well become the 'locus classicus' for groups in all lands, seeking to
rid themselves of their Jewish populations." Wise was worried that
"France, Czecho-Slovokia, or England might conceivably propose a conference on Jewish emigrants and refugees, without exciting suspicion with
respect to their purpose."[12] The Jewish representatives at the November
13 session found themselves unable to reconcile "the imperative necessity" of mass immigration with what they called "the fundamental wrong
in such a policy." Unable to find a "satisfying solution" to this dilemma,
the attendees finally decided "that, at least for the time being, nothing
should be done with regard to this matter."[13]

The other major issue debated by the General Jewish Council was
whether or not to hold public demonstrations against Hitler. The AJCommittee, B'nai B'rith, and JLC succeeded in persuading the AJCongress to
endorse a resolution declaring it "the present sense of the General Jewish

Council that there should be no parades, public demonstrations or protests by Jews.''[14] Established four months earlier for the ostensible purpose of coordinating American Jewish political action, the General Jewish Council had instead become the instrument that insured American Jewish political inaction.

The success of the AJCommittee and its allies in winning the assent of the AJCongress to their ''quietist'' diplomacy climaxed a five-year struggle between the two major camps within the Jewish establishment. At the center of the struggle was the issue of staging public protest rallies against Nazism. The AJCongress scheduled its first ''Stop Hitler Now'' rally for Madison Square Garden on March 22, 1933. The leaders of the other major Jewish organizations feared that the proposed rally would anger the American public. ''I am of the opinion that we cannot be constantly thrusting ourselves before the public without danger to ourselves,'' one AJCommittee leader wrote to a colleague. ''They will get tired of us.''[15] Morris Waldman of the AJCommittee likewise complained that ''great numbers of inarticulate and 'average' Americans are becoming a bit irritated by this struggle within their borders, yet alien to them.'' Concluded Waldman, ''It may be that some Jewish groups have too many times protested against Hitlerism.''[16]

Stephen Wise privately sought to soothe his AJCommittee critics by assuring them that the rally would be conducted in a ''reserved dignified style'' and would avoid ''demagogical hysterical resolutions''; it would also feature ''some outstanding Gentiles,'' he stressed.[17] Indeed, Wise later recalled how ''the easiest thing in the world would have been to rouse that audience...to murderous rage''[18] but that he instead spoke in as ''prudent and cautious'' a manner as possible, careful never to use ''the term 'boycott' or 'reprisal.'''[19] The fact that the rally attracted an overflow crowd of more than 20,000 was indicative of the depth of concern among ordinary Jews, but the failure of Dr. Wise and the other speakers to translate the public's outrage into specific action against Germany reduced the protest from an event of potential political significance to a brief and ultimately forgettable display of emotion. When the AJCongress announced plans to stage an anti-Hitler parade through lower Manhattan on May 10, 1933, the ''quietists'' were again appalled. Alfred Cohen, president of the B'nai B'rith, joined Cyrus Adler of the AJCommittee in issuing a joint public statement bitterly condemning "public agitation in form of mass demonstrations," which, they asserted, "would tend to inflame already highly wrought feelings." The statement said that public demonstrations were "futile" and "serve only as an ineffectual channel for the release of emotion."[20] Yet Stephen Wise again ignored his critics and went ahead with the rally. "Better action without unity than unity without action!" Wise thundered in the editorial columns of *Opinion*.[21]

But the defiant stand Wise had taken in 1933 was nowhere to be found just five years later. In 1933, he initiated dramatic public protests; in 1938, he assented to the General Jewish Council's decision not to protest. In 1933, Wise had scoffed when the AJCommittee claimed that public protests would "furnish the persecutors with a pretext to justify the wrongs they perpetrate," but at the first post-Kristallnacht session of the President's Advisory Committee on Political Refugees, he reported that he and his colleagues in the General Jewish Council were urging a moratorium on Jewish demonstrations "in the belief that such protests might stimulate further action by the German Government."[22] In short, Wise had been co-opted.

Despite the Kristallnacht savagery, Wise showed no change of heart about U.S. immigration policy. At the December 8, 1938, meeting of the PACPR, State Department official Theodore C. Achilles reaffirmed the Roosevelt administration's opposition to any "legislative proposals involving changes in quotas." The minutes of the meeting record no criticism or dissent by Dr. Wise; in fact, the committee members, Wise included, "accepted in principle" the position outlined by Achilles.[23] (Ironically, Wise wrote a letter that very day in which he suggested resettling German Jewish refugees in the Soviet Union, of all places.[24])

The decision by the General Jewish Council to refrain from protests on behalf of German Jewry aroused criticism in the Jewish press. One journal editorialized:

> [W]hat leadership has the General Council for Jewish Rights manifested in the latest crisis? Have the constituent organizations and individual members been called upon to express their protest in some concrete fashion? Has any attempt been made to mobilize the masses in organized protest and to translate their indignation into effective action? . . . The General Council was formed "for the defense of equal rights of Jews in this country and abroad." Are we to assume that the

Council's chief weapon of defense in the present tragic emergency is
the issuance of a public statement deploring the tragedy and appealing
for the preservation of democracy? Is this how the equal rights of Jews
are to be defended?

The editorial concluded by appealing to its readers to write or
telephone GJC headquarters and demand that the Council initiate
"effective action."[25]

The AJCongress prided itself on its early anti-Hitler activism as well
as on its claim to represent the feelings of the American Jewish
masses. It could hardly ignore accusations that it had failed to
respond to Kristallnacht. Thus *Congress Weekly* was forced to publish
a lengthy editorial defending AJCongress policy from its critics. The
very headline of the editorial, "What Is the Congress Doing?"
implied that this question was on the minds of more than a few
American Jews. The editorial began:

> The policy of Jewish restraint adopted by the Congress in union with
> Jewish bodies in the General Council. . . did not raise any doubts as to
> the militancy of the Congress among the groups who for twenty years
> have learned to trust it. But there are elements whose patience broke
> under the mental and emotional burden of the last two weeks and
> these kept on inquiring: What is the Congress doing? To these the
> answer was given in the report rendered at the meeting of the Ad-
> ministrative Committee on the night of November 20 and at the Con-
> ference of organizations on the night of November 24.[26]

But the AJCongress had adopted no new position nor advocated any
new methods of action at either meeting. The first meaningful initiative on the German Jewish crisis would be taken instead by two non-
Jewish congressmen.

Early in 1939, Sen. Robert Wagner (D-New York) and Rep. Edith
Rogers (D-Massachusetts) jointly introduced legislation providing for
the nonquota admission of 20,000 German refugee children to the
United States over a two-year period. Joint Senate-House hearings on
the measure were scheduled to open on April 20. Far right and restrictionist groups lobbied hard against the bill throughout the spring.
Jewish organizations, however, refused to publicly press for its adoption. Stephen Wise, for one, specifically pressured some of his col-

leagues in the American Jewish leadership to refrain from public agitation on behalf of the Wagner-Rogers bill.[27] Privately, Wise sought to win endorsement of the measure from some non-Jewish politicians such as Governor Thomas E. Dewey of New York.[28] When Dewey refused to appear at the Wagner-Rogers hearings to testify in its favor, Wise was furious. "It was a real disappointment to see that T.D. never appeared at the hearings," Wise complained to Dewey aide Murray Garfein. "He was needed," Wise added, "and the strange thing to me is that he was in Washington that day and could so easily have said a word for [the] measure."[29] (Six years earlier, Rep. Samuel Dickstein must have been thinking precisely the same thing—about Stephen Wise.)

Wise and Sidney Hollander, president of the National Council of Jewish Federations, were the only Jewish leaders willing to testify at the Wagner-Rogers hearings. Hollander had no illusions about the desperate plight of Germany's Jews. Having just recently returned from a trip to Germany, he reported bluntly: "I talked to men and women of different races and different faiths, but from all the story was the same. With neighboring countries already crowded with refugees, and far-off lands able to absorb but a limited number, nothing lay ahead but extermination."[30] Yet Hollander sought to downplay the Jewish factor in the debate over the bill. "Jews have been persecuted, but they are not the only victims," he testified. "Concentration camps were established there for others before any were built for Jews." He stressed that Jews would not be the main beneficiaries of the measures: "Statements have been made. . . that if this bill is passed it will benefit primarily Jewish children. I have no reason to believe this is true. If it were, I doubt if I would so strongly urge passage of this bill." Hollander concluded by emphasizing his loyalty to America: "If I thought for a moment that this would involve a lessening of support for those in this country, or even a straining of the funds needed here, I would hesitate to sponsor this bill."[31]

Stephen Wise's testimony was characterized by a similar defensiveness. "I want to make it plain," he asserted,

that, so far as I am concerned, there is no intention whatsoever to depart from the immigration laws which at present obtain. I have heard no sane person propose any departure from the existing law now

57

in force. After all, this is a limited proposal. It is a proposal that deals with a rather limited number of children, 10,000 children for a period of two years.[32]

Wise emphasized:

If there is any conflict between our duty to those children and our duty to our country, speaking for myself as a citizen, I should say, of course, that our country comes first; and if children cannot be helped, they cannot be helped, because we should not undertake to do anything that would be hurtful to the interests of our country.[33]

Questioned by one of the congressmen about the idea of expanding the Wagner-Rogers bill to include German Jewish refugee children stranded in Poland, England, or Czechoslovakia, Wise responded:

Hard as it may be to answer your question, Congressman, I feel that the country and the Congress should not be asked to do more than take care of a limited number of children. The bill provides for 10,000 each year for a period of two years. After all, we cannot take care of all of them. Germany has a population of five or six hundred thousand Jews.[34]

After the hearings had concluded, the AJCongress again found itself having to defend to the Jewish public its failure to lobby on behalf of Wagner-Rogers during the crucial weeks prior to the congressional session. "There was a great deal of necessary caution exercised on the part of responsible Jewish organizations while a Commission of the United States Congress was studying the Wagner-Rogers Bill," editorialized AJC's *Congress Bulletin,* which itself had published nothing about Wagner-Rogers during the period prior to the hearings.[35] The fact that the bill was reported favorably out of the Joint House-Senate Subcommittee on Immigration was less a cause for celebration among AJCongress leaders than it was a cause for concern that non-Jews might accuse American Jewish organizations of exercising undue influence on the subcommittee. "No reactionary group can accuse any liberal or Jewish organization of having shaped the decision of the Sub-Committee," an editorial in the AJCongress weekly declared hopefully. "The names of those who testified are on record."[36] Indeed they were. The fact that Jewish support for the bill was so meager and halfhearted no doubt helped guarantee that Wagner-Rogers would never make it out of the Senate or House immigration committees.

Before the Wagner-Rogers controversy had faded from public memory, the Jewish refugee question was again staring the American Jewish leadership in the face. On May 27, the German steamship *St. Louis* cruised into the harbor at Havana, Cuba, with 930 Jewish immigrants aboard. The voyage of the *St. Louis* was no mere happenstance. Hitler was calling the free world's bluff. For more than six years, the Führer had endured the frequent and sometimes harsh criticism of the Roosevelt administration over his treatment of German Jewry. In a speech to his parliament on January 30, 1939, Hitler employed bitter sarcasm as he noted the obvious discrepancy between the complaints about his persecution of the Jews and the paucity of offers to accept Jewish refugees. "It is a shameful example to observe today how the entire democratic world dissolves in tears of pity but then, in spite of its obvious duty to help, closes its heart to the poor, tortured people," the Führer declared.[37] The Nazi publication *Der Weltkampf* echoed Hitler's theme: "We are saying openly that we do not want the Jews, while the democracies keep on claiming that they are willing to receive them—and then leave them out in the cold."[38] The time had come to call Roosevelt's bluff. The *St. Louis* would test America's willingness to match its words with deeds.

When the *St. Louis* docked at Havana, the Cuban officials declared the passengers' immigration visas invalid. All but thirty were refused the right to disembark. On May 30, complex bargaining began between American Jewish negotiators—chiefly Lawrence Berenson of the American Jewish Joint Distribution Committee and Celia Razovsky of the National Council of Jewish Women—and Cuban president Laredo Bru. Long hours passed with no sign that Cuba would relent. On board the *St. Louis,* tensions rose. Passenger Max Loehwe attempted suicide by slashing his wrists and jumping overboard. Captain Gustav Schroeder warned of a possible mass suicide if the ship were forced to return to Hitler's Europe.[39] On June 2, American Jewish leaders opened their morning newspapers to learn that Laredo Bru had ordered the *St. Louis* to leave Cuban territorial waters at once. Many of the passengers were "sobbing desperately" as the steamship lifted anchor, the *New York Times* reported. One passenger was quoted as saying, "If we are returned to Germany, it will mean the concentration camp for most of us."[40] The *St. Louis* did not return to Germany. Instead it remained in the waters between Cuba and Florida, "apparently steaming in aimless circles," according to the *Washington Post*.[41] When the ship came within three miles of Miami Beach, it was confronted by two Coast Guard planes and a patrol boat which followed it until it withdrew to a position some ten miles from the Florida Keys. The plight of the *St. Louis* was no secret. On five of the first eight days of June, its tale was told on the front page of the *New York Times*. Three of those five articles described the *St. Louis* as idling hopefully near the Miami coast.[42]

Yet none of the leaders of the major American Jewish organizations called for the Roosevelt administration to grant sanctuary to the refugees. None of the publications of the major Jewish groups demanded American intervention. In his private correspondence at the time, Stephen Wise implied that his fear of what he called "the really rising tide of anti-Semitism" helped shape his reluctance to demand that the United States take in more refugees.[43]

The *St. Louis* episode was a painfully embarrassing reminder of the hesitancy and impotence of the American Jewish leadership in the face of domestic restrictionism. It threatened to undermine the claims of groups like the AJCommittee and AJCongress that they were actively defending Jewish rights. Hence, as the *St. Louis* chugged slowly back toward Hitler's inferno, the major Jewish organizations took action to insure that there would be no repetition of the incident. The AJCommittee's journal, *Contemporary Jewish Record,* published a lengthy statement from the JDC executive committee warning would-be refugees against seeking refuge in the West. It was "dangerous and undesirable," the appeal declared, for refugees to set out in search of Western havens unless they had ironclad guarantees of admission into a particular country. Irregular immigration "aggravates immeasurably the situation of the native Jewish populations in the countries to which these emigrants have gone," the warning asserted.[44] *Contemporary Jewish Record* also reprinted—without comment or criticism—an editorial from the Galveston, Texas, *News,* defending American immigration policy on the grounds that "worldwide unemployment makes it difficult to find places anywhere for impoverished immigrants."[45] The *Record*'s news section buried the chronicles of the *St. Louis*. It mentioned Cuba's refusal to grant admission to the refugees, and the negotiations of the JDC, followed by the news that the *St. Louis* was forced to leave Cuban waters on June 1. It then reported that on June 13 agreement was reached for the refugees to enter Belgium, France, Britain, and the Netherlands. But it omitted the fact that for three full days the *St. Louis* had deliberately hovered off the American coast.[46] The AJCongress's *Congress Bulletin* likewise downplayed the fact that the ship had reached the very gates of the United States, only to be turned away while U.S. Jewish leaders looked on in silence. The June 9 edition of *CB* did include excerpts from a message sent by the passengers, but it relegated to the back page, and to tiny, almost illegible print, the portion of the text that read, "There was great excitement when the Florida coast was sighted and hope that we might be able to enter that beautiful land."[47]

Post-*St. Louis* editorials in *Congress Bulletin* suggested that the AJCongress leadership was sensitive to charges that it had done nothing to secure American intervention on behalf of the refugees. One editorial conceded that the episode had "raised in many minds the question of the effectiveness of the Jewish leadership. In an editorial on June 2 the *Day* very bluntly declares that 'if the Jewish leaders are so helpless that they can do nothing at such a critical moment, let them go and make room for others.'"[48] As it had done after the Kristallnacht pogroms, the AJCongress leadership sought to explain away its silence over the *St. Louis* tragedy. This time it sought to cast the blame upon those Jewish organizations that had opposed its 1938 scheme for elections to a single all-inclusive Jewish defense agency:

It happened because none of [the] powerful and responsible organizations was ready to establish and recognize any authority above itself. . . . It happened because they obstinately refused to build an all-Jewish central agency for migration problems. . . .

The tragedy of the *St. Louis* and other boats tells the world of today and the generations of tomorrow a shameful story of Jewish disintegration and division in the face of disasters, parts of which could have been forestalled. The leaders of the nationalist camp will not carry the brunt of the blame. For years they have been sounding the warning and calling for unification of effort and centralization of guidance. It is those whose fear of nationalism makes them resist any centralization who will answer for what was humanly possible to do but was not attempted."[49]

The following week, *Congress Bulletin* offered a different argument to rationalize the silence of Jewish leaders. Now the villain was restrictionist public opinion:

> It didn't even occur to Jews to appeal to the American government to find a way of saving the hapless passengers of the *St. Louis* from the hands of the fascist bandits. This was not because the Roosevelt Administration is any less friendly to Jews. Even the Cuban government, which meted out such cruel treatment to people who had complied with the formalities of entry, is deserving of some claim to understanding. The plain fact of the matter is that the government was simply afraid of the demagogic political agitation of the fascists.[50]

The AJCongress was not the only major American Jewish organization to which it "didn't even occur" to appeal to the U.S. government. Reform Judaism's Central Conference of American Rabbis began its fiftieth anniversary convention in Washington as the *St. Louis* pitifully made its way across the Atlantic back to Germany, yet not a word was spoken about the crisis. Ironically, CCAR president Max Currick praised President Roosevelt for "his statesmanly vision and clarity of utterance in defense of human freedom."[51] During the ensuing five days, sessions of the convention were devoted to "urging continued investigation of subversive movements in this country"; protesting England's Palestine policy; discussing "Ways of Fortifying Religious Life"; and complaining about extreme right-wing propaganda activities. It was as if the *St. Louis* did not exist. Conservative Judaism's Rabbinical Assembly of America, meeting less than two weeks after the *St. Louis* returned to Europe, likewise passed a bevy of resolutions but omitted any reference to the incident.[52]

The deafening silence of the American Jewish leadership during the *St. Louis* crisis sent a powerful message to Hitler. The nations of the free world might shed crocodile tears over his treatment of the Jews, but they would take no concrete action on their behalf; the Jews of the free world might wax indignant over the persecution of their co-religionists, but they were afraid to protest the failure of their governments to do anything about it. The Führer could now rest assured that he could deal with the Jews as he pleased.

However
Imminent
Be Their Peril

4

The Nazi invasion of Poland on September 1, 1939, extended the domain of Hitlerian persecution to include the largest European Jewish community of all: 3 million Polish Jews suddenly found themselves in the grip of Nazi terror.

Initial reports in the Western press about the suffering of Polish Jewry may have been viewed by the American Jewish leadership in the context of the travails of war. As early as December of that year, however, the Jewish Telegraphic Agency reported horrifying massacres of civilians that far exceeded the bounds of conventional warfare. "Nazis entered the Polish town of Ostrovie near Warsaw," JTA reported on December 8, "forced all the Jewish men to dig a large pit and then lined them up before the ditch and shot them down from behind with machine-guns so that their bodies fell into the newly-dug grave."[1] Five days later, it reported the news that "400 Jews had been massacred in the Polish town of Likov and several hundred in Kalushin."[2] On December 18, JTA disclosed that "a quarter of a million Jews have been wiped out by military operations, executions, disease and starvation...at least 80% of the remainder have been reduced to complete beggary."[3] There is no evidence to suggest that

American Jewish leaders doubted the authenticity of the massacre reports. "In the matter of the treatment of Jews in Nazi-over-run Poland," Stephen Wise wrote in *Opinion* in February 1940, "we face a spectacle of daily torture and horror such as men have not beheld since the days of Gengis Khan."[4]

But the sudden and dramatic intensification of European Jewish suffering failed to inspire new or dramatic initiatives by the American Jewish leadership to alleviate the Jewish refugee crisis. Divisiveness and lethargy still characterized the organized Jewish world. The eruption of the Polish crisis did prompt Stephen Wise to suggest that the AJCongress, AJCommittee, B'nai B'rith, and Jewish Labor Committee unite into a single Jewish organization for the duration of the war. But the latter three refused because they suspected that the Wise proposal was a ruse designed to grant the AJCongress hegemony in Jewish organizational life.

The General Jewish Council continued to function, but in name only. Leaders of the AJCongress privately longed for a pretext to withdraw their organization from the Council. They were reluctant to publicly ally themselves with other GJC member groups lest the Congress come to be regarded as just one among many Jewish groups. When the AJCongress decided to hold a "Stop Hitler Now" rally in December 1939, it refused to permit the Jewish Labor Committee to co-sponsor the demonstration for fear that such a partnership might diminish the amount of credit the Congress would be given. Permitting the JLC co-sponsorship would be "tragic" for the AJCongress, according to Stephen Wise's aide, Lillie Shultz. She warned Wise that a rally under the exclusive auspices of the AJCongress was "absolutely essential to revive public interest in its work." It would also be "the first step out of the psychological bondage of the General Jewish Council," she stressed.[5]

Some AJCongress leaders expected nothing but trouble from their competitors on the General Jewish Council. AJCongress vice-president Louis Lipsky told Wise:

It is quite clear that the Congress will soon be facing a planned, underground attack which will come from the American Jewish Committee, the Jewish Labor Committee, and possibly the B'nai B'rith...we should avoid initiating an attack, defend ourselves strongly whenever attacked, but devote ourselves principally to the business of building up the structure and influence of the Congress.[6]

This atmosphere of mistrust, mutual recriminations, and determined pursuit of organizational self-interest made unified action almost impossible.

The steadily worsening situation in Europe did not prompt American Jewish leaders to reconsider their opposition to settling refugees in the United States or its possessions. Indeed, some Jewish leaders consciously ignored opportunities for such settlement. On November 18, 1938, the Legislative Assembly of the Virgin Islands, a U.S. territory, adopted a resolution offering the Islands as a haven for refugees. The Secretary of the Interior, Harold Ickes, was attracted by the idea. Ickes's first attempt to discuss the plan with President Roosevelt was unsuccessful: "The President said that he had written me a memorandum on the subject which I found when I returned to my office. In his memorandum he rather slapped my ears back by telling me that refugee matters were for him and the State Department to decide." But when Ickes later raised the issue in a conversation with FDR, he discovered that the President's opposition was based largely on a misunderstanding:

> It was clear that he had not quite understood our proposition. He thought that the refugees would have to have work to support themselves in the Virgin Islands. He thought that if certain conditions were met, it might be all right to go ahead with the plan.

Ickes explained to Roosevelt that there had already been negotiations between the Departments of Interior and State over the scheme, which "had resulted in a meeting of minds on all points." All that was left to be determined, according to Ickes, was the opinion of the Department of Justice as to whether or not the plan "came within our laws." But before that could be done, Ickes complained, Secretary of State Cordell Hull "had personally stopped proceedings at that point."[7] Hull, an elderly Southern conservative, had little sympathy for the plight of the Jews in Europe. Even at the height of the Holocaust, he was still referring to the "projected extermination" of European Jewry.[8] Hull left refugee matters in the hands of Assistant Secretary of State Breckinridge Long, a longtime State Department bureaucrat who harbored deep anti-Jewish prejudices and bitterly opposed any increase in refugee immigration to the United States. Long described Jews seeking to leave Germany as "so-called refugees."[9] Long pressed U.S. naval officials to declare the Virgin Islands a "restricted area" so as to block attempts to settle refugees there.[10] Ickes's proposal for the Islands was ultimately scuttled when President Roosevelt decided to accept the argument of Long and other State Department restrictionists that "all kinds of undesirables and spies" would enter the United States territory in the guise of refugees. "I have sympathy," FDR told Ickes. "I cannot, however, do anything which would conceivably hurt the future of present American citizens."[11]

Stephen Wise defended Roosevelt's hard-line position and vowed to campaign for him in the 1940 presidential election despite FDR's attitude. In a letter to a colleague in September 1940, Wise wrote:

> What I am afraid lies back of the whole thing is the fear of the Skipper's friends in the State Department that any large admission of radicals to the United States might be used effectively against him in the campaign. Cruel as I may seem, as I have said to you before, his re-election is much more important for everything that is worthwhile and that counts than the admission of a few people, however imminent be their peril.[12]

Meanwhile, the possibility of settling Jewish refugees in Alaska was under serious consideration. In November 1938, Secretary of the Interior Ickes told reporters he was "considering" the idea of using Alaska as a haven for the persecuted, although he added that he "would not go so far as to say he would recommend the proposal to the President."[13] When Ickes broached the issue during a conversation with the President the following year, he discovered that Roosevelt was interested in the scheme but was concerned lest too many Jews be granted entry:

> The President's idea is that we ought to try to take care of ten thousand settlers a year in Alaska for the next five years. . . . Of this ten thousand he would have five thousand from the United States, and those from foreign lands would be admitted in the same ratio in which they can come into this country, based upon the quota law. He estimated that, on this basis, not more than ten per cent would be Jews, and thus we would be able to avoid the undoubted criticism that we would be subjected to if there were an undue proportion of Jews.

Although Ickes himself conceived of the idea in much more generous terms, he was pleased to find that the President had at least some sympathy for the project. Quietly he began discussing the plan with potential supporters and contacting wealthy American Jews who might help finance refugee resettlement in Alaska.[14] In January 1940, the proposal was publicly endorsed by Anthony J. Dimond, the non-voting representative of Alaska on Capitol Hill. Dimond said that Alaska "will gladly welcome refugees" and dismissed fears that refugee immigration would stir up racial prejudice among the Alaskan populace: "We take a man for what he is and not for what his forefathers were or where they came from."[15]

Dimond, like other non-Jewish proponents of the scheme, was motivated by a desire to further the economic development of the Alaska territory. Although the entire population of Alaska was less than 70,000, surveys had estimated that the region could support as many as 12 million. It boasted 42 million acres of arable land, more than 22 million acres of pasture, 10,000 square miles of coal, and numerous other mineral deposits which had resisted exploitation largely because Alaska's difficult winter climate discouraged potential settlers. New strategic considerations gave further ammunition to the Alaska development lobby. Aggressive Japan was only six hundred miles from the Alaskan shore; the Soviet Union—at that moment allied with Nazi Germany and fresh from its conquests of eastern Poland and the Baltic nations—was just sixty-five miles away. With southern Alaska barely seven hundred miles from Seattle, an enemy occupation force in Alaska would be within easy bombing range of America's entire Pacific Coast.

In May 1940, Sen. William King, a member of the Senate Committee on Territories and Insular Affairs, and Rep. Frank Havenner introduced joint legislation designed to open up Alaska to development by European immigrants. The King-Havenner bill (S. 3577 and H.R. 5971) meant to establish limited-dividend corporations which would invest private funds in the development of various local industries. The corporations would have the right to import laborers, half of them European refugees and half American citizens.[16] Immigrant laborers were necessary, according to King's explanation of the measure, because few American citizens would find Alaska a sufficiently attractive place in which to settle. Refugees, on the other hand, "in meeting the problems of frontier life, would not be thinking of the comforts of life in the States that they had sacrificed, but in terms of the savagery and hopelessness of the conditions abroad from which they had been rescued."[17] The only disadvantage from the Jewish point of view was that the King bill provided that the selection of immigrants be conducted according to the existing quota limitations for each country.

King-Havenner won the support of both the Department of Labor and the Department of the Interior. Secretary of the Interior Ickes appeared before the Committee on Territories and Insular Affairs on May 13 to present a ringing endorsement of the proposed bill. "[I]f a proposition is good for business and good for the national defense and good for the American people we ought not to turn it down merely because it has some humanitarian by-products," Ickes declared. "[T]he word 'humanitarian' is in bad odor these days, and I don't suggest that this committee take any action at all on humanitarian grounds." Ickes outlined the strategic advantages of the Alaska development project:

> An unpopulated country, rich in natural resources and poorly defended, offers a standing temptation to overpopulated, resource-hungry and militarized nations. There are few territories in the world as rich in resources and as capable of absorbing a new population as Alaska. The industrial development in populating Alaska by American and immigrant stock, carefully selected to insure physical hardihood and loyalty to American institutions, would constitute an important contribution to the defense of American territory in general.[18]

The major American Jewish organizations refrained from endorsing the King bill out of fear that they would be accused of trying to flood the United States with foreigners. Stephen Wise wrote to a colleague of his opposition to the idea of bringing European Jewish refugees to Alaska. "[J]ust because small numbers of Jews might settle there" was no reason to support the Alaska scheme, Wise wrote. He was concerned that talk of settling refugees in Alaska "makes a wrong and hurtful impression to have it appear that Jews are taking over some part of the country for settlement."[19] The only American Jewish group to back the King bill was the tiny Poale Zion, or Labor Zionists of America, which was willing to temporarily set aside its preference for settlement in Palestine, in light of the urgent need to provide a haven for European Jews. The Labor Zionist monthly, *Jewish Frontier,* urged "responsible Jewish bodies in America" to "take a serious interest in this Bill" and to press for the removal of the provision linking immigration selection to the quota laws.[20] The absence of major Jewish support for the measure left the field wide open for the restrictionist forces. Sen. Robert R. Reynolds (D-North Carolina) denounced the King-Havenner proposal as an attempt to bring in through "the back door" hordes of foreigners who "would deprive the American citizens of their daily bread." Colonel John Thomas Taylor, spokesman for the American Legion, warned that the prospective refugees were "fifth columnists" who "did not have the courage and patriotism to remain in their motherlands and fight their own battles over there."[21] Opposition from the restrictionists, seconded by the State Department, succeeded in killing the King-Havenner bill in subcommittee.

The death of the King proposal was not, however, the death of the Alaska development idea. On January 29, 1941, Rep. Samuel Dickstein submitted House Resolution 2791, "providing for the utilization of unfilled immigration quotas in order to colonize Alaska for purposes of national defense and as a market for surplus production."[22] Dickstein proposed to combine all unused immigration quotas from the previous six years in order to facilitate the entry of refugees to colonize the Alaska territory. Entry would be granted only to refugees who could demonstrate "that they had not engaged in subversive activities in their native lands, that they had lost their native citizenship rights, that they had useful and productive occupations which they intended to pursue and that they would remain in the territory a minimum of five years." Dickstein did not hide the fact that his interest in the matter stemmed largely from his concern for the plight of European Jewish refugees. He openly declared that his resolution was meant to "call Hitler's bluff" by disproving the Führer's claims that the Western world was not interested in accommodating the Jews any more than Germany was.[23] Yet American Jewish support for the Dickstein bill was virtually nonexistent. The Labor Zionists' *Jewish Frontier* again endorsed the Alaska plan: "As Jews, we are especially interested that the government should allow a larger number of European refugees to enter if not the United States, at least Alaska." The Labor Zionist journal went even further this time, arguing that "American progressive circles" should in fact "demand openly and courageously the repeal of the 1924 immigration laws and the introduction, instead, of more humane as well as more practical regulations which would be in keeping with the best of American traditions.''[24] But the editor of *Jewish Frontier* was alone in his stand. The reaction of the major American Jewish organizations was the same deafening silence that had greeted the King measure of the previous year. Dickstein's Alaska proposal, like King's, was buried in subcommittee.[25]

Another scheme that was bandied about at that time was the possibility of settling Jewish refugees in the Japanese Empire. Although this plan never reached the stage of serious consideration, the circumstances surrounding the proposal shed further light on Stephen Wise's attitude. During the late 1930s, officials of the Hirohito regime seriously weighed the idea of offering Manchuria, the Japanese-occupied region of northern China, as a haven for Jewish refugees. The Japanese believed that American Jews had influence on the Roosevelt administration and hoped that by winning favor with American Jewry they would be able to secure vitally needed economic assistance from the United States.

Mitsuzo Tamura, an unofficial emissary for the Japanese, met with Wise at the latter's office in New York early in 1940. Tamura was well aware that Wise had condemned the Japanese invasion of Manchuria as "criminal aggression" and had urged the Roosevelt administration to do everything "short of war or what may lead to war that will make it impossible for Japan to continue its relentless and criminal war against China." Yet Tamura hoped he could convince Wise that Japan might be Jewry's salvation. "[T]housands of Jews could be rescued from the brutality and death they were now condemned to suffer in Europe," he implored Wise. What Japan sought in return, Tamura explained, was "America's exporting to Japan items such as fuel oil, heavy machinery and scrap metal." According to Tamura's account of the conversation, Wise scornfully rejected the offer. "Wouldn't you think, Mr. Tamura, that it might be a rather unpatriotic thing for American Jews to do, even to discuss the future export of these items to a non-allied country?" Tamura quoted Wise. Wise also rebuffed Tamura's suggestion that he visit Manchuria "and see for yourself how some Jews are now living in the Japanese Empire and how so many more could be settled there safely and happily."[26]

Following the Nazi conquest of Poland in September 1939, France and Great Britain declared war on the Germans. There ensued an eight-month-long "phony war," as Hitler plotted but repeatedly postponed his invasions of England and France. Finally, in the spring of 1940, the German armies marched through Western Europe. In April, they attacked Norway and Denmark; in May, they captured Holland and Belgium; in June, France fell. Another 350,000 Jews were in Hitler's grasp—more than half a million, if those remaining in Vichy France are included.

As the ravages of war swept Europe, isolationist sentiment swept America. Many Americans still believed that their country had been tricked into joining the First World War, and an official congressional inquiry had spent much of 1934 investigating allegations that the munitions industry had helped drag the United States into the fray. During the interwar years, isolationist senators like Burton K. Wheeler of Idaho, Ernest Lundeen of Minnesota, and Gerald P. Nye of North Dakota railed against supposed Jewish attempts to push America into a conflict with Germany.[27]

When prominent non-Jews warned American Jewish leaders not to agitate for U.S. intervention on behalf of Europe's Jews, they took the warnings seriously. The American ambassador to Great Britain, Joseph Kennedy (father of John F. Kennedy), is said to have told a Jewish leader:

> There [are] still people of sense who at the back of their minds [have] the idea that the Jews would like Germany to be punished by defeat in a war...I tell you on the authority of no less a person than Franklin Delano Roosevelt that if the United States is dragged into war with Germany there might even be a pogrom in the U.S.A.[28]

Equally frightening was the public accusation by flying hero Charles Lindbergh that American Jews sought to drag the United States into war with Germany. Speaking to an audience of 8,000 at an "America First" rally in Des Moines on September 13, 1941, Lindbergh named American Jews as "the second major group pressing America towards the war." He also decried what he said was the Jews' "large ownership and influence in our motion pictures, our press, our radio and our Government." Lindbergh threatened: "Instead of agitating for war, the Jewish groups in this country should be opposing it in every possible

71

way, for they will be among the first to feel its consequences. Tolerance is a virtue that depends upon peace and strength. History shows that it cannot survive war and devastation."[29] To compound matters, Lindbergh's slurs were seconded by an editorial in the *Chicago Tribune,* which ominously noted that the only ward in Chicago "that voted for war" in a recent public opinion survey "was a predominantly Jewish community." The editor continued:

> Americans have but one demand that they may rightfully make of American Jews. . . . It is that they think and act as Americans. This does not mean that they should abandon religion, or customs, or sentimental ties. It does mean that in political matters, and particularly in matters touching our foreign relations, they should be wholly American and not members of any racial group.[30]

Ironically, American Jewish leaders had for years been going out of their way to avoid unseemly agitation for American action against Hitler. "[N]o Jew on earth has asked any nation to take up arms against Hitler," Stephen Wise wrote to a non-Jewish colleague in 1941.[31] Morris Waldman of the AJCommittee urged Wise: "We should exercise the greatest caution in avoiding giving the impression that we Jews have special interests in the present situation. . .Jews in Europe are not the only victims of the present turmoil."[32] A feature article in the AJCommittee's journal, *Contemporary Jewish Record,* specifically cautioned American Jews:

> [A]t the present moment there is one misconception which has become exceedingly dangerous and which must be vigorously attacked, namely, the misconception that Jews are war-mongers. Every American wants above all things to keep this country out of war. [Therefore] rabbis and Jews in public life should express themselves in no uncertain terms along the lines of their beliefs, namely, that Americans must think of America first. The test of every proposition must be whether or not it makes for the security, happiness and well-being, not of a particular group, but of the American people as a whole, and, beyond that, of the world at large. American Jews are Americans, and if in the present crisis they *show* that they are *acting* as such, they will do much to deflect the impact of the war-monger propaganda which is being released against them.[33]

The Lindbergh speech redoubled American Jewish fears of local anti-Semitism and elicited another round of statements from the major American Jewish organizations pledging Jewish loyalty to America and its policies. In a joint statement, the AJCommittee and Jewish Labor Committee asserted that they did not regard Hitler's atrocities as a particular Jewish concern: "We will not put even what he considers our 'interests' before those of our country—since our interests and those of our country are one and indivisible,"[34] the groups vowed. The official AJCongress response to Lindbergh was similar:

> For our fellow-Americans of faiths differing from our own and of other racial ancestries, we have a message. Surely it is needless to state that we are of and for America as truly as any other group within the nation, however it define itself. We have no viewpoint or attitude in relation to foreign affairs that is not determined solely by American interests, the needs and interests of our own free country.
>
> ...The Governing Council of the American Jewish Congress wishes to make clear that, far from "agitating for war," Jewish groups have, since the beginning of Hitler's attack not only on them but on all religion and on humanity itself, exerted the utmost restraint.[35]

Meanwhile, the news from Europe was grim. When savage pogroms swept Rumania during the pro-Nazi "Iron Guard" rebellion of January 1941, an eyewitness correspondent for the Jewish Telegraphic Agency reported every gruesome detail:

> Jewish leaders believe their dead throughout the country would exceed 2,000.... Unknown hundreds of Jews will never be found, however, because of the manner in which they were put to death....
>
> Dozens of Jews—women and children as well as men—were literally burned alive...beaten senseless in the streets, robbed, doused with gasoline and set afire.
>
> Trusted friends have told me, and officials have confirmed, numerous cases of Jewish women whose breasts were cut off, not to mention sadistic mutilations like gouged-out eyes, brandings and bone-breakings.
>
> Perhaps the most horrifying single episode of the pogrom was the "kosher butchering" last Wednesday night of more than 200 Jews in the municipal slaughterhouse.[36]

Such reports were trifling compared to the news of mass slaughter in Eastern Europe that summer.

In early 1941, probably in January or February, Hitler gave the order for the physical extermination of the Jewish people. When the Nazis invaded Soviet Russia on June 22, 1941, the annihilation of European Jewry began. Mobile Nazi execution squads, known as the Einsatzgruppen, followed the advancing German troops through the Ukraine, massacring hundreds of thousands of Jews in just a few months' time. The massacres were no secret. Reports reached the West within weeks. As early as July, the Jewish Telegraphic Agency *Daily Bulletin* described mass executions which had been carried out in Minsk, Brest-Litovsk, Prezemyl, and the Volynian region.[37] There were similar reports in August.[38]

"Time may pass before the ghastly details come to be known," Stephen Wise wrote in the August *Opinion*. "But certain it is,

> by their own claims as well as admissions, that the Nazis have most ruthlessly set the torch to the homes of all Jews in their martial path. Apparently Jews have suffered most, according to their own grisly tale, in such places in Roumania as Jassy, where, according to one report 700 Jews were led out and shot.[39]

On October 2, the JTA reported how thousands of Jews in Nazi-occupied territory were "simply mowed down by machine-guns."[40] Three weeks later, JTA described how 10,000 Jews were slaughtered in the Kaments-Podoski region.[41] On November 16, JTA reported that "fifty-two thousand Jews, including men, women, and children, were systematically and methodically put to death in Kiev following the Nazi occupation of the Ukrainian capitol" and that "similar measures, though on a small scale, have been taken in other conquered towns."[42]

By this time, *Congress Weekly* was referring to the ongoing slaughter as "cold-blooded extermination" and "outright annihilation." The leaders of the AJCongress gave no indication that they doubted the accuracy of the massacre reports:

> From Kovno in the North to Odessa in the South, a wave of outright slaughter, mass deportations and incarceration of Jews in concentration camps is taking a heavy toll of our people. Some 15,000 Jews of Hun-

gary and Galicia were banished to the Ukraine and murdered in cold blood. Their bodies fill the waters of the Dniester.

. . . These are no "atrocity-stories." The Jewish press is not alone in reporting these mass massacres. They are confirmed by authoritative reports in the general press in America and England. Yet no voice has been raised either in this country or in Great Britain to express the horror of free humanity at this cold-blooded extermination of a people.[43]

Yet as the news from Europe went from bad to worse, Stephen Wise's own *Opinion* moved the massacre reports from the lead editorial columns to the "news briefs" in the back pages. Confined to page twenty-two of the December 1941 *Opinion* were two shocking paragraphs about "Germany's officially sponsored program of Jewish extermination":

When Odessa fell, victory parades throughout Rumania turned into orgies of murder and pillage of Jews. Some reports state that 100,000 Jews were murdered; the British Broadcasting Co. estimates 25,000. Either figure makes all previous pogroms appear like childsplay.

Newly-German-occupied Ukraine has her pogroms carefully and systematically stimulated by Germany example, outrivalling Petlura's massacres in 1920. New York Times correspondent cables that corpses of Jews are floating on the Dniester River and the reports of the slain go from 8,000 to 15,000.[44]

The February 1942 *Opinion* allotted exactly one sentence each to the massacre of 52,000 Jews in Kiev and 60,000 in Bessarabia and Bukowina.[45]

The Jewish media was the source of the most detailed reports, but it was by no means the exclusive source for early Holocaust news. *Life* magazine, for example featured in its February 23, 1942, edition a two-page photo spread of what it described as the "methodical massacre" of Polish Jewry.[46]

Widely circulated in March was one of the most horrifying reports yet:

"The field was heaving like a sea." This sentence occurred first in an eye-witness report to Moscow from the city of Borisov, and then repeated in an eye-witness report brought by a representative of the

Joint Distribution Committee from the vicinity of Kiev. In the city of Borisov the Nazis had ordered Jews to dig a communal grave, into which 7,000 men, women and children—some shot to death, others only wounded—were thrown and covered with earth, and it was by the living breath of those interred that the field was heaving like the sea. Another 8,000 Jews were brought to the city from neighboring towns and the burial of corpses and living alike in a common grave was repeated. In the district of Kiev no less than 240,000 Jews, according to the J.D.C. report, found their death in common graves, and the field was again "heaving like the sea."

Months ago it was reported that some 50,000 Jews had been put to death in Kiev in the manner thus described. The human mind found it impossible to believe that even Hitler's plans of extermination should employ such methods of mass murder. But the reports persist, Hitler maintains his ceaseless threats that the Jews will be destroyed, and, following the massacres in Borisov, the Nazi paper in White Russia wrote: "The Jewish problem in White Russia is now solved, but there are still five million Jews left in the United States." One may still hope that the number of those murdered has been exaggerated in the report, but there is no longer any reason to doubt the veracity of the fact. No imagination could invent this conception of the "field heaving like a living sea" with the breath of those buried alive. Only men who saw it with their own eyes could bring it back.[47]

The staff of *Congress Weekly*, however, did not deem the report significant enough to earn more than the second editorial in the March 20 issue. The massacres of 86,000 Jews in Minsk, 52,000 in Kiev, and 25,000 in Odessa merited only a passing reference in the second editorial of the May 1 edition.[48]

May brought fresh reports of atrocities. The JTA reported on May 8 of the torture-murders of "at least 100,000 Serbians and Jews, including men, women and children" in occupied Yugoslavia. Jews were "entirely exterminated from the towns of Subtica, Horgos, Sombor, Backa-Topola and Novi-Sad."[49] Three days later, JTA published excerpts from a speech by Nahum Goldmann (the co-chairman of the World Jewish Congress) referring to "the slaughter of hundreds of thousands of Jews in German-occupied territories."[50] On May 13, an eyewitness described life in the Warsaw ghetto as "a veritable hell on earth."[51] The terrifying news reports contrasted oddly with the activities of the American Jewish Congress, which was engrossed in planning a "War Emergency Conference" in Chicago for May 16-18. The ongoing slaughter of European Jewry was absent from the conference agenda:

> Sunday morning is to be devoted to a series of round-table discussions on economic discrimination, the strengthening of democracy against subversive propaganda, a program of law and legislation, the organization of the American Jewish community, youth activities, inter-American Jewish unity, post-war reconstruction and the American Jewish war effort.
>
> The plenary session on Sunday afternoon is to be devoted to the program "I Am An American."...
>
> ...The Sunday evening session will take the form of a Dinner Symposium on the New World Order.
>
> ...The Monday morning session will hear the reports of the various round-table discussions....
>
> ...Monday afternoon will feature a discussion on World Jewry, its needs, its outlook and the relation of the American Jewish community to these needs.
>
> ...The War Emergency Session will be concluded on Monday evening, May 18, when resolutions will be adopted and officers for the coming year elected.[52]

On the eve of the conference, the JTA disclosed shocking new information about the Nazi massacres:

> Reliable information reaching here today from Nazi-occupied Lithunia reveals that mass-executions of Jews are taking place in practically every town in the Kaunas and Vilna districts. More than 10,000 Jews have been massacred by the Nazi authorities in five towns alone, the report disclosed.
>
> In the town of Shovli, the report states, approximately 7,000 Jews were massacred by the Nazi authorities. In Troki about 2,000 Jews were executed. More than 1,000 Jews were murdered in Nowo-Wileika.[53]

Yet the resolutions adopted by the AJ Congress War Emergency Session did not mention the European slaughter. They pledged "solidarity with all segments of the Jewish people"; called for the establishment of "an American Jewish Congress war effort division"; denounced racial discrimination in the Army; assailed "the activities of subversive forces which are seeking to separate group from group"; urged "communal reorganization via establishment of individual Jewish community councils"; and demanded postwar rights for Europe's Jews.[54]

The days following the conference brought new accounts of atrocities. "More than 7,000 Greek Jews, including 3,000 children under fourteen years of age, have died from starvation since the Nazi occupation of the country," ran one report. "In Salonika, it is estimated, at least fifty Jews are now dying from hunger every day."[55] From Slovakia, the JTA reported that "unburied corpses of hundreds of Jews are lying in the woods near Bratislava."[56] And there were more gruesome details of the work of the mobile execution squads:

> In Vitebsky the Germans rounded up several thousand Jewish men, women and children and loaded them into leaking boats which were towed to the middle of the Dwina River. . . . When the boats reached midstream, the Nazi soldiers turned a murderous stream of bullets upon the Jews, killing thousands of the prisoners and leaving hundreds of others to drown when their leaking craft sank. . . . In every village those Jews who had been unable to flee were shot and burnt. In the districts of Goublokaje and Wilejka no Jews remained alive.[57]

The Holocaust had begun. Information about the mass slaughter was arriving in the West from three to six months late, but it was arriving nonetheless. American Jewish leaders had no reason to doubt the authenticity of the reports. Yet as the long, dark night of Nazi horror descended upon Europe's Jews, the leaders of the American Jewish community seemed to be turning a deaf ear to the anguished cries of their brethren.

The
Right
To Fight

5

The inactivity of the Jewish leadership created a vacuum that others soon strove to fill. On the eve of America's entry into World War II, a tiny dissident group of ultranationalist Zionists began an independent campaign to mount what they conceived as the proper Jewish response to Nazi persecution: armed Jewish retribution. The idea that the Revisionist Zionists sought to promote was the creation of a full-fledged Jewish army to battle alongside the Allied forces against the Nazis.

Vladimir (Ze'ev) Jabotinsky, the dynamic Russian-born orator who founded and led the Revisionists, arrived in the United States on March 14, 1940, with one goal in mind: to secure the necessary political and financial backing for the creation of a Jewish army. The Jabotinsky army campaign would be the spark that would ignite a series of heated disputes between insurgents and the American Jewish establishment throughout the Holocaust years.

During the First World War, Jabotinsky had successfully lobbied for the creation of a Jewish Legion within the British army. The legion participated in the liberation of Palestine from the Turks and then disbanded at the end of the war. When World War II erupted in

1939, Jabotinsky decided that the time had come to campaign for the recreation of a Jewish fighting force. His Jewish army proposal took on a special, added poignancy this time around, since the Nazis against whom the proposed Jewish force would do battle had proclaimed the destruction of Jewry as their goal.

The Jewish world of 1939 was a far cry from what it had been in 1914. The Eastern European Jewish communities where the Revisionists were most popular—and from which they would presumably seek financial and political support for the army campaign—were no longer accessible as they had been in the days of the Jewish Legion campaign. Russia, under Soviet rule, had been off-limits to Zionist activity for many years; Poland had been conquered by the Nazis in September of 1939. The only remaining Jewish community of significant size was to be found in the United States, home to over 4 million Jews—many of them the children of immigrants from Eastern Europe. In the United States, the Zionist movement had been growing steadily under the leadership of the eloquent and forceful Stephen Wise. This was not necessarily a boon for the Jewish army campaigners, however, because Wise and many of his colleagues in the American Zionist leadership were not at all favorably disposed toward Jabotinsky's ultranationlist brand of Zionism. Wise and company were for the most part liberals who were more inclined to side with Palestine's socialist-oriented Labor Zionists. They held no brief for the militaristic, anti-trade union sentiments of the Revisionists. One American Zionist leader described the Jabotinskyites in 1940 as "a near-fascist minority which is disrupting the unity of Zionism."[1]

Jabotinsky was rudely introduced to the opposition of U.S. Jewish leaders when he sought the endorsement of Lord Lothian, the British ambassador to the United States, for the army drive. When Jabotinsky met Lord Lothian in New York in early June, the ambassador expressed sympathy for the army plan and assented to Jabotinsky's request that he publicly endorse the army proposal at a mass meeting to be held at the Manhattan Center.[2] But when news of Jabotinsky's activities somehow leaked out, a delegation of American Jewish leaders quickly went to Washington to meet Lothian and talk him out of it. Stephen Wise, in his capacity as president of the Emergency Committee for Zionist Affairs (a coalition of leading American Zionist groups), headed the delegation. He was accompanied by American Jewish Congress vice-president Louis Lipsky, Zionist Organization of

America leader Solomon Goldman, Jewish Agency official Eliezer Kaplan, and Isadore Breslau of the American Zionist Bureau. They met Lord Lothian on June 18 and succeeded in convincing him to withhold his intended declaration of support for Jabotinsky's Jewish army proposal. Afterwards, the delegation of Jewish leaders issued a statement to the press declaring:

> As recently as May 10, 1940, the Jewish Agency reiterated its readiness to mobilize four divisions for the defense of Palestine, in the cause of the Allies.
>
> The Zionist organizations of America have given their unqualified support to those proposals. It is understood, of course, that such support could be conditioned by the laws of the United States.
>
> It is unnecessary for us to state that American Zionist organizations are not associated with Mr V. Jabotinsky's activities in any way.[3]

The American Zionist leaders thus had two bones to pick with the Jewish army campaigners. First, there was a substantive disagreement on the nature and role of the Jewish fighting force. The American Zionist leadership preferred the Jewish Agency plan for the Jews of Palestine to fight as a unit of the British army. Convinced that the Allies would be ultimately sympathetic to Zionist aspirations, they sought a Jewish division which would be an integral part of the Allied Forces. The Revisionists, on the other hand, insisted on a fully independent army that, while fighting alongside the Allies, would not be restricted by them, or disarmed after the war. It would encompass Palestinian Jews as well as Jews from other countries, march under its own flag, and—presumably—become the army of the Jewish state-to-be.

The second consideration in the shaping of the Jewish leaders' attitude to the Jewish army plan was a fear that it would create suspicions in the minds of non-Jews about American Jewry's loyalties. The Jewish leaders had declared their "unqualified support" for a Jewish military force, and then explicitly qualified that support as being "conditioned by the laws of the United States." This point was supplemented by a separate statement issued by Isadore Breslau after the delegation's official statement. Breslau stressed that "American neutrality laws forbade enlistment of recruits for foreign armies in this country, and that American Jews would fight only when called upon to do so by their own country."[4] The last thing American Jewish leaders wanted was for non-Jews to suspect that they were bringing to the United States foreign agitators to recruit for some overseas conflict. A decade earlier, in the 1930s, the American Jewish Committee had refused to help sponsor a U.S. speaking tour for Winston Churchill because, Morris Waldman wrote in his memoirs, "we feared that his appearance in the United States on such a mission" might be interpreted as part of some Jewish-British plot "to involve the United States in the European mess."[5]

These fears were still apparent in the early 1940s. During his 1940 tour of the United States, Jabotinsky reported to friends that "the Jews are still shy of saying any decisive word lest they be charged with warmongering.... I have never seen American Jewry so scared of local anti-Semites as they are now."[6] Jabotinsky was not alone in this assessment. Labor Zionist leader David Ben-Gurion, who visited the United States in October of that year, recalled a conversation he had with one American Jewish leader:

> He agreed with all I said, but argued that he could do nothing in public, since he might injure the Jews of America. I asked him, "Which are you first, a Jew or an American?" He replied, "...We are a minority here. If I stand up and demand American aid for Britain, people will say after the war that the dirty Jews got us into it, that it was a Jewish war, that it was for their sakes that our sons died in battle." This fear I found in almost all Zionist circles.[7]

An editorial in *Congress Weekly* openly expressed fears that the Jabotinsky campaign was creating the impression "that the Jewish Army is intended to be composed of Jewish citizens in America, thus raising questions which did not exist of the loyalty of Jews to their country."[8] *New Palestine,* the publication of the Zionist Organization of America, expressed similar concerns. A Jewish military unit might "eventually" include "recruits from neutral lands who are living as refugees in those lands," the ZOA organ suggested. But Jewish army activities in the United States that implied recruitment of American Jewish youths would be "mischievous in their effect on the status of American Jews," it warned.[9]

Jabotinsky died suddenly in New York in August 1940, leaving his band of followers in the United States confused and leaderless. It was not until late 1941 that the group renewed its public activities, this time with twenty-six-year-old Peter Bergson at the helm. Bergson's real name was Hillel Kook, but he operated under the alias in order to avoid embarrassing his uncle, the chief rabbi of Palestine. He was assisted by Samuel Merlin, Yitzhak Ben Ami, Alexander Hadani, Jeremiah Halpern, and Aryeh Ben Eliezer, five young men who, like Bergson, had been affiliated with the militant Irgun Zvai Leumi underground group in Palestine and Europe. All had been dispatched to the United States between 1939 and 1941 to engage in various Revisionist missions. With the death of Jabotinsky and the wartime demobilization of the Irgun, however, the Bergson boys were on their own.

They began working to arouse support for the Jewish army idea, soliciting aid from prominent Jews and non-Jews alike. At a December 4, 1941, public conference in Washington, D.C., the Committee for a Jewish Army of Stateless and Palestinian Jews was officially established. The group's professed aim was

> To bring about, by legal means and in accordance with the laws and foreign policy of the United States, the formation of a Jewish Army, based in Palestine, to fight for the survival of the Jewish people and the preservation of democracy. This army, composed primarily of Palestinian Jews and refugees as well as of volunteers from free countries, will fight on all required battlefields side by side with the United States, Great Britain and the other Allied nations.[10]

This point was reemphasized a month later when Bergson placed a full-page advertisement in the *New York Times,* a publicity tactic that was to become the hallmark of the Bergson group. "JEWS FIGHT FOR THE RIGHT TO FIGHT" barked the ad's banner headline. "The Jews of Palestine and the stateless Jews of the world do not only want to pray— THEY WANT TO FIGHT!!!" it began. The ad went on to demand the creation of a Jewish army, "200,000 strong," and stressed the strategic advantages to the Allies of such a force; the Jewish army, it argued,

> Will consolidate the Allied positions around the Suez Canal;
> Will release a considerable part of the Anzac forces from the Middle East for combat in the Pacific, and thus
> Will strengthen the defenses of this hemisphere.[11]

83

The text was flanked by 133 signatures, including those of three senators, fourteen congressmen, eleven rabbis, five Protestant ministers, and prominent journalists and show business people. Abram Leon Sachar, national director of the B'nai B'rith Hillel Foundations, was also among them—as were several prominent Christian associates of Stephen Wise's, such as Paul Tillich and Reinhold Neibuhr of the Union Theological Seminary. The willingness of so many public figures to be associated with the Revisionists' campaign posed a real problem for the Emergency Committee on Zionist Affairs, the leading Zionist body, which Wise chaired. ECZA officials made a number of attempts to persuade backers of the Bergson group to withdraw their support from the insurgents.[12] At the same time, the Zionist leaders sought to persuade the Bergsonites to abandon their independent course and join the efforts of the major Jewish organizations. In response to overtures from the ECZA, Bergson, on December 3, submitted his "First Proposal Made by the Committee for a Jewish Army to the Emergency Committee on Zionist Affairs." It began:

> Recognizing that all Zionist bodies should now be united in the demand for the formation of the Army, and further recognizing that all political actions directed toward the attainment of this goal should be centralized in the hands of an authoritative body, the Committee for a Jewish Army feels that all possible effort should be made to unify all forces and to widen the base of a common endeavor for the creation of the Army.

Bergson proposed that he would "leave to the Jewish Agency the conduct of political negotiations with the British and American governments" over the Jewish army issue. In exchange, the CJA would be given control of "all activities relating to the formation of the Army," meaning public relations; registration of would-be volunteers; organization and maintenance of training camps; and fund-raising for the project.[13] The CJA proposal thus sought to retain a wide measure of autonomy for the Bergson group within the overall framework of the ECZA. The willingness of the Bergsonites to come under the umbrella of the major Zionist bodies represented a tactical compromise. By themselves, the Bergsonites simply did not have the name recognition, contacts, or influence necessary to have a serious impact on international events. "For the sake of argument," CJA activist Bernard Fineman wrote to Peter Bergson,

> let us imagine that President Roosevelt asked the Committee to discuss the matter of a Jewish Army with him or with the Secretary of State. What Jews could we send whose names would be familiar to him? On the other hand, names like Stephen Wise, Albert Einstein, Rabbi Hillel Silva [sic], etc., are nationally known, and no Jewish movement of importance can be successful that excludes people of this calibre.[14]

The reply of the ECZA to the CJA proposal, however, made it clear that Wise and his colleagues were unwilling to place any significant amount of authority in the hands of the Bergson committee. The ECZA insisted on exercising exclusive control over propaganda efforts on behalf of the Jewish army: "The activity on behalf of the Jewish Army is to be carried forward under the aegis of the Emergency Committee for Zionist Affairs. [The ECZA] cannot relinquish its responsibility for the direction of the effort on behalf of the Jewish Army, the type of propaganda, etc." ECZA secretary Arthur Lourie stressed his group's intention to insure that CJA activities would "be in harmony with the policies of the Emergency Committee." The Bergson group's governing body, Lourie wrote, would have to include "a majority appointed by the Emergency Committee."[15] Gabriel Wechsler, national secretary of the army committee, replied that the CJA would not accept the idea of total ECZA control over its group. Lourie's curt response was, "[M]y Committee feels that no purpose is served by continuing these discussions."[16] But Wechsler was not willing to take no for an answer. He wrote Lourie again, this time offering "equal representation [for the ECZA] on a Committee of Policy as well as in the various executive positions on our Committee." Wechsler explained that "since we are a non-partisan, non-sectarian body, our Committee could not submit to control by your Committee, which is a strictly Zionist body, while nothing prevented your Zionist Committee from accepting representation on our Committee—representation which would give you a full share in the leadership of our work." Lourie did not respond.

The failure of the ECZA to reach an accord with Bergson disturbed even some who were usually sympathetic to the Jewish leadership. Thus Maurice Winograd, an editor of the *Daily Forward* and one of

Stephen Wise's "great admirers" (as he described himself), wrote to Dr. Wise that he was

> overcome by despair whenever new discords set in, dividing us further against ourselves.
>
> Why continue the fight against the Revisionists who have been maligned so cruelly all these years? Surely, you don't believe that Jabotinsky, that great Jew, was a "fascist," or that his followers are anything of the sort. (Would that there were more such "fascists" in the world today.)
>
> Thus, why not make peace, instead of widening the gap to the delight of our enemies in the British Colonial Office and elsewhere. There is plenty of division, plenty of opposition outside the Zionist movement.
>
> No, dear Dr. Wise, this isn't the way for an "Emergency Committee" to act—certainly not in the present crisis.[17]

The Jewish leadership ignored Winograd's complaint and continued working actively against Bergson's committee. By the summer of 1942, an internal memo from the Jewish army group's headquarters to its various chapter directors around the country complained that "a certain Mr. Roessler of Newark, N.J. who had accepted to be a chairman of our local committee, suddenly refused explaining that most of the Zionist leaders of Newark advised him against it." The memo added, "There is a similar situation in Saint Paul, Minnesota and also in several points in the South."[18]

A prominent newspaper publisher in Kansas confided to one of Bergson's men that local B'nai B'rith officials were pressuring him to refuse to print CJA ads. The local B'nai B'rith group, he said, "received a notice from the International B'nai B'rith advising them to do everything in their power to keep the newspapers from publishing any advertising regarding the stateless Jews and the Committee for a Jewish Army."[19]

In their public criticism of the Bergson committee, Stephen Wise and his colleagues tended to avoid debating the merits of the Revisionists' actual proposal. A five-point statement released by Wise in the name of the ECZA on February 17, 1942—immediately on the heels of the suspension of negotiations with the CJA—expressed support for the Jewish Agency's Jewish military unit plan; decried the Bergsonites' separate fund-raising drive as divisive; complained that the Bergson group's campaign was causing ''chaos'' in the Jewish community; and denied all connection between the ECZA and the Committee for a Jewish Army, which it described as being composed of ''persons formerly connected with an extreme section of the Revisionist organization.''[20]

In spite of the Jewish leaders' opposition, however, there is evidence that there was a steady growth in support for the Jewish army drive throughout 1942. One indication of this was the struggle that took place within the Jewish War Veterans organization over whether or not to endorse the Jewish army plan. In January, JWV national director Benjamin Kaufman bluntly refused to back the Bergson committee's campaign. ''[W]e have come to the conclusion that all of our efforts should be directed towards recruiting for the American Army instead,'' he wrote.[21] In May, however, the sizable Kings County [Brooklyn] Council of the JWV voted unanimously to endorse the Bergson army plan. Matters came to a head at the JWV annual convention, held in Scranton, Pennsylvania, from October 9 to October 11. After vigorous lobbying efforts by both sides, a resolution supporting the Jewish army idea was defeated by a vote of twelve to nine in the resolutions committee. Because of the narrow margin of defeat, the resolution was put to a floor vote and there defeated by a vote of just 1,035 to 970, or 51.6 percent to 48.4 percent. The fact that the resolution very nearly passed despite the active opposition of the JWV leadership is indicative of the depth of feeling in favor of the Jewish army campaign among rank-and-file JWV members.

There were further manifestations of the growing support for the army campaign during a July 21, 1942, AJCongress rally in New York called to protest the slaughter in Europe. Senator Henry Cabot Lodge, Jr., one of the guest speakers, unexpectedly called for the immediate formation of a Jewish army. The audience cheered wildly. When former Governor Herbert Lehman of New York spoke against the creation of a separate army, he was met by hisses, boos, and heckling by members of the audience.[22] The Revisionist organ *Zionews* cited this episode as proof of the gap between the Jewish ''masses'' and the leaders of the major Jewish organizations:

The reaction of the audience clearly showed that the Jewish masses have much more sense for realities than those who pretend to be their leaders, and that all the vacillation of Rabbi Wise...could not outweigh the straightforwardness of Senator Lodge's attitude, and the public's reaction to it.

. . . As long as Jewry will not be represented by leaders democratically elected, and directly responsible to the masses, there will always exist the dangerous discrepancy which vitiates all efforts to bring the Jewish problem nearer to a real solution.[23]

Several prominent Jewish publications began to express dissatisfaction with the Jewish leaders' position in the controversy. An editorial in *The Reconstructionist* asked:

If, as is now evident, *all* Zionists agree that a distinct Jewish unit should be organized, and if [the Bergsonites] have taken the initiative, do they not deserve support? And what is the trouble with our leaders that, in times like these, they cannot get together on so vital a question, particularly if they share a common viewpoint?[24]

The *Southern Jewish Weekly* was similarly critical, asking, "When will the authorized Jewish leaders in America take the cotton wadding out of their mouths and speak in public with the forensic force they use across coffee tables?[25]

There seem to have been pockets of Jewish army support even within the major Jewish organizations. Joe Weingarten, a national vice-chairman of the Zionist Organization of America, in August 1942 accepted co-chairmanship of the CJA's Southwest Division. Even Dr. Joseph Tenenbaum, a senior official of the American Jewish Congress and close aide to Stephen Wise, when contacted by the Bergson group, "took a positive stand to our Army plan, and, with some reservation, promised to cooperate," one of the Bergonites reported.[26] The dissatisfaction with the Jewish leadership that was prompting such defections was articulated by Harry Grayer, a former president of the Order Sons of Zion, one of the smaller American Jewish organizations:

Even devoted life-long Zionists have grown weary of resolutions, speeches, declarations, ineffectual repetition of ineffective phrases.

Do we want a Jewish Army to fight with the Allies and defend Palestine, or do we not? We should make up our minds first, and then speak our mind in clear, unequivocal and "undiplomatic" language.

Stop straddling, stalling, temporizing, equivocating. What is this foggy "Jewish Fighting Force Based on Palestine"? What master lexicographer coined that gem of innocuous desuetude?[27]

Bergson's success in attracting support from major political figures also won praise from the American Jewish media. When Sen. Edwin Johnson (D-Colorado) accepted the national chairmanship of the Jewish Army Committee in early 1943, the Independent Jewish Press Service commented:

Whatever else may be said about the Committee for a Jewish Army, it has displayed imagination and enterprise. Only these qualities could have resulted in obtaining Senator Edwin Johnson of Colorado as national chairman of the Committee. . . .

His acceptance of a post to head the controversial work of the Army Committee does his courage as well as his human sympathies credit.[28]

The CJA again splashed its demands across two full pages of the *New York Times* on December 7, 1942. The advertisement was headlined, "A Proclamation of the Moral Rights of the Stateless and Palestinian Jews" and was accompanied by a striking Arthur Szyk illustration of a Jewish soldier in battle. The text of the ad again demanded the creation of a Jewish army, "under their own insignia, on every battlefield of the world to which the United Nations' High Command will assign them."[29] Bergson exploited the colorful, symbolic value of the Jewish army proposal to attract potential supporters. "A Jewish Army marching valiantly to the front would seem like an instrument of divine retribution to the Germans," one ad vowed.[30] Another declared: "Suicide squads of the Jewish Army would engage in desperate commando raids deep into the heart of Germany. Jewish pilots would bomb German cities in reprisals."[31]

Bergson was offering Jews a chance at "revenge and survival," as he put it.[32] Most expressive of this angle of Bergsonite propaganda for the Jewish army was a poem the group distributed in late 1942. On August 17 of that year, *Life* magazine had carried on its cover an impressive photograph of a man identified as Bert "Yank" Levy, a "guerrilla warfare expert" in the United States Army. A poem of admiration, dedicated to Levy, was published in the *Saturday Review* and then reprinted and circulated by the Committee for a Jewish Army:

This is a son of warriors, of the Maccabees
Of David, of deep-thewed Samson, God-given Gideon
No banker this, no Doctor of German philosophy;
This is the Fighting Jew—the dark tense face,
Fierce and aware, lonely, waiting and watching
No banners here, no parades in front of the mayor
With flowers and politicians, no silly boasting
But the Eagles look, that once from the Walls of Jerusalem
Fell like an arrow into the Roman legions.

Jewish leaders had reason to fear the raw emotional appeal that such a campaign could have within the Jewish community. They were justifiably concerned that the Bergson boys could turn those emotions into practical support and create a serious mass movement in Jewish America which would usurp the authority of the major Jewish organizations. ECZA spokesman Arthur Lourie complained that "under the cover of the army idea, the [CJA] is creating an organization, unhappily with considerable success."[33] An official of the AJCommittee likewise privately bemoaned the fact that "the Jewish Army crowd is making great headway."[34]

In December 1942, Wise's ECZA approached the CJA in a new attempt to arrange a merger.[35] Even as tentative negotiations between the ECZA and CJA resumed, however, some factions within the ECZA were warning their constituents against assisting the Army Committee. A letter sent to the membership of the Zionist Organization of America from its leaders warned:

The Jewish Army Committee was organized. . . on the initiative of a group which, though not officially a committee of the Irgun, is composed of persons affiliated with that organization. As you know, the Irgun is the extreme wing of the Revisionist Party which seceded from the World Zionist Organization several years ago. Many of the sponsors of the Jewish Army Committee are non-Jews and non-Zionists. . . who are probably unaware of the fact that the Jewish Agency has been actively concerned with the problem since the war broke out.

Until a decision is reached, Z.O.A. members should refrain from contributing to or aiding the Committee for a Jewish Army.[36]

The negotiations ended inconclusively.

In the meantime, however, events in Europe had taken a dramatic turn for the worse. By the end of 1942, news of the extermination of Europe's Jews had been confirmed beyond any shadow of a doubt, and the quarrels over the Jewish army proposal seemed to pale into insignificance. When the Bergsonites and the American Jewish leaders would clash next, it would be over the life-and-death questions of how to save millions of Jews from Hitler.

The
Awful
Burden

$$\textcircled{6}$$

The first definitive report to document the massacres in Europe as a deliberate Nazi plan to annihilate the Jewish people was smuggled to London by the Jewish Socialist Bund of Poland in May 1942. The Bund Report substantially underestimated the number of Jews slain, putting the figure at 700,000; in fact, by that time a more accurate estimate would have been three times that number. Significantly, the report described the "death mobiles" by which Jews were gassed to death at the Chelmno concentration camp during the early stages of the Holocaust, before the gas chamber technique was perfected:[1]

Report of the Bund Regarding the Persecution of the Jews

From the day the Russo-German war broke out, the Germans embarked on the physical extermination of the Jewish population on Polish soil, using the Ukrainians and the Lithuanian fascists for this job. It began in Eastern Galicia, in the summer months of 1941. The following system was applied everywhere: men, fourteen to sixty years old, were driven to a single place — a square or a cemetery, where they were slaughtered or shot by machine guns or killed by hand grenades. They had to dig their own graves. Children in orphanages, inmates in old-age homes, the sick in hospitals were shot, women were killed in the streets. In many towns the Jews were carried off to "an unknown destination" and killed in adjacent woods. 30,000 Jews were killed in Lwów, 15,000 in Stanislawów, 5,000 in Tarnopol, 2,000 in Zloczów, 4,000 in Brzeżany (there were 18,000 Jews in this town, only 1,700 are left). The same happened in Zborów, Kolomyja, Sambor, Stryj, Drohobycz, Zbaraż, Przemyslany, Kuty, Sniatyn, Zaleszczyki, Brody, Przemyśl, Rawa Ruska and other places.

The murder actions were repeated in these towns many times. In some, they are still in progress—Lwów.

In the months of October and November, the same began to happen in Wilno, in the Wilno area and in Lithuania. 50,000 Jews were killed in Wilno during the month of November. 12,000 are now left in Wilno. The total number of the Jews murdered in a beastly fashion in the Wilno area and in Lithuania is 300,000, according to various estimates.

The killing of the Jews in the area of Slonim started in September. Almost all were murdered in Zyrowice, Lachowicze, Mir, Kossów and other places. In Slonim, the action started on October 15. Over 9,000 Jews were killed. In Równe the killing started during the first days of November. In three days over 15,000 people, men, women and children were killed. In Hancewicze (near Baranowicze) 6,000 Jews were shot. The action of killing Jews embraced all Polish territories beyond the San and the Bug. We have mentioned only some of the localities.

In November–December, the killing of Jews also began in the Polish territories incorporated into the Reich, the so-called Warthegau. The murder was accomplished by gassing in the hamlet of Chelmno, twelve kilometers from the town of Kolo (county of Kolo). A special automobile (a gas chamber) was used. Ninety persons were loaded each time. The victims were buried in special graves, in an opening in the Lubard Woods. The victims themselves had to dig their own graves before being killed. On the average, some one thousand persons were gassed every day. From November 1941 until March 1942, a total of 5,000 persons were gassed at Chelmno, Jewish residents of Kolo, Dabie, Bugaj, Izbica Kujawska, 35,000 Jews from the Lodz ghetto and a number of Gypsies.

The extermination of Jews in the territory of the so-called

Government-General started in February 1942. The beginning: Tarnów, Radom, where Gestapo and SS-men came to the Jewish quarters every day, killing the Jews on the streets, in the courtyards and in the homes. In March, the action of mass expulsion of the Jews out of Lublin started. Children and elderly people in the orphanages and old-age homes were murdered in a beastly fashion along with the patients in the hospital for general and epidemic diseases and numerous residents were killed in the streets and the homes. In all, there were over 2,000 victims. Some 25,000 Jews were carried off in "an unknown direction" out of Lublin, in sealed railway cars. They disappeared without a trace. Some 3,000 Jews were interned in barracks at Majdanek Tatarowy, a suburb of Lublin. No Jew has remained in Lublin. In Kraków, during the last days of March, fifty Jews were picked out from a list and shot in front of the gates. During the night of April 17–18, the Gestapo arranged a blood-bath in Warsaw. They dragged fifty Jews, men and women, from their homes, picking them from a prepared list, and killed them in a beastly fashion in front of their gates. Some they could not locate in their homes. Every day since April 18, they kill a couple of Jews in their homes or in the streets during daytime. This action proceeds according to a prepared list and embraces Jews of all levels in the Warsaw Ghetto. There is talk about more bloody nights. It is estimated that the Germans have already killed 700,000 Polish Jews.

The above facts indicate without any doubt that the criminal German Government has begun to realize Hitler's prophecy that in the last five minutes of the war, whatever its outcome, he will kill all the Jews in Europe. We firmly believe that the Hitlerite Germans will be held fully accountable for their fearful bestialities at the proper time. For the Jewish population, which is going through an unheard-of hell, such consolation is insufficient. Millions of Polish citizens of Jewish extraction are in immediate mortal danger.

We are, therefore, addressing ourselves to the Government of Poland, as the caretaker and representative of the entire population living on the soil of Poland, immediately to take up the necessary steps to prevent the destruction of Polish Jewry. The Polish Government should influence the Governments of the United Nations and the competent factors in those countries immediately to apply the policy of retaliation against the Germans and against the fifth column living in the countries of the United Nations and their allies. The Governments of Poland and the United Nations should let the German Government know of the application of the policy of retaliation. It should know that Germans in the USA and other countries will, already *now,* be held responsible for the beastly extermination of the Jewish population.

We are aware of the fact that we are requesting the Polish Government to apply unusual measures. This is the only possibility of saving millions of Jews from inevitable destruction.

May 1942

An official of the American Jewish Committee attended the Bund press conference in London on June 30 at which the Report was discussed, and reported back to his superiors in New York about the news. Ironically, he remarked that "the reports that seven hundred thousand Jews have been killed may be considered exaggerated and deceiving." But the AJCommittee representative affirmed the widespread conviction that "the Nazis have changed their tactics from persecution and humiliation towards actual physical extermination of the Jewish population in Poland."[2] The American Jewish Congress leadership, which likewise interpreted the Report as confirmation of fears that Hitler was embarking upon a systematic extermination campaign, announced that it would stage a mass protest rally at Madison Square Garden on July 21, 1942. The AJCommittee, on the other hand, refused to deviate from its ten-year policy of opposing public rallies. As one AJCommittee official explained it, "Parades and demonstrations" would only result in "a strengthening of the Nazi propaganda in America and the creation of a counter offensive in this country against the Jews."[3] Rather than co-sponsor the meeting, the AJCommittee's new president, Maurice Wertheim, merely sent a sympathetic telegram to the assembly. This prompted some barbed criticism of the AJCommittee in New York's Yiddish press: "The American Jewish Committee certainly owes an explanation as to what kind of 'Jewish' politics it is carrying on which holds it back from crying out at such a time when the Nazi massacres are more horrible than all massacres of Jews in the past," one newspaper complained.[4]

But the Committee was not alone in its policy of restraint. None of the featured speakers at the AJCongress rally demanded specific American action on behalf of the Jews in Europe. Stephen Wise, for example, stressed that Europe's Jews would be redeemed only "through a victory speedy and complete of the United Nations."[5]

The theory that Europe's Jews should be rescued not through Allied intervention on their behalf but rather solely through Allied military victory over the Nazis was put forward by Roosevelt administration officials as an excuse for their failure to save the Jews. Stephen Wise accepted this view during the early months of the war because he feared that American Jewish demands for special aid to European Jewry would give ammunition to those who accused American Jewry of dragging the United States into the war. Thus when A. Leon Kubowitzki of the World Jewish Congress privately urged Wise to call for a policy of Allied reprisals against the Germans as a response to the massacres of Jews, Wise objected; since the American people had not yet "completely thrown themselves" into the World War, Wise argued, American Jewish leaders should not request that special actions be initiated on behalf of the Jews.[6]

As the summer of 1942 wore on, the news from Europe went from bad to worse. On August 28, Wise received this cable from Gerhart Riegner, the World Jewish Congress representative in Geneva:

> Received alarming report that in Führer's headquarters plan discussed and under consideration according to which all Jews in countries occupied or controlled Germany numbering 3½-4 millions should after deportation and concentration in East be exterminated at one blow to resolve once for all the Jewish question in Europe stop the action reported planned for autumn methods under discussion including prussic acid stop we transmit information with all necessary reservation as exactitude cannot be confirmed stop informant stated to have close connections with highest German authorities and his reports generally speaking reliable.[7]

Wise responded by consulting Under-Secretary of State Sumner Welles, who asked him to refrain from publicizing the information until the State Department could confirm it through its own channels. Wise complied.[8] Meanwhile, a second cable arrived. The authors were Recha and Yitzhak Sternbuch, leaders of the Relief Association for Jewish Refugees, headquartered in Montreux, Switzerland; the conduit was the Polish Consulate in New York; the recipient was Jacob Rosenheim, leader of Agudas Israel, a U.S. Orthodox Jewish group. The message was grim:

According to recently received authentic information, the German authorities have evacuated the last ghetto in Warsaw, bestially murdering about one hundred thousand Jews. Mass murders continue. From the corpses of the murdered, soap and artificial fertilizers are produced. The deportees from other occupied countries will meet the same fate. It must be supposed that only energetic reprisals on the part of America could halt these persecutions. Do whatever you can to cause an American reaction to halt these persecutions. Do whatever you can to produce such a reaction, stirring up statesmen, the press, and the community. Inform Wise, Silver, Lubavitcher, Einstein, Klatzkin, Goldmann, Thomas Mann, and others.[9]

On September 4, representatives from all the major Jewish groups met to consider the two cables. The meeting ended without the attendees reaching agreement on a course of action. It was decided, instead, that a second meeting would be held under the chairmanship of Dr. Wise at the AJCongress offices two days later.[10] At the second meeting, on September 6, a variety of proposals were raised. None, however, was new or significant. They included an appeal to President Roosevelt to denounce the atrocities; an appeal to congressional leaders, church figures, and opinion-makers to condemn the Nazis; and a request that the State Department press neutral countries such as Argentina and Chile "to make representations to the German Government."[11] The only suggestion that substantially departed from the traditional position of the American Jewish leadership was a proposal "that the United States Government should be petitioned to warn Germany with reprisals against German aliens in this country if the massacres will continue."[12] Dr. Wise was not enthusiastic about any of the suggestions. He expressed doubts as to the accuracy of the Sternbuch cable and again mentioned his fears of a rise in anti-Semitism in the United States if there was too much agitation over the situation in Europe. Most of all, he stressed his conviction that the Jewish leadership should adhere to the State Department's demand that the news from Europe not be publicized until the details could be independently confirmed. Not everyone at the meeting accepted Wise's arguments. The representative from the Jewish Labor Committee, for instance, shouted, "If the Polish Jews will be annihilated, I don't care what is going to happen to the Jews here and to you and to your government!" In the end, however, Wise won the group's assent to ap-point a subcommittee of Jewish leaders to decide how to respond to the crisis.[13] The subcommittee, consisting of representatives of the AJCongress, AJCommittee, B'nai B'rith, JLC, and Union of Orthodox Rabbis, met on September 9. The five agreed not to take any action until Wise could meet with Under Secretary Welles again to learn if State had received any further information about the cables. AJCommittee official David Rosenblum, who attended the third meeting, noted to his superiors that the various suggestions raised at the first two meetings ''have been repeatedly resorted to during the last nine years without much effect, and there is no great hope that any of them can or would be effective now.'' Nevertheless, Rosenblum warned, the AJCommittee might soon come under ''pressure to do some of these things again,'' since ''there is the human desire to want to do something in the face of a great impending calamity.''[14]

Long weeks passed as Wise anxiously waited to hear from Welles. The weeks soon became months, and Wise was wracked with self-doubt. ''I don't know whether I am getting to be a Hofjude [court Jew],'' Wise confided to a friend, ''but I find that a good part of my work is to explain to my fellow Jews why our government cannot do all the things asked or expected of it.''[15]

Yet even as Wise waited for ''confirmation'' from the State Department, he and his colleagues already believed that the worst was true. In a letter to Sumner Welles in September, the AJCongress, AJCommittee, B'nai B'rith, and Jewish Labor Committee jointly urged the administration to protest the deportations of Jews from Vichy France. The letter included this line: ''In accordance with the announced policy of the Nazis to exterminate the Jews of Europe, hundreds of thousands of these innocent men, women and children have been killed in brutal mass murder.''[16] Nevertheless, Jewish leaders were not prepared to ask the United States to admit the French Jewish refugees. In September, Rep. Emanuel Celler proposed a congressional resolution authorizing the State and Justice departments to admit as refugees anyone living in France on September 15 ''upon proof being shown that said intended immigrants are refugees fleeing round-up, internment, castigation and punishment and other religious persecutions inspired or conducted by Nazi authorities or French officials under compulsion.'' The major Jewish organizations refused to lobby on behalf of the bill, which died in committee.

Samuel Margoshes, the AJCongress vice-president who was editor of the Yiddish-language daily *The Day,* defended the silence of the Jewish establishment on the grounds that the immigration question was an "extremely delicate" issue, a matter which Jews could not tamper with until there was evidence of "change in the attitude of both the government and the public towards immigration in the United States, rendering the whole subject less touchy."[17]

On November 24, Under Secretary of State Welles called Stephen Wise in to confirm the Riegner cable and release him from his pledge of silence. At a press conference that very afternoon, Wise disclosed the text of the cable to the world media. Wise's announcement was featured on the front pages of numerous newspapers around the nation the next morning, although some dailies were less generous (the *New York Times,* for example, placed it on page ten).

The subcommittee of Jewish leaders met in New York several days later (on November 30) and decided to dispatch a special delegation to meet with President Roosevelt. Wise then wrote to the President to ask if he was "prepared to receive a small delegation, which would include representatives of the American Jewish Committee, the American Jewish Congress, the B'nai B'rith." Wise stressed his reluctance to take up the President's valuable time:

> I do not wish to add an atom to the awful burden which you are bearing with magic and, as I believe, heaven-inspired strength at this time. But you do know that the most overwhelming disaster of Jewish history has befallen Jews in the form of the Hitler mass-massacres.
>
> I have had cables and underground advices for some months, telling of these things. I succeeded, together with the heads of other Jewish organizations, in keeping these out of the press. . . . The State Department has now received what it believes to be confirmation of these unspeakable horrors and has approved of my giving the facts to the press. The organizations banded together in the Conference of which I am chairman, feel that they wish to present to you a memorandum on this situation. . . . We hope above all that you will speak a word which may bring solace and hope to millions of Jews who mourn, and be an expression of the conscience of the American people.[18]

Roosevelt was indeed willing to say a "word," but not much more. On December 8, FDR met at the White House with Wise, Maurice

Wertheim of the AJCommittee, Adolf Held of the Jewish Labor Committee, Israel Goldstein of the Synagogue Council of America, Henry
Monsky of B'nai B'rith, and Rabbi Israel Rosenberg, chairman of the
Union of Orthodox Rabbis. The Jewish leaders presented Roosevelt
with a twenty-page booklet entitled "Blue-Print for Extermination,"
which provided country-by-country details on the slaughter of
Europe's Jews. Roosevelt expressed his shock and sympathy over the
plight of the persecuted Jews, but would make no promise of U.S.
action on their behalf. He would go no further than to authorize the
delegation to prepare a statement, in his name, acknowledging the
Nazi atrocities and expressing his revulsion at them. In the statement
that the Jewish leaders prepared and released to the press, however,
they went somewhat further; they quoted the President as promising
that the Allies "are prepared to take every possible step" to halt the
slaughter and to "save those who may still be saved."[19] Wise expressed enthusiasm over the meeting. He wrote to an associate, "We
ought to distribute cards throughout the country bearing just four letters, TGFR (Thank God For Roosevelt), and as the Psalmist would
have said, thank Him every day and every hour."[20]

Despite the overwhelming tragedy that had clearly engulfed world
Jewry, the meeting with Roosevelt was virtually the sum total of
public action by the American Jewish leadership in response to the
Riegner cable. The months of December, January, and February passed with hardly a whimper from the major American Jewish organizations. The only organized community-wide action was a national day
of fasting proclaimed for December 2. That prompted *The
Reconstructionist* to publish an angry editorial headlined "Fasting Is
Not Enough," which charged:

> The response of the Jewish people to the call to prayer and fasting in
> lamentations over the Jews exterminated by the Nazis was widespread
> and spontaneous. We participated in it, as we believe most Jews did
> who wanted to express their kinship with their fellow Jews in Nazi-
> dom. . . . [But] we raise a question as to the desirability of fasting and
> prayer when unaccompanied by any suggestion of an outlet to action
> for the emotions evoked.
>
> . . . To engage in religious ritual, to evoke mass emotion without
> channeling that emotion into a program of action, is dangerous on two
> counts. In the first place, it encourages that sentimental attitude which

finds so much solace in the lamentation over evil that it makes for complacency with evil. In the second place, by encouraging the illusion that prayer and fasting are effective in themselves, it leads to dangerous disillusionment, despair and defeatism when they prove ineffective.

In the future, it would be well if our leaders, before calling us to prayer and "affliction of soul," would suggest a course of action to which our ritualistic expression of mass emotion might stimulate us.[21]

The
Paramount
Consideration

7

The leaders of the American Jewish Committee gathered for their annual meeting in January 1943, at the very peak of the Holocaust. Yet the "Statement of Views" adopted unanimously and issued at the conclusion of the meeting ignored the Nazi annihilation of European Jewry. The twelve-paragraph statement began with a resounding affirmation of Jewish loyalty to America:

> At this time when our country is engaged in an epoch-making war, we, who are united with our brethren of all faiths in the common bond of American citizenship, pledge every effort and every sacrifice to the winning of the war, the achievement for the whole world of the Four Freedoms and the blessings of the Atlantic Charter and the establishment of a just and enduring peace.

The statement's only reference to the Jews of Europe was its call for postwar rights—for the "repatriation and rehabilitation" of the refugees, and "the complete restoration and safeguarding of their equal civil and religious rights."[1]

On January 20, the AJCongress announced that it would sponsor yet another "Stop Hitler Now" rally at Madison Square Garden, on the evening of February 2. The precise impetus for this rally is a matter of some dispute. At a December 29, 1942, meeting of the AJCongress leadership, the idea of staging a protest meeting seems to have been raised in response to information that Bergson's Committee for a Jewish Army was planning to hold such a demonstration. The minutes note, "The matter of holding a Madison Square Garden meeting was revived, in view of the information that the Jewish Army Committee is planning a similar meeting."[2] No doubt the last thing Stephen Wise wanted was for the Bergsonites to be seen as spearheading the Jewish community's response to the Holocaust, stealing away the mantle of leadership from the established Jewish organizations.

In December 1942, Bergson and his colleagues had decided on a dramatic shift in emphasis. Although they would continue to function as the Committee for a Jewish Army, the new focus of their activities was the plight of the Jews in Europe. Their first proposed project was a pageant entitled "We Will Never Die." Its author was Ben Hecht, an acclaimed playwright who had little interest in Jewish affairs until his imagination was fired by the sensationalist tactics of the Bergson crowd. On January 26, Hecht dispatched invitations to thirty-three Jewish groups to participate in a meeting at his hotel suite in New York in order to "co-operate in the organization of an all-Jewish mass demonstration at Madison Square Garden featuring a pageant dramatizing the German war of extermination against the Jews."[3] Although the meeting was widely attended, none of the participants would make a commitment to co-sponsor the pageant. The AJCommittee representative at the meeting considered the project meritorious, but recommended that the AJCommittee steer clear of the Bergson militants nonetheless. "Obviously, we as a Committee should have nothing to do with this venture," the memo recommended.[4]

One result of the meeting may have been that when it was disclosed that the pageant would not get under way until early March, the AJCongress staff realized that it could postpone its own Madison Square Garden rally without having to fear that the Bergsonites would beat them to it. What is clear is that the Congress did then delay its rally until March 1, and gave no explicit reason for the postponement.

When the Bergsonites learned that the AJCongress planned its Madison Square Garden rally for approximately the same date as the opening performance of their pageant, they decided to propose that the two projects be combined. CJA national secretary Gabriel Wechsler wrote to AJCongress vice-president Louis Lipsky and "offered the Congress joint sponsorship in 'We Will Never Die,'" with the pageant performance to be followed by a "political mass meeting." A copy of the pageant script was provided to Lipsky in order to demonstrate "that there were no ideological differences between this presentation and the American Jewish Congress." According to the Bergson boys, the AJCongress leaders both rejected the offer and formally "decided as a matter of policy to hamper and destroy any activities of our Committee no matter how worthwhile."[5]

Hecht recalled that Stephen Wise then telephoned him to try to persuade him to abandon the pageant project. "I must ask you to cancel this pageant and discontinue all your further activities in behalf of the Jews," Wise is said to have urged. He added, "If you wish hereafter to work for the Jewish Cause, you will please consult me and let me advise you."[6] Hecht and Bergson ignored Wise's opposition and went about organizing the opening performance of "We Will Never Die." In a real political coup, they succeeded in convincing Governor Thomas E. Dewey of New York to declare March 9, the scheduled opening of the pageant, a Day of Mourning for European Jewry. According to the Bergsonites, Wise tried to persuade Dewey to revoke the proclamation. Samuel Merlin charged that "A high-ranking and respected official of the [American Jewish] Congress wrote to Governor Dewey asking him not to declare March 9 a day of mourning as 'We Will Never Die' was run by persons who were irresponsible and that such action by the Governor would offend the great mass of American Jewry."[7] Isaac Zaar, a Bergson group activist, recalled the incident in almost identical language.[8] According to Hecht's version, Wise himself brought a delegation of "twelve important Jews" to Albany to influence Dewey to cancel the declaration and even threatened him with a loss of the Jewish vote in his reelection campaign if he did not sever all ties with the "dangerous and irresponsible racketeers who are bringing terrible disgrace on our already harassed people."[9]

Ironically, even as the AJCongress was beginning what was to become a years-long battle against the Bergson militants, its own leaders were adopting more militant positions on issues relating to the rescue of Europe's Jews. They were not yet going so far as to specifically criticize the Roosevelt administration or its restrictionist immigration policies, but there were the first stirrings. On the eve of the March 1 rally,

Stephen Wise wrote in *Opinion:* "Children must be saved. Havens of refuge must be provided for those who are able to escape. Immigration regulations must for a time be waived or suspended."[10] The AJCongress was not yet willing to challenge Roosevelt, but an editorial in *Congress Weekly* did ask: "[I]t is our American patriotism, our love for this country and its institutions, our belief in the historic role assigned to America in the leadership of humanity, which prompts the question, *Why is the Congress of the United States silent?*"[11] Wise made his most militant declaration at a speech in Detroit the day before the rally. He told the audience at the Casa Temple, "I do not believe my country is so poor in spirit as to deny refuge to such handfuls as may escape the Hitler morgue and come to our shores."[12]

The March 1 meeting marked the first tentative attempt by the American Jewish leadership to advocate some sort of change in U.S. immigration policy. Over 37,000 people heard the sponsors —including every major Jewish group as well as a host of smaller ones, the only exception being the AJCommittee—issue an eleven-point declaration, including a limited call for changes in U.S. immigration policy:

> The procedure that now prevails in the administration of existing immigration law in the United States, which acts as deterrent and retardation of legal immigration under the established quotas, should be revised and adjusted to the war conditions and in order that refugees from Nazi-occupied territories may find sanctuaries here within such quotas.[13]

Although this went further than anything else suggested by American Jewish leaders since the rise of Hitler, it was still inadequate in relation to the magnitude of the European crisis. For even if a more liberal administrative procedure was implemented, the maximum number of Jews from Greater Germany and Poland who could be admitted would have been less than 28,000 annually. The minimalist approach adopted by the AJCongress at its March 1 rally was pleasing to Joseph Proskauer, the sixty six year old former judge who had just succeeded Maurice Wertheim as president of the American Jewish Committee. Proskauer praised the March 1 rally for its conservative tone: "It was decently conducted; it was addressed by prominent speakers; it was not flamboyant or vulgar and was the complete antithesis in these respects of a subsequent mass meeting that was held under the auspices of the Jewish Army Group."[14]

The most significant outcome of the March 1 rally was a willingness on the part of all the major Jewish organizations to have their representatives cooperate under the auspices of a newly formed Joint Emergency Committee on European Jewish Affairs. Included as members were the AJCongress, AJCommittee, B'nai B'rith, JLC, Synagogue Council of America, Union of Orthodox Rabbis, American Emergency Committee for Zionist Affairs, and Agudas Israel. One group which was not included was Bergson's Committee for a Jewish Army. At the first meeting of the JEC, on March 15, it was decided to inform the CJA "that its presence was not desired."[15] In an *Opinion* editorial hailing the establishment of the Joint Emergency Committee, Stephen Wise felt compelled to explain why the Bergsonites were being prevented from joining the new coalition:

> [T]hings have been said and done by the Jewish Army Committee which are—to lapse into understatement—gravely menacing to the unity and security of American Jewish life. If a sobering sense of responsibility should come to those who have elevated themselves to the place of heads of the Jewish Army Committee, it may become possible to deal with them, but only after they have ceased to publish their glaring, garish, sometimes misleading advertisements in the daily press.[16]

Not content to simply deny the Bergsonites membership in the Joint Committee, however, the major Jewish groups set out to actively obstruct their separatist activities. The decision to campaign against Bergson was no doubt fueled by the increasing success with which Bergson's projects were meeting. His pageant, "We Will Never Die," was a tremendous success in its two-performance opening night at the Garden, playing to a packed house and winning rave reviews in the major newspapers. The Jewish leadership must have been especially alarmed by signs that some community leaders seemed to be contemplating cooperating with the pageant project. For example, Richard Gutstadt, director of the B'nai B'rith's Anti-Defamation League in Chicago, wrote to an AJCommittee official to suggest that "there may be a basis for some collaboration" between the Jewish establishment and the dissidents on this particular project. "Proffers will, I assume, undoubtedly be made for some joint sponsorship, and I should prefer that an affair of such magnitude should have its presentation accompanied by a fine dignity and excellent sponsorship."[17] The Gutstadt letter prompted inquiries from other community figures as to whether or not "there has been some change of feeling with reference to the Committee for a Jewish Army, and also with reference to the presentation of the pageant in the various communities."[18]

There had, in fact, been no change of feeling at all. As "We Will Never Die" and its crew took to the road to begin a national tour, the Jewish leadership's attacks followed along. In Kingston, New York, a scheduled performance of the pageant was called off after pressure from the American Jewish Congress and the Zionist Organization of America. In Gary, Indiana, "all of the Jewish organizations met" after learning of a plan to present "We Will Never Die" locally, and "unanimously agreed to present a demand to the American Legion [the local sponsoring group] that it be stopped." In Buffalo, AJCongress officials interfered in attempts to organize a benefit luncheon for "We Will Never Die" and "even managed to produce a scandal at the luncheon itself," a Bergson activist recalled. "All entries and halls of the Hotel Statler were watched by their men who stopped everyone going into the luncheon room and succeeded in convincing most of them not to join us at the luncheon."[19]

The Jewish leaders were horrified when they learned that Bergson was planning to publish a newspaper advertisement featuring a Ben Hecht poem "saying that there's going to be a very happy Christmas this year because by December there just wouldn't be any Jews left for the Christian world to spit at," according to a journalist who caught wind of the controversy.[20] In his memoirs, Hecht attributed the anger over the advertisement to the B'nai B'rith, whose leaders argued "that if we print such a full page ad in The Times, the American State Department will raise Hell with the Jews of America." Bergson warned Hecht that, according to Joseph Proskauer of the American Jewish Committee, "such an anti-Christian attitude could well bring on Jewish pogroms in the U.S.A."[21]

The unceasing flow of atrocity reports and the increased activity by Jewish organizations helped fuel a growing public sympathy for the Jews of Europe. This sympathy did not escape the attention of Allied policymakers, who scrambled to preempt pro-refugee agitation. In January and February, the British Foreign Office and U.S. State

Department exchanged barbed notes blaming each other for not providing havens for refugees. Finally, in a memorandum dated February 25, State Department officials suggested that British and American representatives confer in Ottawa to discuss the refugee controversy. The British accepted the proposal. Later, the site of the talks was changed to Bermuda, to which the public and media would have limited access due to wartime travel restrictions. The Roosevelt administration prepared for the Bermuda conference with the intention of adhering strictly to its traditional immigration policy. Secretary of State Cordell Hull made this clear in a March 3 note to his British counterparts, citing as the continued basis of U.S. policy Myron Taylor's declaration at Evian (in 1938) opposing the "dumping of unfortunate peoples in large numbers." The man chosen to head the United States delegation to Bermuda was Dr. Harold Dodds, president of Princeton University and someone who could be counted on to loyally defend administration policy. Another key member of the delegation was Rep. Sol Bloom (D-New York) who, although himself Jewish, had staunchly defended Roosevelt's refugee policies. (Behind the scenes, Bloom had been actively pressing State Department officials to have Peter Bergson deported from the United States on the ground that Bergson's militant activities "would eventually provoke sufficient antagonism among the citizens of the United States to cause anti-Semitic pogroms."[22]) Joining Bloom on the U.S. delegation was Sen. Scott Lucas (D-Illinois). A three-man advisory delegation was to include George Warren of the President's Advisory Committee on Political Refugees, George Backer of the Jewish rehabilitation group ORT, and Robert Alexander of the State Department's Visa Division.

As preparations got under way for the April 19 opening of the Bermuda conference, the first murmurs of criticism were heard in the American Jewish community. A columnist for Stephen Wise's *Opinion* questioned the purpose of the gathering, and noted warnings in the press that it would be an Evian-style farce:

> Besides, one wonders why another conference at all? What is needed now—and now before it is too late and all in vain—is that the United States and Great Britain declare openly to Germany for the whole world to hear: "You say you don't want the Jews. Very well, then, we will take them off your hands." This is the core of the whole matter. All else is detail. *The Nation* already calls this suggested conference

another Evian, warning not to expect anything because the United States Government did nothing while the Jews are being exterminated in Europe.[23]

Criticism was not reserved for the Allies. American Jewish leaders, too, were targeted. The Independent Jewish Press Service *Bulletin* featured an editorial with some harsh things to say about the performance of the Jewish establishment:

Now let's be frank about this, our dear Leaders. Isn't it a fact that for ten years you have been trooping up to the State Department with bated breath and hat in hand—and getting the run-around? Politely, of course.

Then why didn't you report back to us, the Jewish people of America, so that we could try to do something about it before it was too late? What could we have done? We could have done what other Americans do when their kinsmen are threatened with danger and death. We could have brought pressure to bear on Congress, on the President, on the State Department—*mass* pressure, not just the backstairs "diplomacy" of your hush policy. It is too easy for a government official to say No when he knows it isn't going any further.

When you found that you were getting nowhere with your backstage wire-pulling you should have stood up and said so, loud and clear, so that every Jew in America could hear it, and every Gentile too. That would have been the democratic thing to do. Then we, the people, could have done the next democratic thing. We could have organized a mass movement to back you up. Instead of doing that you hushed up your failure.[24]

In another sign of growing restlessness within the Jewish community, a group of students from the Conservative rabbinical institution, the Jewish Theological Seminary, issued a declaration entitled "Retribution Is Not Enough," which was published in *The Reconstructionist*. "We Jews who live in the serenity of America have failed to grasp the immensity of the tragedy which has befallen our people, and this failure is perhaps the greatest part of the tragedy," the students wrote. "What have the rabbis and leaders...done to arouse themselves and their communities to the demands of the hour? What have the rabbinical bodies...attempted in order to impress upon

110

their congregations the necessity for action now?'' The appeal concluded with a six-point program for practical action, including a demand for the rescue of Jews from countries threatened with Nazi invasion; ''pressure on the United Nations to obtain refuge for Jews,'' with a specific demand ''that the United States allow Jews to settle in the Virgin Islands.... If the United States will not change its immigration laws, then efforts should be made to establish internment camps here for those refugees until the war ends''; pressure on the Allies ''to open up Palestine for large-scale immigration''; a demand for Allied food shipments to starving Jewish populations in Europe; the creation of ''a Jewish army to be composed of Palestinian and stateless Jews''; and a demand that the Allies ''fully publicize the atrocities against the Jews.''[25] In a follow-up editorial, *The Reconstructionist*'s staff gave ''hearty endorsement'' to the students' call. ''It may not be feasible to carry through the whole program outlined by the Seminary students,'' the editorial conceded, ''but we must do everything humanly possible in this situation.''[26]

The Jewish establishment was not immune to such complaints. The problem of grassroots Jewish dissatisfaction as well as the ongoing slaughter in Europe were both on the agenda of the Jewish leaders as they deliberated over what position to take with regard to Bermuda. In a series of meetings during March and April, representatives of the groups comprising the Joint Emergency Committee on European Jewish Affairs hammered out a memorandum to be sent to each of the delegates to the Bermuda gathering as well as to Under Secretary of State Sumner Welles. The introduction to the paper included some rare implicit criticism of Allied apathy. ''So far as is known,'' the memo asserted, ''the United Nations have as yet taken no decisive action to rescue as many of the victims marked for death as could be saved.'' The body of the statement, however, merely incorporated the proposals adopted at the March 1 rally, including the call for the Allies to negotiate with the Nazis in order to secure free Jewish emigration from Europe; for the establishment of ''a number of Sanctuaries'' in unspecified ''Allied and neutral countries''; and for England to permit unlimited Jewish immigration to Palestine. The Jewish leaders ignored the demand of the Jewish Theological Seminary students that the United States be urged to permit refugees to settle in the Virgin Islands. The only reference in the memo to the issue of refugees entering the United States was a reiteration of the call made at the March 1 rally for a change in the administration of U.S. immigration procedures, "within the quotas."[27]

Although the final text of the memorandum was temperate, the mood within the Joint Emergency Committee was not. There were outbursts of dissent over the tradition of fealty to the Roosevelt administration's position. Carl Sherman of the American Jewish Congress complained that if the JEC "acquiesced to the wishes" of the State Department, it would be bound to U.S. policy and thus "our meetings are useless." Henry Montor, of the United Palestine Appeal, suggested a day of lobbying of congressmen by Jews from all across America. Dr. Israel Goldstein, of the Synagogue Council of America, asserted that "public opinion is ahead of the government's attitude and we have to press the State Department with our maximum demands." Nahum Goldmann, of the World Jewish Congress, warned against suggestions that the JEC ask for permission to send its own representative to Bermuda; he feared that the presence of Jewish "experts" there would be used by the Allies as "an alibi" for inaction.[28]

When the Roosevelt administration ignored the JEC's recommendations for Bermuda, Goldmann was furious. He demanded that the JEC sponsor a mass meeting of "1,000 to 2,000 representatives of all Jewish organizations," to which the media would be invited, to publicize "the failure of our efforts to have our large program discussed at the Bermuda Conference." According to the minutes of the April 18 JEC meeting, Goldmann "expressed the view that the time has come to change our policy. We have to oppose the American and British governments' attitude and act accordingly in our mass meetings and elsewhere. We have to insist on the fulfillment of our program."[29]

But Goldmann and the others who were inclined toward greater activism were a minority within the Joint Emergency Committee. Stephen Wise ran roughshod over the dissidents' proposals, engineering a "compromise" according to which their suggestions were referred to a subcommittee consisting of the Joint Committee's five co-chairmen. A central figure in this five-man quietist faction was Joseph Proskauer of the AJCommittee. Proskauer later reported to his colleagues that although "the spirit I encountered at the first meeting [of the JEC] was to rely entirely on the mass meeting technique," he was later able to "change all this" and persuade a majority on the Committee to put their faith in private meetings with government officials.[30]

Despite the efforts of Wise and Proskauer to stymie rumblings of militancy within their ranks and to dissociate themselves from the antics of the Bergson group, senior Roosevelt administration officials made little distinction between the various Jewish groups. In a diary entry from the first day of the Bermuda conference, Assistant Secretary of State Breckinridge Long attributed to Wise a series of activities sponsored by the Bergsonites—including a Senate resolution introduced by the national chairman of the Bergson Group and full-page advertisements sponsored by Bergson:

> One Jewish faction under the leadership of Rabbi Stephen Wise has been so assiduous in pushing their particular cause—in letters and telegrams to the President, the Secretary and Welles—in public meetings to arouse emotions—in full page advertisements—in resolutions to be presented to the conference—that they are apt to produce a reaction against their interest. Many public men haved signed their broadsides and Johnson of Colorado introduced their resolution into the Senate.[31]

The actual proceedings of the Bermuda conference were never made public, but it became clear immediately upon the close of the meeting that there had been no dramatic change in Allied policy toward the Jews. Within the American Jewish leadership, reaction was mixed. Dr. Israel Goldstein, president of the Synagogue Council of America, declared the conference "not only a failure, but a mockery."[32] But Goldstein was in the minority. The response among most leaders of the major Jewish organizations was far milder. Stephen Wise wrote in *Opinion* that Bermuda had been "a woeful failure," but he pointedly avoided criticizing President Roosevelt or his administration. In a private note to Nahum Goldmann, Wise strongly cautioned against any public criticism of FDR:

> It is very easy to hold press conferences and to call meetings, but we must in advance consider what it will lead to—that it will shut every door and leave us utterly without hope of relief as far as FDR is concerned. He is still our friend, even though he does not move as expeditiously as we would wish. But he moves as fast as he can, in view of the Congress on his hands, a bitterly hostile and in a very real sense partially anti-Semitic Congress.[33]

In a second letter to Goldmann, Wise complained that "wild people" in the Joint Emergency Committee were interested in "calling President Roosevelt and the State Department names." Wise feared that such action might arouse anti-Semitism in the United States. To declare "that the President and our government will not do anything for the refugees," Wise wrote, "is morally and perhaps even physically suicidal."[34] Like the AJCongress, the AJCommittee was reluctant to challenge the Roosevelt administration over the results of Bermuda. Its journal, *Contemporary Jewish Record,* published no criticism of the American performance at the refugee gathering.[35]

The official U.S. position, as articulated at Bermuda and afterwards, was that the best way to rescue European Jews was through successful prosecution of the war effort. This position inevitably put American Jewish leaders on the defensive, since it carried with it the implication that rescue advocates were more interested in Jewish needs than in a swift Allied victory over the Axis. American Jewish leaders faced an ongoing conflict over whether or not to advocate aid to Jewish refugees at the risk of provoking accusations of disloyalty against American Jews. Some Jewish groups came down squarely on the side of the administration's "rescue through victory" stand. An editorial in the official journal of the B'nai B'rith declared, in early 1943: "There is only one way to stop the Nazi massacres and that is by crushing the Nazis in battle, wholly, completely, and irrevocably, without questions, without 'negotiations,' without asking for quarter or giving it. Meanwhile—everything for Victory!"[36]

Officials of the AJCommittee shared this defeatist attitude toward rescue. "I am not sure that very much can be done except to lick Hitler and stop Hitler," wrote one.[37] "[I]f anything could possibly be done, say, to stop Hitler from murdering Jews or anybody else, it would long ago have been done by the British and American Governments," counseled another. "The truth is, however, that the only way to stop Hitler is to defeat him in battle." This particular paragraph, included in the original draft of a letter sent by an aide of Morris Waldman, was omitted from the final draft.[38] But in a memorandum for an official AJCommittee position paper on the war, Waldman himself was even blunter:

[T]he paramount consideration for us Jews should be to do everything possible to help the democratic forces in this titanic struggle and to do

114

nothing that will embarrass or weaken those forces. This should be the fundamental principle, the essential criterion of our Jewish interests and activities, the consideration to which all such interests must be subordinated, regardless of the extent and nature of our sacrifices.[39]

But the slow pace of the Allied advances, the unceasing massacres of European Jewry, and the bitter disappointment of Bermuda left some Jewish leaders wondering just how viable the "rescue through victory" position really was. When the Joint Emergency Committee met on May 24 to draft a letter to Sumner Welles about the failure of the Bermuda conference, the mood was increasingly militant. A minority of those in attendance still recoiled at the idea of Jews opposing the policies of the U.S. government; Joseph Proskauer disapproved of one draft because the "whole tone of the letter" was critical of the State Department, and Harris Perlstein of the Jewish Welfare Fund argued that Jews should not criticize the American government "in view of the fact that American soldiers were giving their lives." But the final wording that the majority approved implicitly challenged the "rescue through victory" concept: "To relegate the rescue of the Jews of Europe, the only people marked for total extermination, to the day of victory is...virtually to doom them to the fate which Hitler has marked out for them."[40]

While the Jewish leaders confined their criticism to a private letter, others took bolder stands. Rep. Emanuel Celler openly declared on the floor of the House of Representatives that "victory is not the only solution":

Victory, the spokesmen [for the Allies] say, is the only solution. In the meantime, let the millions guilty of no wrongdoing be trampled to death, their lives snuffed out by lethal gases and guns, the women outraged and the children mangled. After victory, the disembodied spirits will not present so difficult a problem; the dead no longer need food, drink and asylum.[41]

Peter Bergson likewise criticized the Allies and scoffed at the idea that the rescue of Europe's Jews should be subordinated to the war effort. Bergson pulled few punches and heeded few of his opponents. Sen. Scott Lucas, one of the American delegates to Bermuda, had warned

Bergson privately that criticism of the U.S. position at Bermuda might cause anti-Semitism. "[W]e are playing with dynamite," Lucas wrote.[42] Bergson was not impressed. As soon as the conference concluded, Bergson placed in the *New York Times* another of what Stephen Wise called his "lurid and garish" full-page advertisements. "To 5,000,000 Jews in the Nazi Death Trap, Bermuda Was a 'Cruel Mockery,'" the headline bluntly proclaimed. "Not only were ways and means to save the remaining four million Jews in Europe not devised" at Bermuda, the advertisement charged, "but their problem was not even touched upon, put on the agenda, or discussed."[43] Although the ad was signed by the "Committee for a Jewish Army of Stateless and Palestinian Jews," it made clear that the Jewish Army proposal would be taking a back seat to Bergson's chief demand: the creation of a special Allied rescue agency to save Jews from Hitler. The ad's two demands were:

1. Immediate utilization of all existing possibilities of transfer of Jews from Hitler-dominated countries to Palestine or to any temporary refuge and the initiation of all further possibilities in this program.
2. The immediate creation of a Jewish army of stateless and Palestinian Jews, including "suicide" Commando squads, and Air Squadrons for retaliatory bombing, which will raid deep into Germany, thus participating as an entity in the war and bringing their message of hope to Hitler's victims.[44]

While the Bergson group worked through the newspapers and the public, the Joint Emergency Committee sought to utilize conventional channels; it decided to seek a direct audience with President Roosevelt to discuss the outcome of the Bermuda gathering. On April 28, Stephen Wise wrote to the President, in the name of the AJCongress, AJCommittee, B'nai B'rith, and JLC, requesting an appointment "in the light of the continuing annihilation of our fellow Jews and the negative results of the Bermuda Conference." Wise stressed that the group would ask for U.S. intervention "without, of course, to the slightest degree impairing our war effort."[45] But Wise's polite request fell on deaf ears. Two weeks passed before Wise was even accorded the dignity of a reply from the President's secretary. The reply was negative. Wise's many years of loyal service to "the Chief" had yielded few dividends. At one of the most crucial moments in recent Jewish history, Wise's faith in FDR had proven to be badly misplaced.

There
May
Be No
Jews
Left To Save

8

There was significant movement toward Jewish interorganizational unity in early 1943. The terrible slaughter in Europe was an important impetus. It overshadowed everything American Jews did, making the petty quarrels that divided the various Jewish factions seem criminally irresponsible. The intensified domestic competition posed by the Bergson activists was also a factor. It forced the major Jewish organizations to realize that a failure to close ranks could mean surrender of the mantle of communal leadership to the young upstarts whom they so feared and despised.

Despite the confirmation in 1942 of the hideous details of the Holocaust, the issue of rescue was absent from the agenda when eighty Jewish leaders representing all the major groups met in Pittsburgh in late January. The conferees issued a declaration which called for the convening of an "American Jewish Assembly." The assembly would be held "within five months" and would have as its aims:

(a) to consider and recommend action on problems relating to the rights and status of Jews in the postwar world.

(b) to consider and recommend action upon all matters looking to

117

the implementation of the rights of the Jewish people with respect to Palestine.

(c) to elect a delegation to carry out the program of the American Jewish Assembly in cooperation with the duly accredited representatives of Jews throughout the world.[1]

Henry Monsky of the B'nai B'rith, in a speech to the gathering, urged that American Jewry's "first and primary responsibility to be discharged, at whatever price and sacrifice, in cooperation with all groups that make up the United Nations, is to win the war."[2]

Neither the steady stream of news reports about the ongoing massacres nor the obvious failure of the Bermuda conference persuaded the Jewish leaders to alter the proposed agenda of the assembly. The official announcement of the forthcoming conference, issued in April, blandly repeated the three-point program adopted four months earlier in Pittsburgh.[3]

In June, the AJCongress formulated a ten-point program which it hoped the gathering would adopt. The proposals did not, however, include any mention of rescuing Jews from Hitler:

1. The recognition of the right of the Jewish people to be heard at the peace conference.

2. The assurance of equal rights, such as obtain in the United States and as are set forth in the Four Freedoms and the Atlantic Charter, for every individual Jew in all countries of the world.

3. The recognition of Jewish group rights in all lands where such rights are accorded to others.

4. Compensation and reparation for losses suffered by Jews in Germany and Nazi-occuped territories.

5. Freedom to return to the lands from which the Jews were driven by the Nazis and opportunities for migration and settlement in other lands for Jews who cannot or do not wish to return to their former homes.

6. The trial and punishment of the criminals responsible for the torture and murder of the Jews, as well as others, in Germany and Nazi-occupied territories.

7. The establishment of an appropriate United Nations agency responsible for the rehabilitation of the Jews.

8. The outlawing of anti-Semitism by international regulation.

9. The establishment of Palestine as a Jewish Commonwealth through free immigration under Jewish administration and control.

10. The implementation of this program by the American Jewish community in cooperation with the accredited representatives of the Jewish communities of the world.[4]

The June 18 edition of *Congress Weekly* was devoted entirely to the upcoming conference. Five lengthy articles discussed the purpose and significance of the gathering; none urged either rescue initiatives nor the possibility of more Jewish refugee immigration to the United States.[5]

In July, Stephen Wise penned his final pre-conference "Forecast." He listed the objectives of the assembly as a united Jewish agreement

respecting three leading problems. One, the status of Jews in the post-war world, including the right of repatriations. . . two, the indefensible right of expatriate Jews to migrate to the lands, large or small, within the United Nations, and, finally, the duty of the United Nations to make it possible for Jews as a people to rebuild their Jewish National Home.[6]

The assembly plan had drawn early opposition from the leaders of the American Jewish Committee, who were

opposed to the convoking of any such large body on the ground that it would tend to increase anti-Semitism in the U.S. very greatly; that anti-Semitism was already growing appreciably in Washington and other parts of the country, and that such a large Jewish gathering would be bound to have that result.[7]

Later, however, AJCommittee president Joseph Proskauer softened his position, insisting only upon "the change of name from 'Assembly' to 'Conference,' so that the public will not be misled into believing that the Jews have set up a political organization." When the conference sponsors subsequently agreed to change its name from "assembly," the AJCommittee withdrew its opposition. Organizational unity apparently had been achieved. Nevertheless, the Jewish public exhibited little enthusiasm for the conference, as one *Congress Weekly* columnist conceded:

It is not difficult to understand the initial reaction of distrust, and even of fear, regarding the entire idea of the Conference. Jews, ordinary Jews with sound national instincts, asked apprehensively when they first heard of the Conference: "What! Another organization! Is this the solution for a people that stands on the brink of annihilation?"[8]

Grassroots pressure for meaningful action seemed to be building. A Maryland rabbi wrote to one of the organizers of the AJConference that the emphasis on postwar problems "is a very laudable initiative but the problem of saving millions of Jews who are yet in Europe and are facing annihilation, will not be touched upon."[9] Rabbi Meyer Berlin, leader of the religious Zionist movement in Palestine, appeared at the July 15 meeting of the Joint Emergency Committee. According to the minutes, he

> complained bitterly about the indifference, inadequate action and lack of feeling on the part of the American Jews compared with the Palestine Jews. They engage in street demonstrations, sign huge petitions, close shops and also manifest their feelings by other means. They are discouraged by the silence of the American Jews.[10]

Stephen Wise was on the defensive. He replied to Berlin by asserting that he and his colleagues had already done for European Jewry "everything that was practically possible."[11] Ironically, Wise was backed by Nahum Goldmann. In April, Goldmann had urged mass protests and vociferous criticism of the Allies. By July, he was deeply pessimistic about the efficacy of public protests. At the July 15 meeting, Goldmann declared that mass meetings were "futile"; he recommended instead that the Jewish leaders concentrate on influencing small groups of Gentiles to express their sympathy with the plight of Europe's Jews.[12]

Wise and Goldmann were repeatedly challenged by colleagues who demanded militant action. At the August 10 meeting of the JEC, Maurice Wertheim of the AJCommittee proposed a "march on Washington" by Jewish leaders to dramatize their demands.[13] At the same meeting, AJCongress deputy Lillie Shultz boldly suggested the use of election-year Jewish political pressure to force concessions from the Roosevelt administration on the refugee question. The minutes of the meeting report:

> The time has come, she said, to be critical of lack of action and in view of the fact that this is the eve of a presidential election year, ways can be found

to indicate to the administration, and possibly through the political parties that the large and influential Jewish communities will find a way of registering at the polls its [sic] dissatisfaction over the failure of the administration to take any effective steps to save the Jews of Europe.[14]

Wise could not ignore such rumblings indefinitely. If he failed to address them, his position of leadership in the community would be threatened. A week before the scheduled opening of the American Jewish Conference in August, *Congress Weekly* for the first time addressed the conspicuous absence from the conference agenda of the European Holocaust. "The primary task of the American Jewish Conference," the *CW* editorial maintained, "is to deal with the postwar Jewish situation." But for the first time it declared, "[I]t is safe to presume that the pressing question of immediate rescue action will be a principal item on the agenda." Why the postwar situation was "primary" while the raging Holocaust merely "a principal item" was not explained. The editorial reflected the confused attitude of the AJCongress leadership, as it shifted back and forth between its disappointment over U.S. policy and its fear of openly criticizing it. On the one hand, it noted, the President's position was that "the final defeat of Hitler" is the only way by which "the Jewish people of Europe may be saved." But, it added, "To raise again the question of taking more effective measures than those agreed upon at the Bermuda Conference might appear to contradict the wishes of the highest authority of the land." Nevertheless, it concluded, it was the duty of the AJConference to "suggest" to the President "that if action is delayed until 'the final defeat of Hitler,' there may be no Jews left in Europe to save."[15] It was the closest that the AJCongress had yet come to actually challenging FDR.

This spirit of protest was not, however, carried over into the proceedings of the AJConference when it convened two weeks later. In his opening speech, Stephen Wise called upon the conference "to demand of the United Nations that not another hour be lost rescuing from the lands in the hands of Hitler the remaining Jews." Wise even implicitly criticized U.S. policy when he asserted that "the ways of rescue will be found, provided the United Nations, led by our own, have the will to rescue our harassed, despoiled, tortured brothers."[16] But in the very next breath, Wise deflated the significance of his own remarks by warmly praising the President:

As a spokesman of the Conference at its opening hour, I choose to register my unchanged faith in the deep humanity of the foremost leader of free men in the world today, Franklin Delano Roosevelt. This body of delegated and widely representative American Jews, dedicated to the triumph of our Nation's cause, declares its deep and unchangeable confidence in the integrity and goodwill of its Commander-in-Chief.[17]

On the second day of the gathering, Joseph Weinberg of the Jewish Labor Committee and Israel Goldstein, representing the Zionist Organization of America, called for Allied food shipments to Jews in occupied Europe and a "stern warning" by the Allies of "retribution" for Nazi atrocities.[18] Goldstein was the only featured speaker to explicitly demand specific action on behalf of European Jewry. He went even further and directly addressed American Jewry's unwillingness to take action on the rescue question:

Let us forthrightly admit that we American Jews, as a community of five millions, have not been stirred deeply enough, have not exercised ourselves passionately enough, have not risked enough of our convenience and our social and civic relations, have not been ready enough to shake the bonds of so-called amicability in order to lay our troubles upon the conscience of our Christian neighbors and fellow citizens.[19]

The only other protest of this nature came from Dr. Maurice Perlzweig, chairman of the British Section of the World Jewish Congress and a member of the AJConference's Committee on the Rescue of European Jewry. (The committee had been established at the very last moment prior to the conference in response to domestic criticism that the Jewish leadership interpreted as "an indication that the delegates and the community wanted action in this field."[20]) Perlzweig, speaking to the opening meeting of the Rescue Committee, expressed bitterness over the conference's emphasis on postwar matters and the Palestine controversy: "[U]nless we do our job in the Rescue Committee, there may be no Jews for whom a post-war scheme of things will be necessary . . . and the whole question of immigration into Palestine may become irrelevant as far as Europe is concerned."[21] But Perlzweig's attitude was not shared by the conference organizers or the speakers whom they selected to address the gathering. The other speakers spoke vaguely of the need for "the United Nations" to provide havens or to take unspecified action to rescue Jews; none called for direct U.S. intervention on behalf of the Jews or a change in American immigration policy to grant sanctuary to large numbers of refugees.

By the third day of the conference, the delegates were deeply embroiled in an acrimonious debate over whether or not to pass a resolution in favor of the creation of a Jewish commonwealth in Palestine. Stephen Wise spearheaded the pro-Zionist lobbying effort. Wise was ideologically committed to Zionism. He helped found the Federation of American Zionists and was a leader of its successor, the Zionist Organization of America. For Wise and the other Zionists within the Jewish establishment, the Palestine solution also offered an easy way out of an otherwise embarrassing dilemma. Jewish leaders did not have to demand that America serve as a haven for Jewish refugees; Palestine could serve that purpose. Jewish leaders did not have to be in the uncomfortable position of criticizing their own government; they could point an accusing finger at the British instead. But Palestine was no longer a realistic option. Back in 1935, the British Mandate authorities administering the Holy Land had permitted a record 55,407 Jewish refugees to enter. Local Arabs were infuriated at the Jewish influx. Their rioting prompted a total reversal in British immigration policy. The number of Jews granted entry dropped to 26,796 in 1936 and 9,441 in 1937. A British white paper of May 15, 1939, clamped a near-total lid on Jewish immigration for the next five years. The restrictive British policy did not dampen the Zionist enthusiasm of Stephen Wise and his colleagues, but it did make their clamor for Palestine as the solution to the Jewish refugee crisis an untenable proposition.

Not only was Palestine impractical, it had the potential to shatter the fragile Jewish organizational unity which the American Jewish Assembly ostensibly sought to promote. Yet the Zionist delegates pressed the issue despite the knowledge that it could provoke a fatal split with the anti-Zionist American Jewish Committee. On its fourth day the conference voted overwhelmingly in favor of a pro-Zionist Palestine resolution, and the AJCommittee announced its withdrawal. On September 2, the final session of the American Jewish Conference issued resolutions on a myriad of subjects, including a perfunctory call for rescue of Jews from Hitler. Interestingly, the Jewish Telegraphic Agency *Daily Bulletin* quoted extensively from the resolutions on relief and postwar rights but did not even mention the resolution on rescue—an omission that says much about the significance the delegates themselves attached to the rescue issue.[22] An editorial in *Congress Weekly* itself conceded that the AJConference's rescue resolution left something to be desired. If the resolution had no impact on Allied policy, *CW* asserted, it would be because "the resolution was adopted unanimously, but with a unanimity lacking the force of a rebuke to the democracies and an appeal *de profundis* to the justice of humanity."[23]

The Jewish leadership was hardpressed to explain just what it was that the conference had accomplished. An essay in *Congress Weekly* admitted that there were many American Jewish "skeptics" who "shake their heads gloomily, and wonder what on earth has been achieved by more speeches and more resolutions." *CW* readers were assured, however, that "the passing of a number of resolutions is not invariably merely a vocal or mathematical exercise; nor is speech-making inevitably a substitute for action; though a drug on the market, it need not always be an opiate.... An outspoken resolution for a Jewish Commonwealth is in itself an act of decision."[24] This was Stephen Wise's chief argument as well. He hailed as a "major event" the adoption "by more than 99% vote in favor of Palestine as a Jewish Commonwealth."[25] Some Jewish periodicals, however, found the stress on Palestine an odd contrast with the seeming disinterest in the Holocaust. The Cincinnati weekly *Every Friday* editorialized:

> [W]hen the future historian...will go through the records of the recent gathering of the American Jewish Conference, he will be shocked to find that the action of the Conference on the Rescue of Jews from Hitler Europe was within the limits as prescribed by "proper Salon-etiquette," while its actions on the establishment of a Jewish Commonwealth in Palestine was [sic] accompanied by dramatic demonstrations and emotions ad libitum.[26]

Although the Jewish leaders were unwilling to clash with the policies of the Roosevelt administration, some public figures and congressional leaders were less hesitant. On September 9, Thomas Curran and William Fullen, presidents of the Republican and Democratic national clubs respectively, issued an unprecedented joint statement calling for the unrestricted entry to the United States, for a temporary period, of refugees from religious persecution. Five days later, Rep. Samuel Dickstein offered House Joint Resolution 154, a "sense of the Congress" resolution urging the Secretary of State and the Attorney General to take such action. Whereas "countless thousands of innocent persons, of all racial and religious denominations, in many of the countries of continental Europe have been murdered or otherwise ruthlessly persecuted by the Axis Nations," and whereas "unless something is done within the next few months, which months will embrace winter, countless more thousands will be murdered or otherwise ruthlessly persecuted," the Dickstein measure declared, "it is therefore urged that an administrative policy be adopted to admit to the United States for a period not exceeding six months after hostilities have ceased between the Allied and Axis Nations such persons now residing in continental Europe who desire to come to the United States and who can establish to the satisfaction of any American consul before whom they may appear that they are bona fide political or religious refugees." On October 14, Sen. W. Warren Barbour (R-New Jersey) proposed Senate Joint Resolution 85, which was identical to the Dickstein resolution except that it set the maximum number of admissible refugees at 100,000.[27]

The reaction of the major Jewish organizations to the Dickstein and Barbour proposals was not one of instantaneous and unanimous rejection, as had been the case with similar bills ten years earlier, but neither was the persecution of European Jewry limited to harassment and expulsion, as it had been ten years earlier. The problem was now outright annihilation, thousands of lives each day, and the American Jewish response hardly equaled the urgency of the crisis. During the autumn of 1943, *Congress Weekly* editorialized on Dickstein-Barbour just twice, both times confining the matter to a secondary position on the editorial page. "We may hope that their demand of temporary hospitality for all refugees from religious persecution will find ready acceptance by the coming session of Congress," the AJCongress journal averred in September. But then it went on to stress that "what actually prevented the ready extension of American hospitality to refugees in recent years" was not the quota system itself but the administration of the quota regulations. "Even before Congress expresses itself in a legislative act," the editorial asserted, "the administrative authorities can and should remold American policy in this question . . . great changes can and should be made in the ad-

ministrative restrictions which have impeded refugee admission."[28]
In October, *Congress Weekly* stressed that it was supporting the
Dickstein-Barbour resolution because it was "very limited" and
because it emphasized that "the barring of immigration to this country does not rest on the strength of existing laws but on 'practices of
administrative officials.'" The AJCongress weekly concluded that the
adoption of the resolution "will relieve all believers in American
humanitarianism of the painful awareness that some administrative
organs of our Government have chosen to practice inhumanity."[29]
The refusal of the Congress to go beyond such mild criticism may
have stemmed in part from an ongoing fear that substantial Jewish
refugee immigration to the United States would cause anti-Semitism.
In his autobiography, Morris Waldman of the AJCommittee recalled a
senior official of the AJCongress privately complaining to him that
while "there is no hope in the future of Jews in Europe," any attempt at "scattering them in other countries would only tend to
intensify anti-Semitism in those countries."[30]

The AJCommittee was unalterably opposed to the Dickstein Barbour resolutions. An internal memo circulated among the AJCommittee leadership stressed two points. First, it claimed, the resolutions
could not assist Jews in German-occupied countries, because the
Nazis would not grant their release. Second, it was not necessary for
Jews in the neutral countries because "they are in no danger, even
though their conditions of life are not pleasant and they would prefer
to be in the United States."[31] Even as thousands were murdered daily
in the gas chambers of Auschwitz and Treblinka, the leaders of the
American Jewish Committee still refused to criticize the policies of
the Roosevelt administration. Indicative of this fear was a brief correspondence between a Columbus, Ohio, businessman and John
Slawson, who in 1943 became a vice-president of the AJCommittee.
The businessman wrote to inquire as to the accuracy of a remark by
Nahum Goldmann that only eighty Jewish refugees were being permitted to enter the United States each month. Slawson's assistant
replied with a lengthy defense of American immigration policy,
attacking Goldmann's statement as "ludicrous" and "outrageously
inaccurate." The letter claimed that the low immigration figures were
"due very largely to lack of transportation facilities," with "the difficulty of securing visas" only "a secondary factor." In contrast to
Goldmann's statistics, the letter concluded, the actual immigration

figure was "almost 400 per month." Not mentioned by the AJCommittee official was the fact that more than twenty times that number of Jews were being murdered each *day*; even at "400 per month," the number allowed to enter the United States was hopelessly inadequate.[32]

The only Jewish organizations to unequivocally endorse the Dickstein-Barbour initiatives were, once again, the Bergson group and the Labor Zionists of America. Bergson claimed credit for having helped to influence the original refugee statement by the Republican and Democratic leaders, and urged his followers to pressure their congressmen to take action on the proposal.[33] The threat of rising anti-Semitism had not stopped Bergson from publishing his provocative newspaper advertisements; it had not stopped him from publicly criticizing the Bermuda failure; nor would it dissuade him from urging the admission to the United States of large numbers of refugees. As for the Labor Zionists, their journal, *Jewish Frontier,* published a feature editorial sharply criticizing the Roosevelt administration's immigration policy and warmly endorsing the Dickstein-Barbour resolutions. It also reprinted the entire text of both resolutions.[34]

Many months later, long after the Dickstein and Barbour resolutions had been buried and forgotten in congressional subcommittees, an article in *Congress Weekly* noted, "For one reason or another, even though the projects had the support of important men in both parties, they were not adopted." To what extent the silence of organized American Jewry was one of those "reasons" is a question that will forever remain unanswered.

The
Dignity
Of A
People

_9_

The disastrous outcome of the Bermuda refugee conference was the catalyst for an important shift in the priorities and tactics of the Bergson Group. In a letter to his most active members, Bergson explained the "new trend" his organization would be taking: "It has become increasingly clear that the Administration will not yield to appeals made on behalf of the doomed Jews of Europe. As time passes it also becomes more and more evident that if results are to be achieved, more dramatic methods of pressure will have to be used."[1] What Bergson called "a vast clamor for action to be taken by the Jewish masses"[2] began in July 1943 with an Emergency Conference to Save the Jewish People of Europe. Fifteen hundred people packed the Hotel Commodore in New York from July 20 to 25[3] to hear a wide array of military and diplomatic experts demand the establishment of a special United States government agency devoted exclusively to the rescue of European Jews. The Emergency Conference sought to demonstrate that rescue need not be postponed until the attainment of Allied military victory. The conference was in many ways a tremendous success. It enjoyed the endorsement of numerous prominent Americans, senior congressional leaders, administration officials such as Secretary of the Interior Harold Ickes and Secretary of the Treasury Henry Morgenthau, Jr., and even the President's own wife, Eleanor. Most important, the proceedings of the Emergency Conference received generous media attention nationwide. For the first time, the viability of rescue was given serious national exposure. The conference provided the organizational framework for Bergson's latest brainchild, the Emergency Committee to Save the Jewish People of Europe.

In contrast to the major Jewish organizations, the Emergency Committee publicly and explicitly criticized the Roosevelt administration for its apathy during the Holocaust. "Although President Roosevelt is considered by many as the greatest friend the Jewish people ever had, nevertheless he has done less than many of them," the Washington representative of the Emergency Committee bluntly told reporters on August 9. "Not one man has ever been appointed by the United States or Great Britain to help the Jews of Europe."[4]

The most innovative of Bergson's new "dramatic methods of pressure" was a rabbinical March on Washington organized in conjunction with the Union of Orthodox Rabbis. On October 6, three days before Yom Kippur, Bergson led several hundred Orthodox rabbis in a rally on the White House steps to demand U.S. intervention on behalf of the Jews in Europe. The American Jewish leadership had fought Bergson's proposed march tooth and nail. Samuel Rosenman, who was prominent in the AJCommittee as well as an adviser to Roosevelt, disparagingly referred to the clergymen as "a group of rabbis who just recently left the darkest period of the medieval world."[5] He was anxious to "keep the horde from storming Washington."[6] Rosenman later recalled how he "unsuccessfully tried to stop their coming"[7] but had to content himself with persuading the President to avoid the protesters. Rosenman and Stephen Wise privately urged FDR not to meet with any of the demonstrators.[8] The President arranged to be away when the rabbis arrived. FDR could not, however, miss the front page news coverage accorded the demonstration in the Washington newspapers and elsewhere the following morning. The protesting rabbis did meet Vice-President Henry Wallace and a congressional delegation, to whom they presented a petition calling for, among other things, the creation of "a special inter-governmental agency to save the remnant of Israel in Europe, with powers and means to act at once on a large scale."[9]

Dr. Wise condemned the demonstration as a "painful and even lamentable exhibition":

> [W]hen it was found that the President was unable in advance to promise to meet with the rabbis, the parade—for such it was—should not have been arranged.
>
> . . . They who set out to be leaders must bear themselves with a sense of responsibility. There is such a thing as the dignity of a people. It must not be ignored. But the stuntists who arranged the orthodox rabbinical parade are not so much concerned with the results of their pilgrimage as with the stunt impression which it makes.[10]

Yet even Samuel Margoshes, a former Wise deputy, wrote after the rally that "when the recognized leadership is dormant and sleepy there appear forces which accomplish wonders, without the authority and the earmarks of collective responsibility which should be behind every public act of ours in this responsibility-laden hour."[11]

The march of the rabbis was Bergson's opening salvo in the campaign to bring about the creation of a governmental rescue agency. He followed with a series of biting full-page advertisements in newspapers around the country, demanding the establishment of the rescue unit and asking readers to sign a petition to that effect. The ads bore hard-hitting headlines like, "How Well Are You Sleeping? Is There Something You Could Have Done to Save Millions of Innocent People from Torture and Death?" and "They Are Driven to Death Daily but They Can Be Saved."[12] On October 31, the Bergson group staged a rally at Carnegie Hall to honor Sweden and Denmark for giving refuge to some European Jewish refugees. Bergson had invited the Swedish and Danish ambassadors to the United States to attend the rally, but the ambassadors sought out Assistant Secretary of State Breckinridge Long's opinion on the advisability of attending, and Long had referred them to Stephen Wise, who persuaded them to stay away from the dissidents' rally.[13] The Carnegie Hall protest nevertheless kept the rescue issue in the public eye, helping to maintain the momentum of the campaign. Finally, in November, the Bergson effort culminated as Rep. Will Rogers (D-California) and Sen. Guy Gillette (D-Iowa) introduced resolutions in the House and Senate urging "the creation by the President of a commission of diplomatic, economic and military experts to formulate and effectuate a plan of immediate action designed to save the surviving Jewish people of Europe."[14]

The resolution became the focus of a new struggle between the Jewish leaders and the Bergson group. The establishment could not endorse the Bergson-inspired resolution without in effect surrendering its position of authority in the community; on the other hand, to back the resolution would be to concede that they had failed to take the initiative on the rescue issue and that the insurgents had legitimately taken the initiative in their stead. There was serious disagreement between the Wise forces and Bergson over the text of the resolution as well; Wise insisted that any resolution concerning Europe's Jews must contain an affirmation of the Jews' right to immigrate to Palestine—a thorny political matter which Bergson was avoiding for fear that it would cloud the rescue issue. But how could Jewish leaders oppose the rescue resolution without appearing to be opposed to rescue?

Senator Gillette received an early taste of the Jewish leaders' opposition when Dr. Wise and "two or three other Jewish leaders" visited his office prior to the congressional hearings on the issue:

> None of these gentlemen seemed to be enthusiastic for the passage of the resolution and the tenor of the conversation seemed to suggest their belief that the action as proposed by the resolution was not a wise step to take, although they professed very strong interest in everything that would look to the saving of the remnant of the Jewish people in Europe from destruction.[15]

But Gillette stood fast. The resolution was unanimously approved by the Senate Foreign Relations Committee and passed on to the full Senate for action. The measure faced a rougher time in the House of Representatives, however, because of fierce opposition spearheaded by Rep. Sol Bloom (D-New York), the elderly Jewish chairman of the House Foreign Affairs Committee. The Bergson group had led the chorus of Jewish criticism of Bloom's role in the failure of the Bermuda refugee conference. The Gillette-Rogers resolution was another Bergson-inspired slap at Bloom, since the demand to create a new agency to aid European Jewry implicitly reaffirmed the charge that Bermuda had been a "cruel mockery."[16] Bloom insisted on holding full hearings on the Gillette-Rogers resolution, for it would give him an opportunity to hit back at the Bergsonites.

The Bloom hearings opened on Friday morning, November 19. The first witness was Dean Alfange, a leader of the Liberal Party and of Bergson's Emergency Committee to Save the Jewish People of Europe. After allowing Alfange to make an introductory statement, Bloom cut in and called his attention to a telegram about the hearings which the Bergson boys had mailed to their supporters. The text of the telegram was read aloud. The part that especially irked Bloom was a sentence that noted the introduction of the Gillette-Rogers resolution and added, "Imperative to mobilize public opinion throughout country to force passage resolution and enable our office Washington, London, Palestine, England, Turkey to continue work on larger scale."[17] When he read the line about Bergson asking "for contributions to force this committee of Congress to act," Bloom explained, "I immediately called the hearings." Bloom proceeded to grill Alfange about the offensive cable. Alfange finally conceded that "the language is bad, and had it occurred to me, I would not have allowed it to be used."[18] Alfange tried to steer the topic back to the issue of rescue, but Bloom persisted and even made several unkind remarks about Bergson's finances.

The question of the Jewish leadership's opposition to the resolution came up even before any prominent Jewish leaders had a chance to testify. Evidently it was already known to members of the House Foreign Affairs Committee that the Bergson group was at odds with the Wise forces over the bill. Rep. Herman D. Eberharter (D-Pennsylvania) told witness Herbert Moore, a Bergson sympathizer and director of Transradio News Features:

> It seems to me that you ought to be able to appreciate that if these groups who are so vitally interested cannot agree themselves, it must be a very difficult question for a committee like this in a Congress to pass such an important resolution. If these groups are fighting among themselves as to the wisdom of this thing . . . if these groups, the Jewish people themselves, and those interested in their fate in Europe cannot agree as to the wisdom of this, your position is not very sound.[19]

In reply, Moore insisted that the grassroots Jewish public supported the resolution, even if "there are individuals who head groups" who did not. Eberharter persisted:

Well, this committee can certainly not go beyond the heads of these groups. We must rely upon the heads of these groups as representing each particular group. We cannot go and consult every individual in order to come to a conclusion as to the wisdom of passing a resolution of this kind.[20]

When the hearings continued on November 23, it was Peter Bergson's turn to take the witness stand. Bergson, however, had been given no prior notice that he would testify. Spotting Bergson in the room, Bloom asked him to take the stand and, unlike the other witnesses, insisted on swearing him in. A slightly bewildered Bergson readily complied. Bloom began by questioning Bergson about his citizenship, then turned to the ''force passage'' telegram and reread it aloud.

> CHAIRMAN BLOOM: What is your answer, Mr. Bergson?
> MR. BERGSON: Well, if I would have received the telegram, I would probably have sent some money if I had it.[21]

Bloom was not amused. The congressman pressed Bergson about his status in the United States and about the telegram. Bergson eventually conceded that ''instead of saying 'secure,' they used a bad word, called 'force,' and the committee is willing to apologize for using the word 'force'; it should have said 'secure passage of the resolution.'''[22]

Bloom also questioned Bergson concerning Jewish groups that opposed the work of the Emergency Committee to Save the Jewish People of Europe. When Bloom asked whether or not the American Jewish Congress was ''trying to do the same as your organization is doing,'' Bergson hedged and tried to skirt the question. Finally he replied, ''I will say I do not know.'' Bloom pressed Bergson to name those Jewish organizations that opposed his group. Bergson, afraid that talk of Jewish disagreements would endanger the chances for passage of the resolution, tried to imply that the Jewish Agency for Palestine was not opposed to the ECSJPE's activities; he did concede, however, that the American Jewish Committee opposed his efforts.

The sensitive question of Jewish disagreements over the bill had first been raised publicly on November 17, two days before the hearings. A New York radio station had broadcast an editorial authored by Herbert Moore's Transradio News agency, which strongly criticized

Chairman Bloom and the Jewish leaders suspected of privately supporting Bloom against the Gillette-Rogers resolution. The editorial declared:

Large Jewish organizations are said to be identified with the attitude of Congressman Bloom in opposing any action by the United States Government to help rescue their compatriots. However, thus far no spokesman for this group has ventured to explain openly why the policy of rescue is opposed, and it is probable that the congressional hearing now about to begin will uncover the real reason for such opposition.[23]

The dispute over the attitude of the Jewish leadership remained unsettled until it was Stephen Wise's turn to testify at the Bloom hearings. Wise appeared in his capacity as co-chairman of the American Jewish Conference—in effect, as a spokesman for the entire range of established Jewish organizations with the exception of the American Jewish Committee, which had just withdrawn from the Conference because of the Conference's pro-Zionist stand. Wise and his colleagues could not attack the Gillette-Rogers resolution outright. Instead, they sought to criticize the resolution for what it did *not* include: a reference to the Palestine question. As far as Wise and his colleagues in the Zionist leadership were concerned, there was no point in establishing a "rescue" body unless there would be somewhere to settle the Jewish refugees once they were rescued. Wise would therefore seek to amend the resolution to include a demand that the British open the gates of Palestine to Jewish refugee immigration. The Bergsonites were no less devoted to Zionism than Wise, but they wanted to avoid the entire Palestine issue for a specific tactical reason. The Bergsonites feared that although Wise's insistence on adding to the resolution a reference to the right of Jews to immigrate to Palestine might seem "innocent on its face and laudable in its purpose,"[24] in fact the introduction of the acrimonious subject of Palestine could "provoke serious complications."[25] And indeed it did.

Dr. Wise began his testimony by denouncing the Transradio editorial as "an utterly unpardonable misstatement of fact, for which I think only unauthorized, irresponsible, quasi-spokesmen of the other small group of American Jews have chosen to make themselves responsible."[26] Wise paused to make clear that he was totally opposed to that "small group," with its "rashly written and rashly published advertisements asking for help and simultaneously always asking for

135

money"—money, he predicted, for which "there never will be an accounting in any sense worthy of the name."[27] As for the resolution itself:

> Of course we favor it. But one can favor a document without saying
> that it has reached perfection and that there are no blemishes in it or
> inadequacies in it which may be expanded.... I cannot understand
> why... this resolution has no reference to Palestine.
>
> If this resolution is seriously meant by some of the people who stand
> behind it and whose chief purpose is not to create dissatisfaction and
> confusion in American life, they would have spoken of opening the
> doors of Palestine.[28]

As the Bergson group had feared, the Jewish leadership's insistence
on a Palestine amendment contained the seeds of bitter controversy.
Rep. Charles Eaton (R-New Jersey) immediately questioned "the propriety... in the face of this terrific tragedy, of a committee of the House
of Representatives... serving notice on the British Parliament as to what
action they should take in a matter which has been the subject of such
controversy."[29] Rep. Eberharter agreed:

> It seems to me that that is a very controversial question, the question of
> the establishment of the Jewish national state and the home for Jews in
> Palestine... And to mix that question with the question of the present
> and immediate necessity of rescuing the Jews may not be the best thing to
> do.... I think you ought to consider, speaking for the ... American
> Jewish Conference, the advisability of injecting that controversial ques-
> tion into this resolution.[30]

When Rep. Will Rogers, Jr., the co-sponsor of the resolution and a
longtime Bergson group stalwart, also disputed the raising of the Palestine question, Wise spoke up forcefully:

> MR. ROGERS: I doubt the wisdom of injecting the ancient and acrimo-
> nious Palestine question into a resolution specifically involving relief....
>
> RABBI WISE: ... That is one thing I cannot understand. I have noticed
> that the group which you represent [the Bergsonites] in applying for
> funds has spoken of Palestine as a possibility of settlement.
>
> There is an extraordinary discrepancy between the money solicited by
> the committee on behalf of which you have spoken in your statement

today, in which you seem to doubt the wisdom of adding the opening of the doors of Palestine to this resolution. You will admit that there is such a discrepancy, Congressman?

MR. ROGERS: . . . In my opinion I think it is perfectly clear that there are two problems. There is the problem of getting people out, and there is the problem of what to do with them once they are out.

. . . the question of getting them out, that is the purpose to be undertaken by this resolution. . . . It is to have no connection with Palestine. And in my opinion it would be unwise to inject that into the question of relief.

CHAIRMAN BLOOM: Do you want to answer that, Dr. Wise?

RABBI WISE: I don't care to answer it.[31]

Meanwhile, the Jewish leadership went on the offensive. The chief body representing the major Jewish organizations—with the exception of the AJCommittee—was now the American Jewish Conference. In November, the Joint Emergency Committee had voted five to four to dissolve itself and transfer its functions to the Rescue Committee of the AJConference.[32] (Ironically, some Roosevelt administration officials viewed the very creation of the AJConference's Rescue Committee as a tactical maneuver by the Jewish establishment to set up "a rival of the Emergency Committee to Save the Jewish People of Europe."[33]) The Conference's first move, on December 29, was a public attack on Bergson. The Bergson group had no right "to speak for the Jewish people in this country," since it had no "mandate from any constituency" and had thus served merely to "undermine" the "recognized national Jewish agencies," the Conference declared in a detailed press release. It charged that the Jewish army compaign had consisted of "unrealistic agitation" and the publishing of "exaggerated statements" that had "created misunderstanding"; that the rescue campaign was "sensational" and "competitive" and had accomplished nothing except "to bring confusion in the minds of well-meaning people who might otherwise be helpful to the truly representative and responsible bodies in organized Jewry"; that the rescue resolution itself, although sponsored by congressmen with "the highest humanitarian sentiments," had in fact been proposed "in complete disregard of the rescue program which is being actively pressed at Washington by representative Jewish agencies."[34] At the same time, Stephen Wise contacted Interior Secretary Harold Ickes and urged him to resign from his honorary chairmanship of the Washington chapter of the Emergency Committee. Wise assured Ickes that the "irresponsible" Bergsonites "had not done a thing which may result in the saving of a single Jew."[35] (Ickes resisted the pressure.)

The AJConference's well-publicized quarrel with the Gillette-Rogers resolution and its sponsors sparked criticism from various quarters, including the *New York Post,* which declared:

> We hate to see such displays of factional spleen as the American Jewish Conference's attack on the Emergency Committee to Save the Jewish People of Europe. . . .
>
> The Baldwin-Rogers resolution which the Emergency Committee sponsored in Congress is a concrete and specific measure designed to get results now before it is too late. . . the Conference should not damn it lock, stock, and barrel because somebody else put it forward.[36]

Some prominent Christians were likewise alarmed by the Jewish leaders' behavior. An editorial in *The Protestant,* for example, charged that the Jewish establishment had opposed the Bergson group "out of envy of its popularity and achievements."[37]

Stephen Wise's testimony does not appear to have been too well received in the Jewish community, either. The Jewish press overwhelmingly supported the rescue resolution and published stinging criticism of the Jewish establishment. An editorial in the *Jewish Review and Observer* (Cleveland) lambasted the Jewish leaders for doing little more than collecting data on the Nazi atrocities:

> The American Jewish Congress has made a specialty out of collecting such data—probably for a gigantic post-war "kaddish," since statistics will not produce resurrection. . . . What right does the [American Jewish] Conference have to attack the resolution and its sponsors, the Emergency Committee to Save the Jewish People of Europe, for making "rash and exaggerated claims as to what this resolution will accomplish," when the Conference itself has been doing nothing to halt the massacre?[38]

The Reconstructionist pointed out that "many years of ineffective activity on the part of Zionist bodies and philanthropic organizations" had created a vacuum "into which the Emergency Committee rushed."[39] The Yiddish press published especially biting criticism of "the circles who were trying to kill the resolution out of consideration for their own prestige."[40]

The American Jewish Congress was understandably jittery about the growing grassroots backlash over Dr. Wise's testimony. A lead editorial in *Congress Weekly* asserted that the Bergson group "privately constituted and without any public responsibility, has assumed the role of 'savior' with utter disregard of all existing Jewish organizations and their years of effort through and with the government agencies created to deal with the rescue problem. . . . Dr. Wise is a member of the President's Committee on Refugees. He is thoroughly familiar with all the phases and aspects of the situation. He is the spokesman of organized Jewry both as president of the American Jewish Congress and co-chairman of the American Jewish Conference."[41] Two issues later, the AJCongress organ again felt constrained to devote an entire editorial to explaining how "there can be no cooperation between representative Jewish organizations having historic records of achievement and responsible to great Jewish constituencies and fly-by-night groups whose methods and techniques savor of cheap sensationalism."[42] Wise exhibited similar defensiveness in replying to friends who were puzzled at his opposition to Bergson. He wrote to one: "After fifty years, that is to say, a long life of service to my people in every sense, I do not feel called upon to defend my reasons for having nothing whatever to do with a little group of irresponsible and unrepresentative people who set themselves up as saviours of Jewish life."[43]

Although the testimony of Dr. Wise helped bury Gillette-Rogers in the House Foreign Affairs Committee, the rescue resolution was still very much alive—in large measure because of a blunder by the State Department's arch-restrictionist, Breckinridge Long. He appeared before a secret session of the House committee to testify that the United States was in fact doing everything in its power to save Jews. A separate rescue agency was therefore unnecessary, he asserted. According to Long, the United States had already admitted "approximately 580,000 refugees" from Hitler. What Long had done was to substitute the maximum number of refugees theoretically admissible for the number who were actually admitted, which was less than half that number (and many of whom were non-Jews). When Long's testimony was made public on December 10, it sparked a firestorm of angry criticism from Jewish organizations,[44] prominent newspapers, and pro-refugee congressmen like Samuel Dickstein and Emanuel Celler.[45] Although the House committee voted to shelve the resolution, it was scheduled for a full debate in the Senate when the winter recess concluded in late January. Still smarting from the controversy over Long's remarks, the Roosevelt administration braced for more trouble as the date for the Senate hearings approached.

Meanwhile, a group of Treasury Department officials decided to take the initiative. Secretary of the Treasury Henry Morgenthau, Jr., had in recent months become increasingly perturbed over the cruel indifference of the State Department on refugee matters. On January 13, Morgenthau and his aides met to consider how to make headway on the refugee problem and simultaneously spare President Roosevelt further embarrassment. Oscar Cox, director of the Lend-Lease program, bluntly warned of the danger of electoral consequences if the rescue resolution were to come up for an open debate on the floor of the Senate. "[I]n the course of the debate the State Department's position will be ripped open," Cox pointed out, and that would constitute "a direct attack on the Administration including the President for having failed to act in this kind of important situation."[46] Morgenthau concurred. The ongoing controversy over the resolution was "a boiling pot on the Hill," he said. "You can't hold it; it is going to pop, and you have either got to move very fast, or the Congress of the United States will do it for you."[47] As the Treasury officials saw it, the choice for Roosevelt was either to have a nasty confrontation with Congress and the American Jewish community—on the eve of a presidential election—or to take action which would preempt such a conflict. They opted to press for the latter. On January 16, Morgenthau, accompanied by his assistants Randolph Paul and John W. Pehle, presented Roosevelt with a report detailing the obstructionist activities of the State Department on refugee affairs. It was a scathing indictment, drawn up by Paul, Pehle, and their colleague Josiah E. Dubois, Jr., and it originally bore the title "Report on the Acquiescence of this Government in the Murder of Europe's Jews" (in its final form, the title was changed to "A Personal Report to the President"). Morgenthau told the President that "a growing number of responsible people and organizations" were persuaded that there was "plain anti-Semitism motivating the actions of these State Department officials, and, rightly or wrongly, it will require little more in the way of proof for this suspicion to explode into a nasty scandal."[48]

140

Roosevelt needed little convincing. On January 22, he issued an executive order establishing a War Refugee Board which would be responsible for "the development of plans and programs and the inauguration of effective measures for (a) the rescue, transportation, maintenance and relief of the victims of enemy oppression, and (b) the establishment of havens of temporary refuge for such victims."[49] John Pehle was selected as executive director of the new agency. His colleagues in the Treasury Department were appointed to man the WRB staff. (Senator Gillette and Representative Rogers promptly withdrew their rescue resolution, noting that "it would be futile to pass a request for what has already been done."[50])

The question of establishing temporary havens, as mentioned in Roosevelt's order, was crucial. The rescue of Jews from Hitler would be severely hampered if there was no place to put the refugees once they were rescued. As early as April 1943, in the memorandum prepared for the Bermuda conference, the major Jewish organizations had called for the creation of "a number of Sanctuaries" in unnamed "Allied and neutral countries." They had refrained from specifically urging the United States to sponsor such havens on its territory for fear of provoking anti-Semitic outbursts from the anti-immigration crowd. Even after the establishment of the WRB, they hesitated to press for temporary havens in the United States. Their reluctance once again created a vacuum which the Bergson group moved to fill. In February, Bergson presented WRB officials with a lengthy memorandum outlining rescue options. The memo urged the "steady transportation of the Jewish evacuees into neighboring neutral and United States territories," although it did not specifically recommend the United States as one of them; that would come later. The Bergsonites again sought to avoid a fight over the Palestine question; they suggested that "Palestine might well be given particular attention," but went no further.[51] In a speech some days later, Bergson specifically appealed to "American Zionists" to "brush aside political considerations" —that is, the Palestine question— "at a time when thousands of us are dying daily."[52] The American Zionist leadership, however, continued to stress Palestine as the sole solution. Abba Hillel Silver, co-chairman of the American Zionist Emergency Council, declared that the War Refugee Board was "doomed to failure" unless it concentrated on Palestine.[53] The American Jewish Committee sidestepped the havens question altogether. At its annual meeting on January 30, the issue was simply ignored in favor of a discussion of postwar problems.[54]

Treasury Secretary Morgenthau was enthusiastic over the temporary havens proposal; he hailed it as "a magnificent idea."[55] He hesitated to push for direct presidential action, however, after Secretary of War Henry Stimson warned that there might be congressional opposition. At a March 8 meeting of the WRB staff, Morgenthau recommended that the Bergson group be asked to launch a campaign for congressional action on the havens idea. "After all, the thing that made it possible to get the President really to act on this thing was the Resolution which at least had passed the Senate to form this kind of a War Refugee Board, hadn't it?" he noted. "I think six months before [the Resolution] I could not have done it."[56] Some weeks later, Josiah DuBois appeared at a Bergson group meeting and urged his listeners to sponsor a public campaign for havens.

Morgenthau and his aides had no choice but to seek outside pressure on the President if they hoped to get anywhere. When asked at a March 25 press conference "whether the United States would take part in offering haven," FDR replied that "we are taking care of all the refugees who can get out now, in North Africa." Pressed about the willingness of the United States to accept more refugees, Roosevelt replied that "there are not enough to come."[57] The American Jewish Conference replied by praising Roosevelt's remarks at the press conference urging Europeans to temporarily open their frontier to escaping Jews; it ignored his refusal to offer the refugees haven in America.[58] A statement issued by the American Jewish Committee likewise hailed FDR's comments and sidestepped his restrictionist stand.[59]

There were no doubts left as to what was going on in Europe. An editorial in the March 10 edition of *Congress Weekly* bluntly noted: "Trainloads of Jews are still being sent from Western Europe to extermination camps in Poland. Each day lost is a day in which thousands perish." Two weeks later, the President himself publicly declared that the Jews of newly occupied Hungary were "now threatened with annihilation."[60] Nevertheless, the impetus for the establishment of havens in the United States was to come from non-Jewish sources. In the April 13 *New York Post,* columnist Samuel Grafton coined the phrase "free ports" for refugees, drawing an analogy with goods that are temporarily stored in ports free from inspection or customs duties;

the syndicated column appeared in more than forty newspapers around the country. A Gallup poll found fully 70 percent of Americans in favor of establishing temporary havens on U.S. territory. A rumor reached Morgenthau that Governor Thomas E. Dewey of New York, the leading contender for the 1944 Republican presidential nomination, was planning to propose that the United States admit 100,000 Jewish refugees temporarily.[61]

At an April 19 mass meeting called to commemorate the Warsaw ghetto revolt, the American Jewish Conference adopted a resolution urging recognition of "the right of temporary asylum for every surviving Jewish man, woman and child who can escape from the Hitlerite fury into the territories of the United Nations."[62] Although the declaration still fell short of an outright plea for the United States itself to offer haven, it kept the ball rolling.

Finally, in its April 28 edition, *Congress Weekly* backed the "free ports" idea. The *CW* editorial actually defended the restrictionists' rationale for blocking Jewish immigration: "Slight as may be the chance of enemy agents trickling through in the guise of refugees, the government cannot relent on the restrictions of wartime admissions." This said, the editorial concluded that "the establishment of the so-called 'free ports' thus offers the simplest method by which havens can be provided for the refugees on American soil without endangering the safety of this country."[63] This backhanded endorsement was followed, during the next three weeks, by unequivocal endorsements of the free ports idea from a wide range of non-Jewish sources, including the International Labor Organization, the president of the American Federation of Labor, the Congress of Industrial Organizations, the Washington Episcopal Diocese and the *New York Times,* which suggested that "Army camps, vacated as the peak of training passes, could be used" to house refugees.[64] From the floor of the House of Representatives, Rep. Thomas J. Lane (D-Massachusetts) and Rep. Clare Booth Luce (R-Connecticut) urged the Roosevelt administration to take the lead in creating "free ports" on American soil.[65] Bergson's Emergency Committee to Save the Jewish People of Europe, for its part, sent a telegram to President Roosevelt appealing for "the establishment of temporary rescue camps in the United States for Jewish refugees from Europe.[66]

Meanwhile, the War Refugee Board submitted to the President a proposal recommending the establishment of temporary havens, either by executive order or in conjunction with congressional action. While the President weighed the WRB suggestion, bits of information were leaked to the press. On May 14, the Jewish Telegraphic Agency reported "persistent rumors that President Roosevelt is about to inaugurate a system of free ports" for refugees, in view, it said, "of the fact that public sentiment overwhelmingly favors this proposal."[67] In what seems to be a hint that the JTA was receiving its information from someone on the WRB, the report continued:

> In support of the possibility of the establishment of free ports an informed source today gave the following analogy: If shipwrecked victims were found swimming in the waters off our coast, they would be picked up and landed, and there would be no question of their applying for immigration visas. Once landed, they would be cared for until they could be evacuated to their own countries.[68]

Two days later, however, the JTA quoted "authoritative circles" as asserting that "whatever may be done about giving refugees from Europe temporary asylum on United States soil will require the backing of House and Senate leaders." Although there was no legal obstacle to a direct executive order, "official circles" declared, "affirmative action by Congress would place the matter beyond any question or doubt."[69] The Bergson boys knew how to take a hint. They arranged for Senator Gillette to present a resolution backing the free ports idea, and on the same day as its introduction they placed a blunt full-page ad in the *Washington Post,* headlined "25 Square Miles or Two Million Lives, Which Shall It Be?" Gillette left no doubt that his resolution was part of the War Refugee Board-Bergson group maneuvering. "The resolution is, at best, but the expression of the views of the Senate," Gillette told the JTA. "It urges the President to provide temporary havens, and it was introduced to crystallize the opinion of the Senate so that the President might feel free to act." Gillette stressed his hope that the president would act even before congressional consideration of the resolution.[70]

Roosevelt did not take action immediately. On May 30, the President told a press conference that he was "working on the subject of 'free ports,'" but emphasized that he "did not wish to limit the idea to areas in the United States," since there were "many places in the world where refugees might find temporary shelter."[71] On June 2,

Roosevelt told reporters that the administration was "considering taking over army camps which are no longer needed, as temporary shelters for refugees from Europe." Yet when asked specifically whether his May 30 statement had been intended to exclude the United States as a possible refuge site, the President replied that "he believed it to be wasteful and unnecessary to bring these refugees across the ocean from Europe only to return them later."[72] But three days later, John Pehle told a United Jewish Appeal audience in New York that plans to create a free port somewhere in the United States "are going forward at full speed." Pehle did not elaborate.[73]

Amid all of the signs, hints, and rumors, there was continued congressional pressure for the free ports proposal. Between June 2 and June 8, resolutions endorsing free ports for refugees were introduced in the House by Rep. Thomas J. Lane (D-Massachusetts), Rep. Vito Marcantonio (ALP-New York), Rep. Thomas E. Scanlon (D-Pennsylvania), Rep. William Rowan (D-Illinois), Rep. Emanuel Celler (D-New York) and Rep. Samuel Dickstein (D-New York). If the President had been deliberately delaying the establishment of a free port until there was sufficient public pressure to give him a free hand, then he must have welcomed the torrent of congressional activity. But he would soon discover that Representative Dickstein could be more trouble than he was worth.

On June 9, President Roosevelt announced that approximately 1,000 European refugees would be brought to the United States and housed in an "emergency refugee shelter" near Oswego, New York. Although FDR went out of his way to emphasize that the group would include "a reasonable proportion of various categories of persecuted people," in fact 918 of them were Jews.[74] The major Jewish organizations warmly praised the announcement. The American Jewish Conference asserted that "it may yet help to stave off the death sentence which the puppet government of Hungary has decreed for the last surviving Jews of Europe."[75] *Congress Weekly*, in an editorial, conceded that "skeptics" might claim that "the rescue of a thousand souls is somewhat puny compared with the magnitude of the catastrophe and the vastness of this country." Such criticism would be unfair, *CW* suggested, because "there are circumstances which prevent the full expression of the traditional humanity of this Republic...prevailing moods ...bar the admission of larger number of refugees." Therefore, *CW* concluded, it was the "symbolism" of the President's action that was most important.[76] Critics of FDR were few and far between. Marie Syrkin, writing in the July issue of *Jewish Frontier,* was one of those few. "If the thousand refugees to be housed in Fort Ontario will actually prove to be the total number admitted, then the 'free port' so established is impressive neither as a practical measure of alleviation nor even as as a gesture," she wrote, expressing her hope "that the President's announcement was a trial balloon and that prodding by the American people may result in an extension of the original scheme."[77] Some weeks later, the Christian Council on Palestine, representing 2,000 Christian ministers and religious educators, appealed to the President to establish free ports to provide refuge "not to a mere thousand, but to tens of thousands." An editorial in the *New York Times* sounded the same theme. "This is only a tiny fraction of the great mass of homeless people, of many faiths and many races, who have been victims of the Nazi terror," it pointed out. "We hope, ourselves, that more than a mere thousand can be sheltered under an expansion of the present program."[78] The most vociferous criticism came from Rep. Samuel Dickstein. He asserted that the Roosevelt plan was "not enough of a contribution for the United States to make," and hoped that Congress "will act to admit an unlimited number of those escaping Nazi persecution." Dickstein declared that he had no intention of canceling his plans to begin hearings on the free ports resolutions on June 21.[79] But as had happened on every previous occasion that Dickstein pushed for increased refugee immigration to the United States, his free ports proposal received no meaningful support from the major American Jewish organizations. The hearings were repeatedly postponed, and then eventually canceled altogether.[80]

The Bergson group, however, did not let up. At the second national conference of the Emergency Committee to Save the Jewish People of Europe in August, executive secretary Gabriel Wechsler deplored "the limitation of one such shelter in this country."[81] Other speakers urged the establishment of refugee shelters in Palestine. Shortly after the conference, two pro-Bergson congressmen, Sen. Elbert Thomas (D-Utah) and Rep. Andrew Somers (D-New York), introduced a joint resolution calling for the creation of "mass emergency rescue shelters in Palestine." The proposal was essentially a ruse to gain the admission of Jews to Palestine; it was not a plan for refugees to enter Palestine temporarily and then return to Europe at the end of the war, à la Oswego. American Zionist leaders were up in arms nevertheless. At the August 31 meeting of the American Zionist Emergency Council leadership, Nahum Goldmann denounced the bill as a virtual betrayal of Zionism. He pointed to what he called its "implication that [the refugees] will be sent back to their countries of origin after the war," and proposed that the AZEC lobby against it in Congress. Brushing aside one dissenter's suggestion that such lobbying "might be misunderstood and might be regarded as detrimental to possible opportunities for rescuing Jews," the AZEC leaders overwhelmingly approved Goldmann's proposal. Within days, the AZEC had dispatched letters to all eight co-sponsors of the Thomas-Somers resolution, demanding that the measure be dropped. It was.[82]

Our Government Will Do What It Can

10

The creation of the War Refugee Board brought a collective sigh of relief from the leaders of the major American Jewish organizations. Their faith in Franklin Roosevelt, which had been shaken briefly by his apparent indifference to the Holocaust, was now restored. "The action taken by our President promises life to people who were otherwise doomed to destruction," the American Jewish Conference declared.[1] The American Jewish Committee sent FDR a telegram expressing its "profound satisfaction and heartfelt gratitude."[2] An editorial in *Congress Weekly* described the creation of the board as "a healing balm applied to the wound which has long tormented American Jewry." That "wound," according to *Congress Weekly*, was the failure of the Allies "to take any definite steps" to rescue Jews—but now that the WRB had been established, "our first duty is to suppress the painful memories and accept with gratitude" that at long last something had been done.[3]

Even if the old painful memories could be suppressed, however, new painful memories were being created daily. "Trainloads of Jews are still being sent from Western Europe to extermination camps in Poland," *Congress Weekly* reported in March 1944. "Each day lost is a day in which thousands perish.''[4] Events took a particularly dramatic turn for the worse when the Nazis occupied Hungary on March 19. Hungary had been the last European country with a sizable Jewish population to remain untouched by Hitler. Now, suddenly, 760,000 more Jews were in the Nazis' grasp. Some Jewish leaders braced for the worst. ''The retreating Nazis will try to exterminate the Jews before they withdraw,'' Nahum Goldmann publicly warned the day after Hungary was occupied.[5] But the leaders of the AJCommittee seemed markedly less concerned about the Hungarian crisis. On March 21, Morris Waldman wrote to his boss, Joseph Proskauer, concerning Proskauer's intention to seek President Roosevelt's approval for the text of a statement on issues of Jewish concern. Waldman urged Proskauer to refrain from bothering the President over the sensitive Palestine question. ''The object of your visit,'' he wrote, ''should appear to be something new, namely general principles affecting the Peace and the Post War World.'' Almost as an afterthought, Waldman added, ''Naturally, the present plight of the Jews cannot be ignored; therefore a paragraph about them.'' Waldman was especially concerned about a paragraph in Proskauer's draft of the statement reaffirming that Jews would do nothing ''that would interfere with the war effort.'' Waldman cautioned that even the mere mention of that issue might raise ''an oblique accusation that there are Jewish citizens who think otherwise.'' Therefore, Waldman explained, he had corrected Proskauer's draft by deleting the paragraph entirely.[6]

Meanwhile, the news from Hungary was bleak. On March 29, the JTA reported that 10,000 Hungarian Jews had already been seized and deported to concentration camps; by April 5, that figure was given as 55,000. On April 19, the JTA published what it called confirmed reports that the Nazis had begun large-scale deportations of Hungarian Jews to death camps in Poland. In May, information about the deportations to Poland—that is, to Auschwitz—became more frequent. On May 10, the *New York Times* quoted a European diplomat who warned that the Nazis were preparing ''huge gas chambers in which the one million Hungarian Jews are to be exterminated in the same fashion as were the Jews of Poland.''[7] On May 19, an official of the Jewish Agency for Palestine telegrammed Stephen Wise: ''Refugees who reached Palestine yesterday relate terrible facts regarding Jews in Hungary. There is clear evidence that mass extermination is prepared there according methods in Poland. Over 300,000 Jews from Sziget and Carpatho-Russia are already interned in camps and ghettoes."[8] Wise took the information seriously. In the May *Opinion,* he wrote, "Tragic news comes to this country through indisputable channels that three vast extermination camps are being prepared for 600,000 and more Jews and, alas, it is true that, while Hitler never keeps a promise, he seems never to fail to execute the most terrible of his threats." Wise concluded, "Our Government will do what it can."[9] Despite the absence of any evidence that the U.S. administration was willing to go out of its way to save Jews, Wise somehow retained his faith that Roosevelt's humanitarian declarations would be translated into meaningful action. In fact, however, the President had so far done little more than issue a warning that Nazi war criminals would eventually be punished. Wise had praised FDR's warning, declaring that it "will be effective to deter the Nazi hangman,"[10] but by early May, an editorial in *Congress Weekly* was forced to concede the "futility" of "meaningless warnings and threats of retribution to come."[11]

On May 17, the full-scale deportation of Hungarian Jewry began. Thousands were gassed in Auschwitz on May 17, 18, 19, and 20. On May 21, the daily death toll at Auschwitz reached a peak of 12,000 and continued at that rate for many weeks afterward. American Jewish leaders tentatively advanced a number of suggestions for direct Allied intervention. The first was retaliatory bombing. *Congress Weekly* noted that a request from the Jews of Warsaw for retaliatory bombing raids had been "treated as a fantastic encroachment upon the plans and designs of the Allied High Command." Nevertheless, the journal of the AJCongress asked:

> Is immediate retaliation still impossible and fantastic? Is there no way of telling Budapest not with words but with deeds that humanity will not stand for the murder of the last million?.... Can not this Hungarian government be made to learn through fire and devastation that murder begets murder?
>
> Thousands of Allied planes swarm through the European skies every day.... A fleet of Allied planes, raining down the warnings against this inhuman crime together with the more eloquent bombs, may save those lives. Is this, too, a fantastic encroachment upon the plans of the Allied High Command? If it is we must be forgiven for being fools....[12]

The Bergson group likewise appealed for Allied retaliatory strikes. But U.S. officials were not impressed. George Warren, a State

Department adviser on refugees, told Bergson, "Anything designed for purposes of retaliation which would divert military energies even momentarily would be inconsistent with the main purpose of defeating the German armies at the earliest possible moment."[13]

A proposal for the bombing of the railroad lines leading to Auschwitz began to circulate in June. On June 12, Swiss rescue activists cabled Jacob Rosenheim of the Agudas Israel in New York:

> Since April, we received desperate letters and telegrams concerning the deportation of Jews from Hungary and Slovakia to Poland; deportation means, of course, death. Frequently 10,000 to 15,000 persons *a day* are deported. Up to now, about 300,000 persons have been deported.
>
> We have submitted to the American and to the British embassies in Berne the proposal of bombarding the railroad junctions concerned, Kaschau and Pressov, but up to now there is no result of this step. The whole rescue action, commissaries, speeches, pity etc. is without purpose if no decisive steps are undertaken.
>
> Please intervene immediately at President Roosevelt, Churchill and eventually Moscow to obtain the proposed bombarding, which is the only way for rescuing still a remnant of these people.[14]

Rosenheim received the message on June 18, and immediately forwarded copies to the leaders of the major Jewish organizations and to John Pehle of the War Refugee Board. Pehle sent the Rosenheim appeal to the U.S. War Department. On June 26, the Department's Operations Division rejected the request as "impracticable" because it would require "diversion of considerable air support essential to the success of our forces."[15] On July 1, A. Leon Kubowitzki of the World Jewish Congress suggested to Pehle "that the Polish Government in London be approached by this government and requested to instruct its underground to attack the camps of Oswiecim [Auschwitz] and Birkenau and to destroy the instruments of death."[16] The idea of bombing the rail lines or attacking Auschwitz was the subject of some public discussion in the Jewish community. On June 27, a columnist for the Yiddish daily *Morning Journal* criticized the proposal on the grounds that a raid on the death camps themselves would result in the accidental killing of inmates.[17] Five days later, the JTA reported "private advices" that the Hungarian authorities were "anxious to complete the deportation of Jews from the capital [sic] before the principal railway lines leading to and from the city are crippled by allied air attacks.'' The report noted suggestively that ''large-scale deportation of the 250,000 Jews of Budapest would be difficult if rail communications are disrupted.''[18] On July 14, the JTA disclosed that Paul Tofahrn, secretary of the Railwaymen's Branch of the International Federation of Transport Workers, was broadcasting messages to railway workers in Hungary, Poland, and Czechoslovakia, urging them to ''save your unfortunate fellowmen from death in the extermination camps of Poland'' by sabotaging rail equipment being used to transport the Jews.[19] Six days later, the JTA again publicly broached the bombing idea; it reported from London that ''liberal circles are demanding that Britain and the United States act to save the Jews of Hungary by first bombing the extermination camps of Oswiecim and Birkenau in Poland.''[20]

While the bombing idea was circulating in late June and early July, four major American Jewish organizations held their annual conventions. None, however, called for an Allied attack on Auschwitz or on the rail lines leading to it.

The fifth annual convention of Agudas Israel opened in Ferndale, New York, on June 23. Speakers urged ''redoubled efforts on behalf of the Jews of Europe,'' but made no demand for specific U.S. action. The theme of the second day was a call for ''unity of action for the rescue of European Jewry,'' but again there was no specific demand for intervention by the United States.[21] That same afternoon, the fifty-fifth annual convention of the Central Conference of American [Reform] Rabbis began in Cincinnati. The emphasis on opening day was a controversy over a Reform congregation in Houston that had decided to bar from membership Jews who observed traditional dietary rules.[22]

The first preliminary meeting of delegates to the second session of the American Jewish Conference was held on June 25 in New York. The main topic for discussion was ''the future organization and functions of the American Jewish Conference,'' the JTA reported. Among the suggestions debated were proposals that the name be changed back to ''Assembly''; that the emphasis of the second session ''be placed on post-war problems''; and that the Conference be established ''as a permanent body.'' There was no discussion of the American refusal to bomb Auschwitz.[23]

June 26 was the fifth and concluding day of the Agudas Israel gathering; a resolution protesting British policy in Palestine was passed.[24] It was also the fourth day of the CCAR convention; the Reform rabbis elected officers for their organization and adopted resolutions decrying the "segregation of blood of Negro donors," demanding "justice to Japanese-Americans," supporting union strikes, and praising "the great record of American industrial management." The Holocaust was not on the agenda.[25]

Meanwhile, the forty-fourth [Conservative] Rabbinical Assembly convention opened in Lackawaxen, Pennsylvania, that same day; "post-war problems" were the announced focus.[26] When the RA convention drew to a close four days later, the issue of American intervention for Hungary's Jews had still not been raised. The closest the delegates came to considering the European crisis was a resolution praising President Roosevelt for establishing the Oswego free port.[27]

The convention of the [Orthodox] Rabbinical Council of America began at the Hotel Pennsylvania in Manhattan on July 10. The list of "subjects slated for discussion" included "Outlook for Judaism in the United States," "The Future of Palestine," and the "Reconstruction of European Jewry."[28] The Hungarian Jewish crisis was conspicuously absent from the agenda.

But if American Jewish leaders were not pressing for Allied strikes on the death camps, what exactly *were* they doing?

Some Jewish leaders were on vacation. At the peak of the slaughter in Hungary, one vacationing official of the AJCommittee wrote to a colleague of his sorrow "that I was unable to visit you in the country." He added, "We had a very fine time in Provincetown—nice and cool. I hope all three of you are enjoying your vacation."[29]

Some Jewish leaders were trying to convince the Jewish public that they had not been silent while their brethren perished. At a meeting of the Joint Emergency Committee for European Jewish Affairs, Stephen Wise admitted that he was well aware of the misgivings "which had been widely expressed about the inactivity of the Joint Emergency Committee." He insisted that the committee "has had many activities," but most were "of a highly confidential character which cannot be reported even to this Committee."[30] On July 14, the Commission of Rescue of the American Jewish Conference issued a lengthy memorandum insisting that it had "constantly pressed" for action to save Hungarian Jewry. According to the JTA,

154

The statement emphasized that among other things, steps were taken by the American Jewish Conference to mobilize American public opinion in support of an effective rescue program. The Jewish Agency was requested to obtain as many Palestine certificates as possible for Hungarian Jews. Efforts were made to secure visas for Hungarian rabbis. . . . The proposal was made that the Hungarian government be asked by neutral intermediaries for a statement of its intentions with regard to the Jews, and that the Red Cross be permitted access to the concentration camps.

During April, May, and June 1944, many meetings of the American Zionist Emergency Council leadership were dominated not by discussions about the situation in Hungary but rather by scheming about how to keep one step ahead of the Bergsonites. Alarmed that the Bergson boys were attracting attention by placing pro-rescue advertisements in the Yiddish press, AZEC officials debated the idea of publishing similar ads in order to counter Bergson's influence.[39] When the AZEC leaders heard rumors that "the Bergson group is in touch with the War Refugee Board and is probably planning a campaign designed towards having the doors of Turkey opened to refugees," they decided that they themselves "should deal with this problem of Turkey" lest Bergson "be permitted to get ahead of the responsible bodies with a campaign for the admission of refugees into Turkey."[40]

At the peak of the Hungarian crisis, AZEC officials met frequently with prominent politicians—but the subject for discussions was often Bergson rather than Hungary. Herman Shulman of the AZEC met with Wendell Willkie (the 1940 Republican presidential nominee) to persuade him to avoid Bergson. Evidently Shulman was successful. The minutes of the May 15 AZEC session reported, "In the light of his conversations with Mr. Shulman, there was little likelihood that Mr. Willkie would associate himself with the Bergson group."[41] A group of Jewish congressmen contacted the AZEC and "volunteered to form themselves into an informal committee which would render whatever assistance it could when called upon." Laurence Feuer, the AZEC representative in Washington, decided that the activity of the Bergson group "might very well be the first problem to present to them." Feuer spoke to the congressmen at length about the need for them to denounce the Bergson boys. When the congressmen suggested that they might want to interview a Bergson spokesman before issuing any statement, the AZEC board members were furious; they insisted that the congressmen were already "in a position to issue a statement [against Bergson] without further delay."[42]

On July 18, the Hungarian government agreed, under international pressure, to halt the deportations. But the gas chambers of Auschwitz were by no means empty. Now that most of the Hungarian Jews had been annihilated, the incoming cattle cars were packed with Jews from other countries. The Holocaust still raged.

It was not until July 31 that the constituents of the American Jewish Conference, together with the American Jewish Committee, jointly sponsored a protest rally at Madison Square Garden. The extraordinary size of the crowd was indicative of the deep concern among grassroots American Jews. More than 40,000 people packed the Garden and spilled out into the surrounding streets. The resolutions adopted at the rally went further than any previous public statements by the American Jewish leadership. They urged "that the protection of the United States and the other United Nations should be openly extended to the victims; that the territories under their administration should be open to all Jews who can be rescued." For the first time, they publicly called for Allied military action against the death camps: "Military authorities, in cooperation with the underground forces, should make every effort to destroy the implements and facilities of the Nazi executions," they urged.[43] The question that remained unanswered was what the Jewish leaders would do if their appeals were ignored. Would they, for example, threaten to turn those 40,000 protesters into 40,000 potential Republican votes in the forthcoming presidential election?

On August 9, A. Leon Kubowitzki sent the War Department a copy of a letter he had received from a member of the Czech government-in-exile, proposing the bombing of Auschwitz and the railways leading to it. John J. McCloy, the Assistant Secretary of War, replied:

> [S]uch an operation could be executed only by the diversion of considerable air support essential to the success of our forces now engaged in decisive operations elsewhere and would in any case be of such doubtful efficacy that it would not warrant the use of our resources. There has been considerable opinion to the effect that such an effort, even if practicable, might provoke even more vindictive action by the Germans.[44]

The AJConference statement concluded with a cryptic assurance that "in addition to these measures, many other steps have been proposed and partly executed, some of them of a nature that cannot be indicated at this time."[31] On July 17, the AJCommittee, which was no longer a constituent of the AJConference, distributed its own list of "Steps Taken by the American Jewish Committee in Behalf of the Jews in Hungary." The steps consisted almost entirely of memoranda drawn up, telegrams dispatched, or private meetings held with low-ranking officials of the Roosevelt administration. There was no mention of attempts to promote the proposal to bomb the railways to Auschwitz.[32] There was a disturbing discrepancy between what the AJCommittee claimed it was doing to promote rescue and the continued opposition by AJCommittee officials to every realistic proposal for the resettlement of those rescued. Thus a suggestion that Santo Domingo be utilized to relocate 100,000 Jews "who could not find a place of refuge elsewhere" was opposed by Max Gottschalk of the AJCommittee's Overseas Committee on the ground that it was "a defeatist solution because it admits that no other country accepts Jews, to which we can't agree."[33]

Some Jewish leaders were busy trying to convince the Federal authorities to take action against Peter Bergson. Beginning in early 1944, leaders of the AJCommittee actively sought the aid of U.S. officials in quashing Bergson. On January 10, Morris Waldman met with State Department officials to discuss a variety of subjects. One was Bergson. Waldman "inquired whether there was not some way in which the Department could instigate an investigation of Mr. Bergson with a view to curtailing his stay in the United States." Waldman asserted that "upon investigating the Department would find that many of Mr. Bergson's advertisements were little better than racketeering." A State Department officer replied that "any such investigation would undoubtedly have to be carried out by the Federal Bureau of Investigation and...it was very doubtful whether the Department of State would be able to have such an investigation made." Assistant Secretary of State Wallace Murray added that "inevitably the Department would be accused of playing politics if it should make such a move," but suggested that "there was no reason" why the Jewish leaders could not submit such a request directly to the Department of Justice.[34] Nahum Goldmann paid a similar visit to the State Department. On May 19, Goldmann told State officials that "the activities of

Bergson and his colleagues had been a matter of the greatest concern to the official Zionist leadership and that it distressed him to see Bergson received in high places and given facilities by this Government." Goldmann said he "could not see why this Government did not either deport Bergson or draft him." One of the State Department officials evidently inquired as to Stephen Wise's opinion of Bergson; Goldmann replied that Wise "regarded Bergson as equally as great an enemy of the Jews as Hitler, for the reason that his activities could only lead to increased anti-Semitism."[35] Goldmann's request was not ignored. Within days, State Department officials were inquiring of the Federal Bureau of Investigation about Bergson's draft status. D. M. Ladd of the FBI replied to State on May 23 that Selective Service headquarters had already "requested Bergson's induction into the United States Navy expedited since 'this man has been in the hair of Cordell Hull and they would like to have him inducted with the least possible trouble.'"[36] But Bergson had influential friends in Washington. At his request, Rep. Andrew Somers (D-New York) and Rep. Will Rogers, Jr. (D-California) repeatedly wrote to the Selective Service authorities to demand that Bergson be left alone.[37] Goldmann's suggestion that Bergson be deported (rather than merely drafted) made no headway because it posed a potentially sticky political problem for the U.S. authorities. Robert Alexander of the State Department's Visa Division confirmed to the FBI in May that the visitor's visa given to Bergson when he first entered the United States back in 1940 had expired. Bergson's status, according to Alexander, was " 'overstayed' " and therefore there already was "a warrant outstanding for the deportation of Bergson." But it "has not been served," Alexander explained, "because it might make a martyr out of Bergson."[38]

Representatives of all the major Jewish organizations met in Washington on August 11 with John Pehle of the War Refugee Board. The group included Kubowitzki, Eugene Hevesi of the AJCommittee, Bezalel Sherman of the Jewish Labor Committee, I. L. Kenen of the AJConference, and two officials of Agudas Israel. Pehle "flatly rejected as unfeasible the proposal that the extermination installations in Oswieczym [Auschwitz] and elsewhere should be destroyed by bombing or parachutists," Hevesi reported to his superiors. According to Kenen's notes of the meeting, Pehle responded to Kubowitzki's bombing proposal by claiming that the proposal "had been objected to by Jewish organizations because it would result in the extermination of large numbers of Jews there." The alternative, Pehle said, "was to send an underground detachment," but he "expressed doubt that the Poles could muster the strength for such engagements." The notes by Hevesi and Kenen report no protest by the attendees. When the Jewish leaders suggested that Allied planes be used to fly Jewish refugee children out of Hungary, Pehle warned that "public reaction would not be favorable" to such a diversion of Allied military resources. Pehle reminded his guests of a recent incident in which "some Jews, members of a single family, had managed at a large price to fly to Lisbon," using money that had evidently been smuggled to them from Western sources. "There had been a bad reaction because Swiss francs had been made available to the Axis," Pehle asserted.[45] A week later, the groups represented at the meeting presented to Pehle a formal memorandum outlining their recommendations for rescue action. The memo carefully avoided any suggestion that Allied forces should be diverted to bomb the death camps or the railways leading to them.[46]

Jewish leaders seem to have known that the Allied excuses about "diversion of forces" were false. They were apparently aware that Allied bombing raids on German oil installations in Poland had already included targets in and around the Auschwitz complex. When Nahum Goldmann approached a senior British official in October with a new proposal to bomb the death camp, he was told that "the British had to save bombs for military targets and that the only salvation for the Jews would be for the Allies to win the war." Goldmann responded that "the few dozen bombs needed to strike the death camps would not influence the outcome of the war and pointed out that the Royal Air Force was regularly bombing the I. G. Farben factories, a few miles distant from Auschwitz."[47] Goldmann was correct. Since May, the Allies had been conducting massive bombing raids on Nazi industrial complexes throughout Central Europe, and Auschwitz was for the first time within easy striking range. On August 20, Allied bombers had raided a group of eight German synthetic oil and rubber installations near Auschwitz and had struck an industrial site at Auschwitz itself. The fleet of over two hundred U.S. and British fighters had dropped 1,336 five-hundred-pound bombs on the factory sections of Auschwitz, less than five miles from the gas chambers. An identical bombing attack on the industrial installations at Auschwitz had been carried out on September 13 by ninety-six Allied Liberators; one accidental hit on Birkenau itself had killed a large number of German soldiers on leave from the eastern front.[48]

But when Goldmann and Stephen Wise convened a "War Emergency Conference" of the World Jewish Congress in Atlantic City several weeks later, the subject of Allied air strikes on Auschwitz was not on the agenda. Much of the scheduled conference activity focused on the postwar situation instead. The delegates discussed "Relief, Rehabilitation and Reconstruction," "Restoration and Guarantee of Jewish rights," and "Restitution of Property."[49] In his opening address to the conference, Wise felt constrained to once again challenge the old accusation that Jews had dragged America into the battle: "[I]t is never Jews who are war-mongers, but the nations," he declared. "And when we are charged with war-mongering, it is only because we are the first or earliest victims of war, even wars waged within a nation of which we are part as well as of war between nations."[50] Goldmann, in his speech to the gathering, spoke of the Holocaust as if it were an accomplished fact, although he knew full well that a hundred thousand Hungarian Jews were still alive: "Today, speaking before the first international Jewish conference since the outbreak of the war, the report I must make is not one of impending catastrophe such as one sensed at the preliminary world Jewish Conference in Geneva in 1932. It is the report of a disaster which has already occurred. . .a hundred thousand more or less can no longer change the terrible fact that the vast majority of European Jewry has been massacred."[51] A. Leon Kubowitzki was the only speaker to mention that there were still Jews alive in Europe who were next in line for extermination, and to suggest that the conference agenda should include the task of rescue. "We have asked that the instruments of annihilation—the gas chambers, the gas vans, the death baths, the crematoria—be attacked in force either by the underground or by Allied paratroopers," Kubowitzki said. But despite repeated requests that action be taken "to destroy these installations so as, at least, to slow down the tempo" of the slaughter, "nothing was done."[52] Kubowitzki's superiors do not seem to have attached much significance to his recommendations, however; the text of his speech was buried in tiny print on the very last page of the December 1 *Congress Weekly*.[53]

Meanwhile, the JTA reported the latest grim news from Europe:

All Budapest Jews have been deported to Germany, according to a report received here which quotes a person who allegedly witnessed the deportations.

The report says that huge columns of Jewish men, women and children were marched from Budapest to unknown destinations guarded by SS troops. These processions are referred to, the witness said, as "death columns," because of the numerous deaths en route.[54]

On the fourth day of the conference, the Rescue Commission of the World Jewish Congress issued a four-point plan. There was no demand for Allied bombing of the death camps:

1. Continued efforts to effectuate the rescue of all Jews in Hungary through the aid of the Vatican, the Red Cross, and the Governments of Spain, Sweden and Switzerland.

2. Efforts to induce the Hitler Government to treat Jewish nationals the same as those of any other religion or race.

3. Efforts to secure Jews confined in ghettoes or in labor or concentration camps the status of civilian prisoners of war; and secure application of the Geneva Convention Mandate of 1929 to the fullest extent.

4. Preservation by military authorities of the evidence of gas-chambers and other death camps used by the Germans and their satellites to kill Jews.[55]

No sooner had the War Emergency Conference come to a close than preparations were under way for the convening of the second session of the American Jewish Conference. The second session had originally been scheduled to be held in July 1944. It was delayed until December at the request of the Office of Defense Transportation, which cited the government's wartime priority on the use of national transportation facilities. The Interim Committee of the AJConference, which considered the request for postponement, conceded "the emergency nature of the Conference and its concern with the immediate problems of the rescue of the Jews of Europe." But a refusal to postpone the conference session would make it appear that American Jews were more interested in rescuing their co-religionists than in wartime necessities. The Interim Committee therefore concluded that the session should be delayed until December in order to demonstrate "that every major possible cooperation should be extended to governmental authority in support of the war effort."[56]

Just what the AJConference had accomplished during the year between its first and second sessions was unclear. *Congress Weekly* addressed this troubling question by publishing a lengthy feature essay which argued that the AJConference was not, in fact, meant to *do* anything:

[T]he Conference has no "function." All the available functions are already distributed. To grant the Conference the power to act would be to relinquish organizational prerogatives. Even within its accepted area the Conference has almost no room to operate. The three Commissions, of which one is a Conference organ in name only, and another hardly more than in name, were able to do little more than make occasional publicity gestures. . . . In point of fact, the Conference was conceived as a functionless body, and was not intended to survive the first session.[57]

A follow-up essay in *Congress Weekly* offered a "Review and Preview" of the AJConference with similar conclusions. "It is apparent," the author admitted, "that there was a gap of inactivity and helplessness for some months following the enthusiastic session at the Waldorf Astoria" in 1943. He frankly conceded that "the leaders, having a limited mandate, a set of general resolutions in their hands, and no clearly defined terms of reference, were not quite sure what to do with the task entrusted to them."[58]

Stephen Wise was enthusiastic about the forthcoming second session of the AJConference, although his hopes for what it might accomplish had little to do with the ongoing slaughter in Europe:

The Conference will probably agree to authorize its Interim Committee to name such representatives as may be required from time to time to attend those sessions of the delegates of the United Nations at which decisions may be reached with respect to Jewish interests. The problem which will claim the largest measure of attention of the Conference is the inclusion of the American scene within its field of operations.[59]

Some of the delegates who staffed the conference's Committee on the Rescue of European Jewry seemed to agree that the rescue question no longer merited serious attention. "The problem now is largely a matter of relief and rehabilitation," committee co-chairman Henry Shulman told his colleagues when the group met during the conference. "Most of the occupied territories in Europe have already been liberated."[60] This view was seconded by committee member David Pinski, who "thought that very few Jews remained alive in Nazi-occupied territory, and he therefore emphasized the need of rehabilitating those who have already been saved.''[61] Dr. Maurice Perlzweig, the British leader of the World Jewish Congress who had criticized Jewish establishment silence at the first AJConference in 1943, responded by ''pointing out that several hundred thousand Jews were still under Nazi control and that every effort must be made to save as many as possible.''[62] The final resolutions of the Rescue Committee complained that ''so little has been done'' to aid the Jews in Europe, and appealed for the Allies ''to avail themselves of the opportunity for the rescue of Jews from imminent death in ghettoes, internment, concentration and labor camps by exchange of those Jews for Germans held by the Allies.''[63] There was no demand for an Allied attack on the death camps or any other military action which presumably might be interpreted as some sort of ''Jewish interference with the war effort.''

Recalling this period some two decades later, Nahum Goldmann ruefully conceded that fear of ''making waves'' was the reason for the failure of the Jewish leaders to press for Allied action:

> I will never forget the day when I received a cable from the Warsaw Ghetto, addressed to Rabbi Stephen Wise and myself, asking us why the Jewish leaders in the United States had not resolved to hold a day-and-night vigil on the steps of the White House until the President decided to give the order to bomb the extermination camps or the death trains. We refrained from doing this, because most of the Jewish leadership was then of the opinion that we must not disturb the war effort of the Free World against Nazism by stormy protests.[64]

EMANUEL CELLER

CHARLES COUGHLIN

SAMUEL DICKSTEIN

GUY GILLETTE

CORDELL HULL

BRECKINRIDGE LONG

JOHN RANKIN

FRANKLIN D. ROOSEVELT

SAMUEL ROSENMAN

SUMNER WELLES

Somebody
Has
Failed
Us

11

During the 1940s, several American ethnic groups successfully employed political pressure to advance their narrow interests in spite of the opposition of the Roosevelt administration.

In 1941, black leaders used the threat of mass street demonstrations as leverage to extract concessions from the administration on the issue of racial discrimination in hiring. A. Philip Randolph launched the campaign by calling for 10,000 American blacks to march on Washington to demand governmental action against discrimination. "Negro America must bring its power and pressure to bear upon the agencies and representatives of the Federal Government to exact their rights," Randolph told his colleagues.[1] "Such a pilgrimage of 10,000 Negroes would wake up and shock official Washington as it has never been shocked before."[2] Moderate black leaders ordinarily would have shied away from sensationalist protest methods. But the reluctance of President Roosevelt to take demonstrative action on behalf of Negro rights pushed angry moderates into Randolph's camp. As Walter White, president of the National Association for the Advancement of Colored People (NAACP), recalled: "[F]or five months we were given the runaround. Appeal after appeal was made to Washington with little tangible result. Conference after conference was held, and nothing happened.''[3] In March, Randolph officially called for a ''March on Washington'' to be held on July 1. ''Mass power can cause President Roosevelt to issue an Executive Order abolishing discrimination,'' Randolph proclaimed. When the Roosevelt administration failed to approach Randolph to seek a compromise, he upped the ante: in May, he called for 100,000 Negroes to join the march. ''Let the Negro masses march!'' Randolph implored. ''Let the Negro masses speak!''[4] The President at last sought to appease the Negro leaders by sending anti-discrimination circulars to major U.S. defense plants. When this failed to satisfy the black leadership, First Lady Eleanor Roosevelt was dispatched to dissuade Randolph and company. A march on Washington ''will set back the progress which is being made,'' Mrs. Roosevelt argued. She used the same sort of argument that administration officials had used to mollify Jewish anger: the march ''may engender so much bitterness that it will create in Congress even more solid opposition from certain groups than we have had in the past . . . it would be considered an effort to coerce the government and make it do certain things.''[5] Randolph remained stubborn.

Finally, on June 18, FDR met personally with Randolph and White. The President offered to formally order defense plants not to discriminate against Negroes in hiring. Randolph insisted on an executive order abolishing all such discrimination. FDR's response was similar to arguments used to dissuade Jewish groups from lobbying for a relaxed immigration policy: ''If I issue an executive order for you, then there'll be no end to other groups coming in here and asking me to issue executive orders for them, too.''[6] Randolph still refused to budge. Roosevelt turned to White and asked how many blacks would actually march. White confirmed the figure of 100,000.[7] ''Call it off, and we'll talk again,'' the President offered. Randolph refused.[8] Finally, FDR appointed Mayor Fiorello La Guardia of New York to head a five-man committee to draw up ''a plan of remedy for discrimination against Negroes.'' Uncertain as to whether the committee would in fact draft the executive order he was seeking, Randolph left the meeting without having agreed to cancel the march. Six days later, however, Randolph and his colleagues were informed that the President was prepared to issue an executive order banning racial discrimination in defense hiring. Randolph insisted that the wording be broadened to include all government hiring; the administration acceded to his demand.[9] On

June 25, Roosevelt signed Executive Order 8802, banning discrimination in defense industries and government alike, and appointing a Fair Employment Practices Committee to investigate instances of bias.

In 1943-44, Polish Americans skillfully exploited the political fears and weaknesses of the Roosevelt administration in order to influence its policy toward Poland. Roosevelt's vulnerability became apparent after the Republicans scored impressive gains in the congressional elections of 1942, improving their representation in the Senate by ten seats and in the House of Representatives by forty-seven. The 1942 results boosted Republican chances in the upcoming 1944 presidential election: if the Republicans could hold on to the states they had won in 1940, and if those states that went Republican in the 1942 senatorial and gubernatorial races remained Republican in 1944, it would bring the GOP's electoral total to 323—twenty electoral votes more than the minimum necessary to elect their candidate. And the Republican candidate seemed formidable. Governor Thomas E. Dewey of New York captured the GOP nomination by a vote of 1,056 to 1, the most lopsided margin of victory ever for a Republican candidate who was not an incumbent President; and he won the nomination without ever having officially declared his candidacy or embarking on a single campaign tour outside his home state. Fully 60 percent of newspapers and magazines across the country endorsed the Republican. Some public opinion surveys showed that many Americans who intended to vote for Roosevelt would do so only if the World War was still being fought—and by mid-1944, the war certainly appeared to be approaching its finish.[10] Pre-election polls hardly gave FDR comfort: *Newsweek* predicted a close race, with the outcome depending heavily on the contest for Pennsylvania's 35 electoral votes.[11] The *New York Times* forecast Dewey winning at least 150 electoral votes, with many states too close to call.[12] Roosevelt's own staff estimated that Dewey could be expected to win nearly 200 electoral votes.[13] In a conversation with aide Robert Sherwood, FDR projected that of the anticipated 50 million voters, 20 million each would vote for the Democrats and the Republicans, while the remaining 10 million were open to persuasion from either candidate—hardly an optimistic forecast.[14] In short, the Democrats had reason to worry—and Polish Americans, with their millions of votes in key electoral states, had reason to believe that the Democratic administration would be susceptible to pressure.

Even before Polish American political agitation got underway, President Roosevelt was displaying extreme sensitivity to its potential. During his meeting with Josef Stalin in Teheran in November 1943, FDR refused to acquiesce to Russia's claims upon Polish territory. By way of explanation, he pointed out that "there were in the United States six to seven million Americans of Polish extraction" whose votes he did not want to risk losing in the 1944 presidential election.[15]

Roosevelt's aides exhibited a growing concern over Polish-American agitation as November 1944 approached. On February 7, Oscar Cox, Director of the Foreign Economic Administration, sent a memorandum to Harry Hopkins outlining this fear:

> The Russian Polish situation has gotten to a state where it not only is likely to make a solution on the merits impossible, but it may create domestic and political circumstances which are highly undesirable.
>
> The Polish-Americans may be able to start enough of a rumpus to swing over other groups before November of 1944.[16]

Maximilian Wegrzynek, president of the National Committee of Americans of Polish Descent, or KNAPP, "is Dewey's leader among the Poles," aide Jonathan Daniels pointed out in a memo to FDR. Wegrzynek and his colleagues "hope to influence American and Polish foreign policy by propaganda, pressure, and the threat of weaning Polish-American voters from their traditional Democratic voting habits."[17] Administration officials met repeatedly with liberal Polish-Americans to discuss the situation. Thus Vice President Henry Wallace met with Leo Krzycki of the American Polish Labor Council on February 22 and later noted happily in his diary that Krzycki is "very eager to see that Polish nationalism in Europe has no effect whatever on Polish voting within the United States."[18] But, as the administration soon discovered, the pro-Roosevelt elements in the Polish-American community were badly outnumbered. The moderate Polish American Council, the largest Polish organization in the United States, was coming under increasing criticism from its more nationalist constituents. The PAC sought to articulate Polish interests without openly challenging American policy—on January 11 it cried out against "the contemplated partition of Poland by Soviet Russia" but emphasized its "implicit trust in our President, Franklin Delano Roosevelt, that he will not permit the Government of Soviet Russia to despoil the Polish Nation"[19]—but this failed to satisfy the rising tide of nationalist feeling in the community. The Polish-American newspaper *Dziennik Chicagoski* reflected a widespread sentiment when it demanded that the PAC either undertake more forceful political action or make room for a more effective organization that would get the job done.[20] Eventually the PAC succumbed to popular demand. Its leaders conceded that since the PAC had been established as a relief organization and therefore could not engage in overtly political activity, a national Polish congress should be held in Buffalo to prepare a coordinated political offensive. The PAC for the first time expressed a willingness to cooperate with the ultranationalist KNAPP and allow it to participate in the national congress. Roosevelt administration observers watched all of this with understandable anxiety. In a report circulated among senior U.S. officials in April, the Office of Strategic Services warned that the forthcoming Buffalo congress would "bring to full flood a tide of Polish nationalist sentiment in the United States... this is counted upon in a year of presidential election to impel the Administration toward action of some kind favorable to Poland." The congress could produce "a marked disturbance in American politics," the OSS report concluded.[21] A memo circulated by presidential adviser David K. Niles underlined this danger, warning bluntly, "Positive evidence is available to the effect that plans are under way to utilize voting blocs, as a threat to foreign policy decisions of our Government."[22] Adam H. Kulikowski, the publisher of a liberal Polish journal, visited Vice-President Wallace on April 19 to warn that, in his opinion, part of the objective of the forthcoming congress was "to defeat the present administration" because of its failure to stand up for Poland. A worried Wallace quickly telephoned Jonathan Daniels and the two tried, unsuccessfully, to fashion a statement of administration policy that would appease Polish-Americans without unduly interfering in American relations with the Soviet Union.[23]

In the meantime, Stanislaw Mikolajczyk, prime minister of the Polish government-in-exile, was pressing for an invitation from the administration to visit the United States and meet with the President. Responding to the administration's fear that such a visit would exacerbate nationalist sentiment among Polish-Americans, Mikolajczyk promised Secretary of State Cordell Hull that he "would spend no more than a week here and would refrain from speech-making or other public contact with Polish groups in this country." The Polish ambassador in Washington further assured Hull that the prime minister had issued "strict instructions to all Polish officials to refrain from any attempts to inject the Polish question into the domestic political situation here."[24] Roosevelt resisted Mikolajczyk's advances, but FDR's aides grew increasingly concerned about the potential political fallout from his refusal to agree to some sort of meeting. Secretary of State Hull warned in May that "another postponement would tend to give credence to the various rumors to the effect that we were planning to abandon Poland for the sake of placating the Soviet Union."[25]

The President, mindful of this electoral predicament, at last consented. Mikolajczyk arrived on June 5 for a very low-key week of discussions with Roosevelt and his aides. Although urged by some of his advisers to demand that the Polish premier adopt a more conciliatory attitude toward the Soviets, FDR refrained from exerting active pressure.[26] Mikolajczyk kept his promise not to incite Polish-Americans. But the threat of a Polish turn to the Republicans remained very much alive nonetheless. Assistant Secretary of State Breckinridge Long was among those alarmed over the danger. In his diary entry for June 13, Long noted:

> This Polish question is a great problem for us here. Detroit, Chicago, Buffalo etc. contain great settlements which are especially articulate in an election year. I have talked to some of their "leaders" who are reasonable and see the problem from the United States point of view but apparently they are not actual "leaders" for their Buffalo convention popped off in a nationalistic (Polish) direction instead of the American tone indicated by their "statement of principles." . . . The whole problem—not only a just settlement in Europe but a solution (or a position) satisfactory to the Poles here seems difficult—and they *may* hold the balance of power in votes in Illinois, Ohio, and New York—and Pennsylvania—though it is improbable they will control in the last two.[27]

Later that summer, the Roosevelt administration received additional disturbing reports on the subject. Joseph Dasher, chief of the Polish Section of the OSS in London, had spoken with Monsignor Kaczynski, the Polish government-in-exile liaison with the American Catholic Episcopate. Kaczynski reported to Dasher that Archbishop Edward Mooney of Detroit, an important leader of Catholic Polish-Americans, was prepared to endorse Dewey if Roosevelt failed to agree to the airdropping of supplies to Polish combatants in Warsaw. Kaczynski, cleverly exploiting the administration's electoral concerns, told Dasher that "even token aid to Warsaw would create [a] favorable impression. . . . Poles would be appeased and possible far-reaching Catholic political actions avoided."[28] Dasher delivered his account of the interview with Kaczynski to the United States ambassador to Britain, John G. Winant. Winant attached to the Dasher memo a note to Harry Hopkins reporting that he himself had just had a similar visit from Archbishop Francis J. Spellman of New York. Spellman had spent two hours detailing the concerns of American Poles, bluntly charging "that the President was more pro-Russian than pro-English" and that the Administration appeared to be preparing to make concessions to Russia on the Poland issue. The Mooney threat to Polish defections to Dewey should therefore be taken seriously, Winant told Hopkins; "the brutal action of a ruthless enemy is responsible for confusions that impact on sectional opinion at home, and can be used to disadvantage in a political campaign," he feared.[29]

Dewey, for his part, took full advantage of the Polish-American dissatisfaction with Allied policy. In August, he denounced the administration's "unilateral approach to the problems of Poland and Eastern Europe."[30] Within weeks, he was sharpening his criticism, declaring that "the rights of small nations and minorities must not be lost in a cynical peace by which any four powers dominate the earth by force."[31] Dewey made a surprise appearance at New York's Pulaski Day parade in October to proclaim that "the American people will not be satisfied unless we meet the just claims of the Polish people." Dewey urged the 250,000 Polish American marchers—many of them waving placards bearing nationalistic slogans—to "do everything in your power to bring discussion of Poland's fate" to the attention of the general public.[32] Some days later, Dewey again sought to attract Polish-American votes; this time he cited the failure of the Roosevelt administration to secure Soviet recognition of the nationalist Polish government-in-exile, and even implied that the lack of U.S. assistance was responsible for the collapse of the Warsaw uprising.[33]

The President was aware of the Polish threat. He read the report from Joseph Dasher; he knew of the concerns expressed by his senior aides; he watched as his Republican opponent made repeated pitches for the crucial Polish-American vote. The President would have preferred that the Poles compromise with Stalin; he did not want the

171

narrow interests of American minority groups influencing his foreign policy decisions. But electoral necessities forced his hand. Politically, he had no choice but to meet with a delegation of Polish-American activists at the White House on October 11. Charles Rozmarek of the Polish American Congress, accompanied by eight leaders of other Polish groups, delivered what the media described as a "bluntly worded" demand for U.S. recognition of "the just principle of Poland's independence and also her territorial integrity." The President was forced to respond, "You and I are all agreed that Poland must be reconstituted as a great nation."[34] Although his wording was vague, FDR clearly wanted his statement to give the impression of assent to the stand of the Polish delegation. The following week, Roosevelt went even further—he specifically asked Winston Churchill to postpone any public solution of the Polish problem until after the presidential election in November.[35]

Unlike their Polish-American counterparts, American Jewish leaders had always frowned on the idea of Jews using their votes as political leverage. Stephen Wise maintained that the concept of a "Jewish vote" was advanced only by "Jewish political self-seekers who would if they could achieve it, and anti-Jewish groups fully ready to exploit an anti-Jewish weapon even if it must be invented ad hoc." Prior to the 1932 presidential election, Wise went out of his way to proclaim, "There is no Jewish vote...there is not and should never be a Jewish vote."[36] Although Wise was privately disturbed by the Roosevelt administration's failure to take concrete action against Hitler during the early years of the Third Reich (in a letter to a Jewish colleague in late 1933, he complained that "FDR has not lifted a finger on behalf of the Jews of Germany"[37]), he campaigned vigorously on behalf of FDR's 1936 reelection drive. "I shall give the fullest measure of my support to the Roosevelt campaign," Wise declared, "because I believe that President Roosevelt's election is not only essential to the well-being of America, but to the highest interest of the human race."[38] Wise was outraged when "certain Jewish leaders supporting Governor [Alf] Landon," the Republican presidential nominee, suggested that there might be a Jewish protest vote against Roosevelt.[39] Wise was likewise chagrined when the "Jewish vote" issue arose during the 1937 New York City mayoral contest. "Something unsavory threatens in the present election,'' Wise reported to readers of *Opinion*. Candidates were seeking to appeal to Jewish voters by speaking out on issues of specific interest to the Jewish community; this was ''an insult to Jewish intelligence and patriotism that should be sternly resented and fittingly punished,'' Wise editorialized. ''Jews will not vote as Jews.'' In concluding, however, Wise seemed less certain that this would actually be the case and felt obliged to add, ''*Opinion* earnestly pleads with every Jewish citizen of New York to remember that he or she is to vote for a candidate for the office of Mayor on the basis of character and capacity and on no other bases and without reference to any other issue.''[40]

Wise's support for Roosevelt was shared throughout the American Jewish community. Jews were attracted by FDR's liberal New Deal domestic programs; they were impressed by his appointment of prominent Jews to senior positions in the administration; they were delighted by the interventionist slant of his foreign policy, including his criticisms of Hitler. These feelings were cemented by the overall philosophy of the Roosevelt administration, the attitude of social egalitarianism which strongly appealed to religious and racial minority groups. The fact that the political forces opposed to Roosevelt were aligned with the extreme right—sometimes including bigots and ultra-isolationists—further contributed to this sentiment. Hence in the presidential elections of 1936 and 1940, more than 90 percent of American Jewish voters cast their ballots for FDR.

But the failure of the Roosevelt administration to initiate meaningful steps to rescue Jews from Hitler evoked serious rumblings of dissatisfaction as early as August 1943. At the August 10 meeting of the Joint Emergency Committee on European Jewish Affairs, Lillie Shultz of the American Jewish Congress raised the idea of using electoral pressure against the president:

> The time has come. . . to be critical of lack of action and in view of the
> fact that this is the eve of a presidential election year, ways can be found
> to indicate to the administration, and possibly through the political
> parties that the large and influential Jewish communities will find a way
> of registering at the polls its [sic] dissatisfaction over the failure of the
> administration to take any effective steps to save the Jews of Europe.[41]

Shultz's boss, Stephen Wise, evidently suspected that Shultz's remarks represented the sentiment of many in the Jewish community. Himself a Roosevelt stalwart despite FDR's failings on Jewish issues, Wise was increasingly worried that anti-Roosevelt feeling was on the rise among grassroots Jews. On August 24, Wise wrote to Samuel Rosenman of his fears that the forthcoming American Jewish Conference might be the scene of anti-Roosevelt agitation. Rumors had reached Wise in August that the President was on the verge of issuing a statement defending the British policy of barring Jewish refugees from Palestine; the AJConference "would be thrown into a nasty uproar" if the statement was released, Wise warned. The statement would injure the Jewish claim to Palestine; it would arouse anti-Roosevelt resentment among "genuine Liberals all over the country"; and by pitting administration policy against the stated views of the Jewish community, it would have "the terrible implication that we have put second things first, our own Palestine interests above the triumph of the United Nations." Most of all, Wise cautioned, it would solidify anti-Roosevelt sentiment among American Jewish voters:

> There is yet another consideration which I must discuss with you and you will understand me. The President has come to have an unique place everywhere in the hearts of men who would be free, but for many reasons which I need not bring home to you, he has come to have a very, very special place in the hearts of Jews. They rightly look up to him, revere him and love him as an exemplar of that truly just and American spirit which abhors intolerance and feels that Jews have their rightful place of service and honor within the American polity. No one would more deeply sorrow than I, unless it be you, if this feeling of Jewish homage before a sovereign and liberating spirit should be changed. The issuance of that statement might change it. In my opening address at the Conference I shall say what I believe is just with respect to the President, but I fear that regrettably unwise things may be said in the course of the Conference by those who do not understand the immensity of the difficulties and the pressures under which the President rests.[42]

Although the planned statement on Palestine was ultimately averted, it was not long before there were public expressions of Jewish disappointment over administration policy. The first was at Bergson's March of the Rabbis in Washington on October 6, 1943. The rabbis had expected to meet with the President himself, and were deeply disappointed to find that FDR had suddenly gone out of town, leaving presidential secretary Marvin H. McIntyre to greet them. The rabbis made it clear that they interpreted this as the sign of a "chilly reception." The Washington *Times Herald,* which headlined its report of the march "Rabbis Report 'Cold Welcome' at White House," quoted a spokesman for the group as saying that there was "considerable resentment" among the rabbis over FDR's failure to meet with them. One of the rabbis, the *Times Herald* noted, "said that if the matters engaging the President were not of 'the weightiest nature' he would seek to have the entire delegation go on record as protesting the Chief Executive's denial of a personal interview."[43] The Jewish press reported that the rabbis' spokesman, one Rabbi Gold, told McIntyre "that since the President did not deem if sufficiently important to receive the delegation, he [Gold] did not deem it worthwhile reading the petition. He therefore handed the script to the secretary, with the request that he transmit it to the President."[44] Commentators in the Jewish dailies expressed strong disappointment over the incident. "We doubt whether the President would have behaved in this manner toward a few hundred clergymen of the Protestant or the Catholic Church and wouldn't have found five minutes to listen to them," wrote S. Dingol in *The Day.*[45] "Would a similar delegation of five hundred Catholic priests have been thus treated?" asked Shlomo Grodzensky in the *Yiddisher Kempfer.* "Would our President, had they come to intervene for their doomed co-religionists, have sent them to his secretary? No, this would not have happened."[46] Samuel Margoshes, editor of *The Day,* came closest to criticizing the President directly, charging that the rabbis "were snubbed as undoubtedly no other religious representatives of their rank and standing would be, if they made their pilgrimage to the White House. Somebody has failed us, and it was not the Rabbis."[47] There was so much resentment in the community over the incident that a columnist for the *Daily Forward* was prompted to complain: "Lately there has been a tendency in certain circles of our overheated nationalists to talk much evil about Roosevelt. It is almost bordering on his inclusion in the list of enemies of the Jews. In open comment it is voiced that Roosevelt has betrayed the Jews."[48] This sort of resentment was "gaining momentum" among the Jewish masses, according to Eri Jabotinsky of the Bergson group, citing "a very serious census, taken by us (mostly through congregations)."[49]

Jabotinsky interpreted the results of the 1943 race for lieutenant-governor of New York as a reflection of the growing anti-Roosevelt tide among Jewish voters. Joe Hanlet, a Republican, swept to victory in the election for lieutenant-governor, winning by a margin of over 300,000 votes in New York City alone—where Jewish voters comprised a significant portion of the electorate. "The anti-Democratic swing in New York City is partly to be attributed to a growing opposition to the Roosevelt Administration, among the masses of the Jewish population," Jabotinsky wrote to a colleague. The failure of the U.S. administration to pressure Britain to open Palestine to Jewish refugees particularly outraged Jewish voters, he asserted, and "unless a change of governmental policy becomes evident with regard to Palestine, it is very probable that over 50% of Jewish votes will go to a Republican candidate in the forthcoming presidential election."[50] The national implications of the Hanlet victory were obvious. As the Washington News headlined its report, "Joe Hanlet Triumph a Warning to F.D.R."[51] Some campaign officials for the Democratic candidate, William N. Haskell, had labeled the election "a vote-of-confidence test of the Roosevelt Administration," according to the News; if that was the case, then the administration had failed the test miserably in a state that would be crucial to the President's reelection hopes.[52]

Much to the dismay of the administration, the leading Republican contenders for the Republican nomination openly courted the Jewish vote. At a November 1, 1943, Zionist rally in New York, Governor Dewey called for the opening of Palestine to Jewish refugees. Wendell Willkie, the 1940 nominee, openly backed the creation of a Jewish state. In his diary, Vice-President Henry Wallace worried about "how vigorously Willkie is going to town for Palestine."[53]

The administration's opposition to the Gillette-Rogers rescue resolution intensified Jewish anger at Roosevelt, according to Eri Jabotinsky:

[I]t is felt in Democratic as well as in Republican circles that the issue involved, if not handled carefully, may well lose for the Administration a good million of Jewish votes, especially in New York City. This, at the present moment, is an important consideration. The debate around the Resolution has certainly succeeded in awakening widespread Jewish interest, and the failure of this Resolution to be adopted by Congress would certainly create a deep rift between the Jews on the one side and the State Department, even the President, on the other side. It is typical today to hear public orators at Jewish public gatherings saying that Jesus was not the Messiah nor apparently is Roosevelt.[54]

Officials of the British government suspected that FDR's need for Jewish electoral support was becoming a factor in the fashioning of U.S. policy on the refugee question. Britain's hard-line policy on Palestine might "hamper the President's chances of re-election," Winston Churchill noted in a message to Prime Minister Clement Attlee and Foreign Secretary Anthony Eden in early 1944.[55] When Roosevelt responded to the Gillette-Rogers initiative by establishing the War Refugee Board, Eden openly suggested that Roosevelt's primary motivation was "placating the large Jewish vote."[56] After a visit to the United States some weeks later, Herbert Emerson reported to Eden that the WRB had indeed been created as a result "of Jewish pressure, especially from the extremist groups," to which the administration had succumbed because "the Jewish vote is large, and this is particularly the case in New York State, which is of first-rate importance in a Presidential election."[57] Likewise Nahum Goldmann met with British government officials in March 1944 and reported back to his colleagues that the British considered the establishment of the WRB "a political manoeuver in an election year."[58]

Some senior Roosevelt administration officials concurred with this view. In his diary entry about the President's intention to establish the War Refugee Board, Assistant Secretary of State Breckinridge Long wrote: "So our policy increasingly is based in part—a large part—on a domestic situation," that is, the fact that "there are 5 million Jews in the country, of whom 4 million are concentrated in and around New York City." In a diary entry two days after the creation of the WRB, Long wrote: "I think it is a good move—for local political reasons—for there are 4 million Jews in New York and its environs who feel themselves related to the refugees and because of the persecutions of the Jews, and who have been demanding special attention and treatment. This will encourage them to think the persecuted may be saved and possibly satisfy them—politically."[59]

The relative importance which the two major political parties attached to the Jewish vote intensified as the presidential election drew closer. The Republican National Convention in June made an open bid for Jewish votes as it passed a resolution lambasting "the failure of the President to insist that the Mandatory of Palestine carry out the provision of the Balfour-Declaration and of the Mandatory while he pretends to support them."[60] In a June 28 "Dear Chief" letter to Roosevelt, Stephen Wise expressed anger over the Republican action:

"As an American Jew and Zionist, I am deeply ashamed of the reference to you in the Palestine Resolution adopted by the Republican National Convention. It is utterly unjust, and you may be sure that American Jews will come to understand how unjust it is."[61] Militants in the community were furious over Wise's blind loyalty to the President. The Revisionist monthly, *Zionews,* commented: "[T]o Dr. Wise and his friends, partisan politics are more important than truth and the interests of their people and their country."[62]

Yet Wise's partisan support for Roosevelt yielded few dividends. On July 7, Wise urgently telegrammed the President to request a meeting prior to the Democratic National Convention in Chicago; Wise wanted to secure from FDR a statement "indicating your personal and administration support of Zionist program besides your abhorrence of Nazi crimes against Jews and your purpose through War Refugee Board to effectuate maximum rescue Jewish civilians." But FDR's secretary replied that the President had no time for such a meeting.[63]

In September, Wise tried again; this time all he sought from FDR was "your personal affirmation of the Palestine plank in the Chicago platform of the [Democratic] Party." In a letter to the President, Wise hinted of Jewish opposition to FDR's reelection bid if the administration failed to dispel doubts about its support for the Palestine plank:

> I would not press this if I did not know how important it was from certain points of view to see you now. There are things afoot which I do not like, designed to hurt you. These must not be permitted. Nearly everything can be done to avert them if we can talk to you and have from you a word which shall be your personal affirmation of the Palestine plank.[64]

Receiving no response from the President, Wise wrote to Samuel Rosenman:

> I may say to you in confidence that it would be definitely helpful to THE cause if we could see the Chief with the least possible delay, and get from him a statement that would be little more than one of assent to the plank in the Democratic platform, together with some word that would indicate that either in this or his next term of office he will do

what he can to translate that platform declaration into action together with the British Government.

Believe me, dear Judge, that I would not press this as I do if I did not have reason to fear that fullest advantage might be taken of the Chief's failure to speak on this at an early date. It would be a mistake to let that word come just before the elections; the sooner the better, as you well understand.[65]

Rosenman needed little convincing. In a memo to Roosevelt, Rosenman warned of the potential electoral consequences of silence on the Palestine issue: "As you know, the Republicans have made much ado about Palestine—promising 'the world.' While this has not had too much effect, it has had some. My information is that when Dewey gets back to New York, he is going to make quite a play on this subject." Rosenman asked FDR to suggest to the British the "possibility of some new policy of unrestricted immigration of refugees—Christian and Jewish alike."[66] The President rebuffed Rosenman's advice. The most he would do, he said, was "say something about preparations being necessary because I do not want to see an immediate mass influx before the country is ready for it."[67]

Roosevelt's reluctance to make such a declaration was based in part on the views of Secretary of State Cordell Hull, who urged him to "refrain from making statements on Palestine during the campaign that might tend to arouse the Arabs or upset the precarious balance of forces in Palestine itself." Hull sympathized with Arab fears that American Zionists were trying to "take advantage of the political situation in this country to commit both major parties to a course which would not be in accord with the war aims of the United Nations."[68]

Meanwhile, officials of the Democratic Party were openly worried that New York State, with its large Jewish population, might go to Dewey. "New York State's electoral votes are by no means certain for the Dem. Party," a Democratic Party official noted in a memo to a colleague; Dewey could carry upstate New York "by 625,000 to 650,000" votes, another official warned. "I deem it imperative that everything be done to cut this down in order to insure carrying the State for Roosevelt"; he recommended that the President make a special visit to New York and crisscross the state for votes.[69] As late as June 2, a New York Democratic activist was telling FDR aide Stephen

Early: "New York will be the real deciding battle ground in coming Presidential campaign."[70] Just weeks before the election itself, on October 2, a Democratic Party activist warned presidential adviser David K. Niles that "if nothing happens between now and election date, Dewey will carry NY State."[71] James Farley, chairman of the Democratic National Committee, likewise expected "defections from the Democratic ranks" in November.[72]

None of the American Jewish leaders sought to use the Jewish vote as political leverage with the Roosevelt administration in 1944. The lone Jewish voice to publicly suggest that Jews not vote for the President was that of the tiny New Zionist Organization of America, the U.S. branch of the Revisionist Zionist movement. In an "Open Letter to President Roosevelt" which it published on November 2—five days before the election—the NZO challenged FDR's Palestine policy:

> You promise us that action in favor of Jewish Commonwealth will be taken "as soon as practicable." What does this mean? . . . Does it mean that all international problems have to be cleared away before you find it possible to take care of this problem, too? Must the Jews always be the first to suffer and the last to be helped?
> . . . You promise to help "if re-elected." Why? The candidate of the opposition party can make promises contingent only upon election. A President in office does not have to wait for election in order to carry out promises. You have not adjourned the business of government till after re-election. You continue to deal with foreign nations and represent the views of this country as regards American policies. Why, then, if you truly consider Jewish Palestine a just and necessary aim, do you make your action on its behalf contingent upon re-election?[73]

In contrast, Stephen Wise's election message to American Jewry was a warning "not to vote as partisans of a particular racial or religious bloc."[74] There was, however, one instance in which Wise actually recommended Jewish bloc voting: to defeat openly anti-Semitic congressional candidates. "Who would say that Jews who happen to live in a certain Congressional district in Mississippi or Michigan"—where anti-Semitic congressmen were standing for reelection—"ought not to vote against the reelection of a candidate for the House who utilizes his place in Congress . . . to deal foul blows against Jews?"[75] Wise declared. *Congress Weekly* said it was "not only the Jewish but the

American duty of the organized Jewish community'' to vote down anti-Semitic candidates.[76]

Wise endorsed the use of the Jewish vote to defeat candidates whose election might endanger American Jews. But his political shortsightedness and fears about Jews seeming clannish prevented him from endorsing the use of the Jewish vote against a President whose policies endangered European Jews.

Shame
And
Contrition

Conclusion

The response of American Jewish leaders to the Nazi persecutions was profoundly influenced by the peculiarities of immigrant psychology. The founders of the American Jewish Committee were mostly the children of German Jewish immigrants who arrived in the United States during the 1840s and 1850s. The fledgling American Jewish community of the mid-1800s was small enough to avoid attracting much Gentile attention, thus permitting the German newcomers to climb the economic ladder and integrate socially without much difficulty. The majority discarded whichever Jewish religious practices interfered with their integration, and urged their children to do likewise. Assimilation into American society was not necessarily a radical step for immigrants from Germany, since their homeland had been the birthplace of reformist ideologies advocating the abandonment of those Jewish traditions that hampered the socioeconomic progress of modern Jewry.

The hundreds of thousands of Jewish immigrants who suddenly began arriving in the 1880s and 1890s were another breed altogether. These were Jews from Russia, for the most part untouched by political emancipation or religious reforms. Their glaringly Jewish mannerisms, language, dress, and religious behavior were a source of acute embarrassment for the wealthy sophisticates of German Jewish stock. The Germans feared that the clamorous and distinctive ways of the newcomers would irritate non-Jews and thereby jeopardize their own hard-won status in American society. (One of the primary reasons that the Germans established the American Jewish Committee was to insure that American Jewry would be represented publicly by respectable voices, rather than by aggressive Eastern European hotheads.)

Yet the Eastern European immigrants, too, were generally anxious to "Americanize." Most were prepared to sacrifice their religious observance to the extent necessary for acceptance among non-Jews, although their large numbers and concentrated areas of settlements slowed the Americanization process. Those of the Eastern European immigrants who rose to positions of Jewish communal leadership were usually more assimilated than their *landsmen* —and more concerned about the need to curtail whichever Jewish behavior might arouse Gentile hostility. Thus, while the Eastern European members of the American Jewish Congress favored a more aggressive Jewish public posture than that advocated by the AJCommittee, the leaders of the American Jewish Congress were often torn between the demands of their constituents for forthright public action and their own sympathy for many aspects of the more cautious approach of their colleagues at the AJCommittee.

The turmoil of the Depression years added a new layer of distress to the psychology of the immigrant generation. Unemployment promoted fears that newly arrived foreigners were displacing American workers; it also stimulated tensions between different ethnic groups competing for the few jobs available. Economic hardship drove many desperate Americans into the arms of the extreme left, which in turn provoked a backlash of extreme right-wing sentiment that often focused on alleged Jewish support for Bolshevism; the prominence of a handful of Jews in the ranks of the radicals provided further ammunition to Red-baiters. Lingering bitterness over American participation in the First World War helped engender paranoia about Jewish groups supposedly seeking to draw the United States into another overseas conflict.

The leaders of the major American Jewish organizations were united in their belief that such suspicions and hostile allegations could be allayed if Jewish political activity was tailored to conform to the consensus of American public opinion on the issues of the day and if individual Jews were careful to behave with extreme caution. It was, to be sure, fundamentally illogical to demand that Jews modify their behavior, since if the Jewish aim was to become like all other Americans, then there should be roughly the same balance of good and bad among Jews as among non-Jews. The perception of the Jewish leadership, however, was that Jews would have to be *better* than the average Gentile in order to insure that there would be no rousing of anti-Semitism. An editorial in the journal of the American Jewish Congress explained this point:

> At times we resent the idea of having to call upon the Jew to be better than his equals. We claim the right to be equally as "bad" as the others. In a people which considers justice as its traditional heritage, claim to equality of "badness" is never justified. It finds much less justification when there is always someone at hand to label each "bad" Jew as exhibit "A" of the whole Jewish people. At such times the adherence to justice is not only an ethical command—it is a command of the defense strategy which a people must adopt to safeguard its rights.[1]

When Secretary of the Interior Harold Ickes publicly urged wealthy Jews to "exercise extreme caution and great scrupulousness in their social behavior,"[2] the organ of the B'nai B'rith seconded his point:

> Jews, he said, should be particularly meticulous to mind their social behavior because the faults of one Jew are attached to his people. Nobody took this amiss. For most Jews have taken pledge with themselves: "Since any dereliction of mine is visited on my people I have a double duty. In all my ways of life I must observe the highest of personal conduct, first, because, as a Jew, I owe it to my teaching to be a man of noblest character; second because I must so conduct myself that no act of mine will reflect on Jews. Of course, it is unjust that a whole people is made to carry the sins of a few; yet I must see to it that nothing which I do reflects on my people. Thus shall Jews meet the challenge of this injustice." This is the pledge that most Jews have taken to their hearts. They commend their pledge also the minority.[3]

As far as AJCommittee official Sol Stroock was concerned, the problem with some Jews was that they were attracting too much Gentile attention. Stroock told the audience at a youth convention of the United Synagogue of America in 1934 that they should avoid "being vociferous." Anti-Semitism would result if Jews engaged in "mass meetings, speechmaking and keeping names in the newspapers," he asserted."[4]

The Union of American Hebrew Congregations, the central association of Reform temples in the United States, announced in 1938 the launching of a "Truth About the Jew" campaign featuring pamphlets with "correct information about the Jew." Presumably this "correct information" would persuade non-Jews of the folly of anti-Semitism.[5] Stephen Wise's *Opinion* likewise quoted facts and figures to prove to non-Jews the error of bigotry. It responded to the spread of jingles that alleged a lack of Jewish participation in the war effort by trotting out "figures recently released from unimpeachable sources [which] establish the fact that the Jew is represented in the military forces of the United States and of the United Nations in ratios which far exceed his population quota."[6] A prizewinning essay for an *Opinion* contest on "How to Combat Anti-Semitism in America" advocated the utilization of "every organ of education and propaganda" in order to "establish the Jew as American in the mind of America." Information to be imparted would include "Jewish collaboration in the voyage of Columbus. . . the pre-revolutionary Jewish settlements. . . Haym Solomon and the Franks family. . . Jewish participation in every major American development."[7]

If anti-Semites murmured about Jews being overrepresented in certain occupational fields, then perhaps it was time for Jews to change jobs. "Although able Jews have the moral right. . . to enter the professions and all other occupations," wrote a columnist for Wise's *Opinion,* "obviously no more should enter any economic activity than it can provide a living for. Unnecessary friction through over-crowding in the professions should be avoided where possible by wise vocational guidance."[8] An exceptionally blunt exposition of this philosophy appeared in a book, *Mr. Smith, Meet Mr. Cohen,* excerpts of which were approvingly reprinted in *Opinion* in 1940. Directly addressing "Mr. Smith"—the stereotype Gentile—the authors wrote:

You have far more in common with the Cohens across the way than you imagine. All their distinctive traits of character, centers of population, types of occupation—all the differences in background and culture, religion and mannerisms, which we trace in succeeding chapters—are relatively unimportant. What is important, for you and for them, is that you both have been hard hit by ten years of depression; that war will endanger and peace prosper you both; that your health and economic security and national hopes are inextricably bound; that you belong, by and large, to the same political parties, see the same movies, read the same papers; that your children go to the same schools, dance the same jitterbug craze, and face the same problems of finding jobs and making homes.[9]

According to this view, then, anti-Jewish prejudice could be eliminated if it is proven just how similar Jews are to Gentiles. Applying this philosophy of Jewish-Gentile relations to the reality of American Jewish life in the 1940s, the failure of the Jewish leadership to push for the rescue of their brethren in Europe becomes more readily comprehensible. Were "Mr. Smith" to discover that "Mr. Cohen" was lobbying for increased refugee immigration, demanding that the Allies bomb Auschwitz or urging his fellow Jews to vote en masse against the President, he might well suspect that Jews were different from other Americans, that Jews were bent on pursuing their own interests whether or not those interests coincided with the national consensus, perhaps even that Jews were less than loyal citizens of the United States.

Yet the Jewish leaders' fears of provoking such anti-Semitic suspicions frequently conflicted with political reality. While Jewish leaders feared that Jewish support for increased refugee immigration would cause anti-Semitism, in fact Jewish congressmen like Emanuel Celler and Samuel Dickstein had repeatedly called for liberalized immigration without sparking any pogroms. While Jewish leaders feared that Jewish criticism of the President would cause anti-Semitism, in fact the Bergson group had publicly criticized the President without any repercussions. While Jewish leaders feared that Jewish pressure on the U.S. administration would cause anti-Semitism, in fact blacks and Polish-Americans had openly pressured the administration without provoking anti-black or anti-Polish outbursts.

Reviewing the wartime record of the American Jewish leadership, Abba Hillel Silver argued, in 1946, that "much of the failure to achieve results, on the part of the American Jewish organizations which concerned themselves with this problem, was due to their lack of coordination, their working at cross purposes, their tardiness, and the political involvements of some of their leaders which kept them from exposing the do-nothing policy of the Government.''[10]

But Ben Halpern, writing in the Labor Zionist monthly *Jewish Frontier* at the peak of the slaughter, in 1943, summed up the record of American Jewish failure more accurately. While it was true that the leaders of the free world had shirked their moral obligation to rescue Jews from Hitler, Halpern wrote, ''Shame and contrition, because we have not done enough, weigh even more heavily upon the Jews of the free countries. Not only do we have the greater responsibility of kinsmen, but our own weakness may be one of the causes why so little has been done. The history of our times will one day make bitter reading, when it records that some Jews were so morally uncertain that they denied they were obligated to risk their own safety in order to save other Jews who were being done to death abroad.''[11]

Abbreviations

Archival Collections:

AJC	American Jewish Congress Papers, American Jewish Historical Society, Waltham, Mass.
AJCA	American Jewish Committee Archives, YIVO Institute for Jewish Research,New York
AZEC	American Zionist Emergency Council Papers, Zionist Archives, New York
CA	Cyrus Adler Papers, Jewish Theological Seminary, New York
DNC	Democratic National Committee Papers, Hyde Park, N.Y.
FBI	Records of the Federal Bureau of Investigation, Washington, D.C.
FDR	Franklin Delano Roosevelt Papers, Hyde Park, N.Y.
HH	Harry Hopkins Papers, Hyde Park, N.Y.
JD-NYPL	Jewish Division, New York Public Library
JGM	James G. MacDonald Papers, Columbia University, New York
LDB	Louis D. Brandeis Papers, Princeton University, Princeton, N.J.
MZ	Metzudat Ze'ev (Jabotinsky Institute), Tel Aviv
NA	National Archives, Washington, D.C.
OC	Oscar Cox Papers, Hyde Park, N.Y.
PSGP	Palestine Statehood Group Papers, Yale University, New Haven, Conn.
SR	Samuel Rosenman Papers, Hyde Park, N.Y.
SSW-AJA	Stephen S. Wise Papers, American Jewish Archives, Cincinnati, Ohio
SSW-AJHS	Stephen S. Wise Papers, American Jewish Historical Society, Waltham, Mass.
WRB	War Refugee Board Papers, Hyde Park, N.Y.
ZA	Zionist Archives, New York

Periodicals:

AJH	American Jewish History
AmJ	American Jewish Archives
CB	Congress Bulletin
CJR	Contemporary Jewish Record
Com	Commentary
CW	Congress Weekly
DAJ	Dimensions in American Judaism
DF	Daily Forward
DT	Daily Tribune
EF	Every Friday
ID	In the Dispersion
IJPS	Independent Jewish Press Service
JCH	Journal of Contemporary History
JF	Jewish Frontier
JTA	Jewish Telegraphic Agency Daily News Bulletin
JW	Jewish Week
Mid	Midstream
MJ	Morning Journal
NJM	National Jewish Monthly
NP	New Palestine
NR	The New Republic
NYHT	New York Herald Tribune
NYP	New York Post
NYT	New York Times
Op	Opinion
Rec	The Reconstructionist
TA	The Answer
TD	The Day
WN	Washington News
WP	Washington Post
WT	Washington Times Herald
YK	Yiddisher Kempfer
Zio	Zionews

Footnotes

Prologue: Death in London, Silence in New York

[1] "The Last Stand" (editorial), *JF,* June 1943.

[2] Slightly different versions of the Polish Jewish leaders' message to Karski are to be found in Karski's *Story of a Secret State* (Boston: Houghton, Mifflin, 1943); in the account Karski gave to Walter Lacqueur in 1979 which was published in Lacqueur's *The Terrible Secret* (Boston: Little, Brown, 1980); in "The Last Stand," op. cit.; in "Zygelbojm Inquest Adjourned For Three Weeks," *JTA,* May 19, 1943, p. 3; and in *NP,* November 17, 1944, p. 28.

[3] See "Zygelbojm Inquest Adjourned For Three Weeks," op. cit.

[4] For text, see "Pole's Suicide Note Pleads for Jews," *NYT,* June 4, 1943, p. 7.

[5] "The Martyrdom of Szamul Sygielbojm" (editorial), *Rec,* June 25, 1943, p. 1.

[6] Theodore Lewis, "Men and Events: Do American Jews Really Care?," *Op,* July 1943, p. 15.

[7] "Abroad: Chronicles of the Week," *CW,* May 21, 1943, p. 2; David Ewen, "The Passing of Joseph Achron," ibid., p. 6.

[8] "Chronicles," *CJR,* August 1943, p. 410.

[9] "Resistance!: Jewish Comment," *CW,* June 18, 1943.

[10] "In the Spirit of Dedication," *CW,* August 20, 1943, p. 3.

Chapter 1: "A Dignified Silence"

[1] "Text of Father Coughlin's Radio Address in Answer to the Attack of Gen. Johnson," *NYT,* March 12, 1935, p. 13.

[2] Leaders of the Democratic Party blamed "Father Coughlin and the Hearst newspapers" for triggering an avalanche of 40,000 telegrams to key senators in the last days before the vote. According to one leading proponent of the World Court proposal, the telegrams "had a very forceful influence" on wavering senators. See "Senate Beats World Court, 52-36, 7 Less Than 2/3 Vote; Defeat for the President," *NYT,* January 30, 1935, p. 1.

[3] "Taft Captures 47 Seats, Borah 5; 15 Coughlin Candidates Win in Ohio," *NYT,* May 14, 1936, p. 1.

[4] The victim was Rep. E. Michael Edelstein (D-New York).

[5] "Jews Urged to Aid in Defense Abroad," *NYT,* March 17, 1935, p. 34.

[6] "Jews Become Copy" (editorial), *Op,* February 1936, p. 8.

[7] Adler to Lazaron, April 13, 1939, in Ira Robinson, ed., *Cyrus Adler: Selected Letters,* 2 vols. (Philadelphia-New York: Jewish Publication Society of America, 1985), p. 262.

[8] "State Department Calls for Full Report on German Situation from U.S. Embassy and Consulate Following Visit by Wise, Deutsch," *JTA,* March 23, 1933, p. 1.

[9] Ibid.

[10] "Nazi Persecution Stressed by Wise," *NYT,* March 22, 1933, p. 8.

[11] "State Department Calls...," op. cit.

[12] "Admission to U.S. of Relatives of American Citizens, Refugees of German Persecutions, Directed in Resolution by Dickstein," *JTA,* March 23, 1933, p. 1.

[13] Adler to Ginzberg, April 7, 1933, reprinted in Robinson, op. cit., p. 258.

[14] Adler to Dickstein, March 28, 1933, reprinted in Michael N. Dobkowski, ed., *The Politics of Indifference: A Documentary History of Holocaust Victims in America* (Washington, D.C.: University Press of America, 1982), p. 316.

[15] "Hope of a New Deal for Immigrants" (editorial), *NJM,* April 1933, p. 195.

[16] Noted in *JTA,* March 31, 1933, p. 3.

[17] "Carr Fights Easing of Curbs on Aliens," *NYT,* March 30, 1933, p. 2.

[18] "Rabbis Advocate Freedom of Ideas," *NYT,* May 8, 1933, p. 32.

[19] "Review of Refusals of Visas by Consular Officials; Hearings Before the Committee on Immigration and Naturalization—House of Representatives, 73rd Congress, 1st Session; Hearing No. 73.1.2 (Revised and Completed), May 18, 23, 1933" (Washington, D.C.: U.S. Government Printing Office, 1933), pp. 2, 5, 6.

[20] Ibid., p. 6.

[21] "Wants Alien Curbs on Refugees Eased," *NYT,* April 14, 1933, p. 17.

[22] "Change Opposed in Alien Quotas," *NYT,* March 4, 1935, p. 4.

[23] Henry Pratt Fairchild, "Should the Jews Come In?" (correspondence), *NR,* January 25, 1939, p. 344.

[24] "The Anti-Germany Boycott: A Statement of the Position of the American Jewish Committee (For the confidential information of Sustaining Members of the Committee. Not for publication.)," cited in Moshe Gottlieb, *The Anti-Nazi Boycott Movement in the American Jewish Community, 1933-1941*; Ph.D. dissertation, Brandeis University, 1967, pp. 514-515.

[25] Morris Waldman, *Nor By Power* (New York: International Universities Press, 1953), p. 49.

[26] "Proskauer Opposes Anti-Reich Agitation," *NYT,* December 11, 1934, p. 2.

[27] Telegram, Cyrus Adler to Oscar Wasserman, March 30, 1933; File: "Germany: Boycott (Demonstrations and Protest Meetings), 1933-36, 42-43; Box 5, AJCA.

[28] Joseph Herbach, B'nai B'rith and the Boycott," *NJM,* November 1933, p. 56.

[29] Solomon Grayzel, "How Shall We Confront Modern Anti-Jewish Movements?," *Proceedings of the Rabbinical Assembly of America* (New York: Ap Press, 1935), p. 109.

[30] "Empire Setting Revived in New Reichstag Meeting; Hull Asks Data on Raids," *NYT,* March 22, 1933, p. 1.

[31] Wise to Gottheils, March 20, 1933; Box 947, SSW-AJA.

[32] Wise to Mack, April 15, 1933. Cited in Carl Hermann Voss, "Let Stephen Wise Speak for Himself," *DAJ,* Fall 1968, p. 37.

[33] Wise to Gottheils, April 17, 1933; Box 947, SSW-AJA.

[34] "Anti-Nazi Protest March Through New York Voted by American Jewish Congress," *JTA,* April 21, 1933, p. 1.

[35] "Administrative Committee Meeting, Thursday evening, August 17, 1933"; File: Administrative Committee Minutes—1933; Box 2, AJC.

[36] John Haynes Holmes, "The Jews of Germany Are Doomed!," *Op,* August 1935, p. 10.

[37] Harold Fields, "Our Interest in Immigration Legislation," *Op,* June 1935, pp. 10, 12.

[38] "Deportation of Criminals, Preservation of Family Units, Permit Non-criminal Aliens to Legalize Their Status; Hearing Before the Committee on Immigration, United States Senate, 74th Congress, 2nd Session, on S. 2969; Part 3, March 3, 1936" (Washington, D.C.: U.S. Government Printing Office, 1936), p. 180.

[39] Ibid., p. 171.

[40] Text of letter reprinted in "Jews In Action: Five Years of the Jewish People's Committee," p. 6; JD-NYPL. Also see Schneiderman to Wallach, June 4, 1937; AJCA.

[41] Naomi Cohen, *Not Free To Desist: The American Jewish Committee, 1906-1966* (Philadelphia: Jewish Publication Society of America, 1967), pp. 222-24.

[42] Letter, Deutsch to American Jewish Committee, December 21, 1934;

File: American Jewish Congress: American Jewish Committee, 1933-44; Box 1, AJCA.

[43] Quoted in "Judge Proskauer Traduces the Jewish People: An Editorial," *Op*, March 1935, p. 5.

[44] Ibid.

[45] James Marshall, "Phantom Sovereignty and the Jewish Nazis," *Op*, February 1935, p. 22.

[46] Jerome Michael, "Phantom Issues," *Op*, February 1935, pp. 21-22.

[47] "Forward or Backward" (editorial), *Op*, April 1935, p. 8.

[48] In "Communists, Take Note" (editorial), *CB*, March 13, 1936, p. 2.

[49] "A One Way Ballot: A Reply to the American Jewish Committee and a Proposal for a Real Plebiscite," *CB*, June 5, 1936, p. 4.

[50] Quoted from *Rec* in "Press Assails Opposition to Congress as Cowardly," *CB*, June 12, 1936, p. 7.

[51] From the May 22, 1936, *San Francisco Jewish Tribune*, quoted in *CB*, June 5, 1936, p. 7; also see "The World Jewish Congress: An Answer to the American Jewish Committee by the National Administrative Committee of the American Jewish Congress" (New York: American Jewish Congress, June 1936).

[52] "The American Jewish Referendum," *CB*, May 6, 1938, p. 2.

[53] Cohen, op. cit., pp. 224-25.

[54] "Jewish Committee to Shun Plebiscite," *NYT*, June 2, 1938, p. 8.

[55] Horace M. Kallen, "Toward the Americanization of the Jew," *CB*, June 17, 1938, p. 4.

[56] "The Congress Election" (editorial), *Op*, June 1938, p. 3.

[57] See *CB*, May 20, 1938, p. 4.

[58] "Referendum Question," *CB*, May 20, 1938, p. 1.

[59] Memo, Wise to Lipsky and Shultz, June 7, 1938; File: AJCongress; SSW-AJHS.

Chapter 2: "Even If Some Hardship Results"

[1] Quoted in Arthur Morse, *While Six Million Died: A Chronicle of American Apathy* (New York: Random House, 1968), p. 167.

[2] Ibid., p. 166.

[3] "The Refugee Conference" (editorial), *Op*, May 1938, p. 6.

[4] Memorandum, Harry Schneiderman to Morris Waldman, "Subject: Proposed Immigration Legislation, April 5, 1935"; File: Immigration, 1936-39; Box 6, AJCA.

[5] Memorandum, Morris Waldman to Sol Stroock, June 9, 1938; File: "Immigration: Refugees, Evian Conference"; Box 7, AJCA.

[6] Leo Stein to Erwin Last, April 12, 1938; File: Immigration, 1936-39; Box 6, AJCA

[7] Memorandum, Harry Schneiderman to Morris Waldman, "Subject: Proposed Immigration Legislation, April 5, 1938"; File: Immigration, 1936-39; Box 6, AJCA.

[8] Celler withdrew gracefully, insisting that he would introduce the measure in a forthcoming session of Congress. See John Elliot, "Conferees Talk of Stimson as Refugee Chief," *NYHT,* July 12, 1938, p. 8.

[9] Memorandum, Rabbi Abels to Morris Waldman and Harry Schneiderman, April 29, 1938; File: Immigration, 1936-39; Box 6, AJCA.

[10] "Minutes of the First Meeting of the Advisory Committee on Political Refugees, at the Department of State, Monday, May 16, 1938," pp. 4-5; File: President's Advisory Committee on Political Refugees; SSW-AJHS.

[11] Ibid., p. 6.

[12] Quoted in "What Can We Do?," CW, December 17, 1943, p. 12.

[13] "No Human Dumping" (editorial), *Op,* August 1938, p. 4.

[14] "Review of Events," *CJR,* September 1938, p. 42.

[15] Harold James, "People in Flight: The German Refugees at the Outbreak of the War," *CJR,* September-October 1939, pp. 31-42.

[16] Jonah B. Wise to Louis D. Brandeis, August 26, 1938; Reel 107, LDB.

[17] "Administrative Committee, Minutes of Meeting, Tuesday, March 13, 1934—8:30 P.M.," pp. 6-7; I-77, AJC.

[18] Morris Waldman to Max Sloss, June 7, 1938; File: "American Jewish Congress: American Jewish Committee, 1933-44"; Box 1, AJCA.

Chapter 3: "As Heartless As It May Seem"

[1] Ralph W. Barnes, "160,000 Germans Seeking Visas to Enter U.S.; 500 Appeal Daily," *NYHT,* November 29, 1938, p. 1.

[2] Lucy S. Dawidowicz, *The War Against the Jews, 1933-1945* (New York: Holt, Rinehart and Winston, 1975), p. 18.

[3] Nora Levin, *The Holocaust: The Destruction of European Jewry, 1933-1945* (New York: Schocken Books, 1975), p. 199.

[4] Levin, op. cit., p. 200; Lucy S. Dawidowicz (op. cit., p. 158) interprets the Madagascar plan as a scheme to provide "the privacy that the Germans wanted for the Final Solution."

[5] Levin, op. cit., pp. 181-82.

[6] "Wants Alien Curbs on Refugees Eased," *NYT,* April 14, 1933, p. 17.

[7] Telegram, Adler to Hull, October 24, 1938, and Hull to Adler, October 29, 1938; Box 5—Correspondence 1933-1939; CA.

[8] Letter, Adler to Waldman, January 5, 1939; File: "Immigration— 1936-39"; Box 6, AJCA.

[9] Untitled and undated memorandum; File: "Refugees—Facts and Figures, 1938-39"; AJCA.

[10] Samuel Rosenman to FDR, December 5, 1938; Personal Correspondence File; FDR.

[11] General Jewish Council minutes, December 18, 1938.

[12] "Dealing Responsibly With Poland" (editorial), *Op,* November 1936, p. 4.

[13] General Jewish Council minutes, December 18, 1938.

[14] Ibid.

[15] Cohen, op. cit.

[16] Morris Waldman, "Effects of Hitlerism in America," *Proceedings of the Rabbinical Assembly of America* (New York: Ap Press, 1934), p. 117.

[17] Incoming Cablegram, Rosen to J. C. Hyman, March 21, 1933; File: Germany: Boycott (Demonstrations and Protest Meetings), 1933-36, 42-43; Box 5, AJCA.

[18] Wise to Mack, March 29, 1933, in Carl Hermann Voss, ed. *Stephen S. Wise: Servant of the People; Selected Letters* (Philadelphia: Jewish Publication Society of America, 1969), pp. 181-82.

[19] Wise to Ruth Mack Brunswick, April 6, 1933, in ibid., p. 183.

[20] "Frown on Parades as Hitler Protest," *NYT,* April 28, 1933, p. 9.

[21] "The Price of Unity" (editorial), *Op,* June 1933, p. 4.

[22] "Eleventh Meeting of the President's Advisory Committee on Political Refugees"; File: PACPR; SSW-AJHS.

[23] "Thirteenth Meeting of the President's Advisory Committee on Political Refugees"; File: PACPR; SSW-AJHS.

[24] Wise to James G. McDonald, December 8, 1938; File: President's Advisory Committee on Political Refugees—Wise, Stephen S.; JGM.

[25] "Paging the General Council for Jewish Rights!," *Rec,* December 2, 1938, p. 4.

[26] "What Is the Congress Doing?" (editorial), *CB,* November 25, 1938, p. 2.

[27] This is evident from a letter from L. Auer to Wise, May 16, 1939; Box 97, SSW-AJHS.

[28] Letter, Wise to Garfein, April 26, 1939; File: Refugee Children; SSW-AJHS.

[29] Letter, Wise to Garfein, May 9, 1939; File: Refugee Children; SSW-AJHS.

[30] "Admission of German Refugee Children. Joint Hearings Before a Subcommittee of the Committee on Immigration United States Senate and a Subcommittee of the Committee on Immigration and Naturalization, House of Representatives; 76th Congress, 1st Session, on S.J. Res. 64 and H.J. Res. 168—Joint Resolutions to Authorize the Admission into the United States of a Limited Number of German Refugee Children, April 20, 21, 22, and 24, 1939" (Washington, D.C.: U.S. Government Printing Office, 1939), p. 92.

[31] Ibid., p. 95.

[32] Ibid., p. 155.

[33] Ibid.

[34] Ibid., pp. 158-59.

[35] "For the Refugee Children" (editorial), *CB*, May 12, 1939, p. 4.

[36] Ibid.

[37] Quoted in Levin, op. cit., p. 127. For a more detailed description of the voyage of the *St. Louis,* see Gordon Thomas and Max Morgan Witts, *Voyage of the Damned* (Greenwich, Conn.: Fawcett, 1974).

[38] Quoted in Morse, op. cit., p. 288.

[39] "Unable to Land in Cuba, Refugee Tries Suicide," *NYT,* May 31, 1939, p. 8; "Fear Suidice Wave on Refugees' Ship," *NYT,* June 1, 1939, p. 16.

[40] R. Hart Phillips, "Cuba Orders Liner and Refugees to Go," *NYT,* June 2, 1939, p. 1.

[41] "Exile Ship Circles As Cuba Weighs Fate," *WP,* June 6, 1939, p. 1.

[42] R. Hart Phillips, "907 Refugees Quit Cuba on Liner; Ship Reported Hovering Off Coast," *NYT,* June 3, 1939, p. 1; "Cuba May Relent on 907 Refugees," *NYT,* June 4, 1939, p. 39; "Refugee Ship Idles Off Florida Coast," *NYT,* June 5, 1939, p. 1; "Cuba Opens Doors to 907 on St. Louis," *NYT,* June 6, 1939, p. 1; R. Hart Phillips, "Cuba Recloses Door to Refugees; 48 Hour Limit on Offer Expires," *NYT,* June 7, 1939, p. 1; "Cuba Again Asked to Admit Emigres," *NYT,* June 8, 1939, p. 1.

[43] Wise to Krensky, May 26, 1939, cited in Voss, *Stephen S. Wise,* p. 233.

[44] "The S.S. *St. Louis* Tragedy" (Statement by the Executive Committee of the Joint Distribution Committee), *CJR,* July-August 1939, p. 97.

[45] Ibid., p. 99.

[46] Ibid., p. 127.

[47] "Refugees en Route to Reich After Being Rejected by Cuba," *CB,* June 9, 1939, p. 1.

[48] "Tragedies on the Seas" (editorial), *CB,* June 9, 1939, p. 4.

[49] Ibid.

[50] Jacob Lestschinsky, "Where Do We Stand?," *CB*, June 16, 1939, p. 5.

[51] "Roosevelt Upholds Faith in 'Liberty of Conscience' as Reform Rabbis Open Parley in Capitol," *JTA*, June 14, 1939, pp. 3-4; "Rabbis' Parley Raps Britain's Palestine Policy, European Persecution," *JTA*, June 15, 1939, pp. 4-5; "Washington Banquet Marks 50th Anniversary of Reform Rabbis' Group," *JTA*, June 16, 1939, p. 4; "Reform Rabbis Urged to Back Neutrality Act Penalizing Treaty-Breaking Nations," *JTA*, June 18, 1939, p. 4; "Rabbis Term Coughlin Propaganda Threat to Democracy, Assail 'Isms,'" *JTA*, June 19, 1939, p. 5; "C.C.A.R. Elects Leipziger President, Reaffirms Faith in Democracy," *JTA*, June 20, 1939, p. 5.

[52] *Proceedings of the Rabbinical Assembly of America—Asbury Park, New Jersey, July 3-6, 1939* (New York: Ap Press, 1939), p. 170.

Chapter 4: "However Imminent Be Their Peril"

[1] "Nazis Machine-Gun All Jews In Town Near Warsaw, Refugees Report," *JTA*, December 8, 1939, p. 1.

[2] "Nazis Machine-Gun 400 Jews In Polish Town on Sniping Charge," *JTA*, December 14, 1939, p. 1.

[3] See *JTA*, December 18, 1939, pp. 1-2.

[4] "Appalling Horrors" (editorial), *Op*, February 1940, p. 4.

[5] Memo, Shultz to Wise, November 29, 1939, p. 2; P-134, Box 93, SSW-AJHS.

[6] Letter, Lipsky to Wise, April 10, 1941; SSW-AJHS. The AJCongress itself was wracked by bitter intraorganizational disputes, with a faction led by Wise at one point pitted against a Lipsky faction. In 1940, Joseph Shubow, a Wise loyalist, assured Wise: "If Lipsky and his minions who have dragged the movement into the gutter must be liquidated, please count on me as joining." (See Shubow to Wise, May 31, 1940; Box 942, SSW-AJHS.)

[7] *The Secret Diary of Harold L. Ickes, Volume 3: The Lowering Clouds 1939-1941* (New York: Simon and Schuster, 1954), pp. 398-99; Nathan R. Margold, "Memorandum for Secretary Ickes," December 26, 1940; Box 18, File: Interior Dept.-Virgin I., 1940; OF-6q, FDR.

[8] *The Memoirs of Cordell Hull,* volume 2 (New York: Macmillan, 1948), pp. 1538-39.

[9] Fred L. Israel, ed., *The War Diary of Breckinridge Long: Selections from the Years 1939-1944* (Lincoln: University of Nebraska Press, 1966), p. 173.

[10] Ibid., p. 196.

[11] Quoted in Herbert Druks, *The Failure to Rescue* (New York: Robert Spellman, 1977), p.16.

[12] Wise to Otto Nathan, September 17, 1940. Cited in Voss, *Stephen S. Wise*, p. 242.

[13] "Ickes Suggests Alaskan Haven For Reich Jews," *NYHT,* November 24, 1938, p. 7.

[14] *Secret Diary,* op. cit., pp. 56-57.

[15] "Alaskan Leader Welcomes Refugee Colonization, But Opposes Entry Rule Changes," *JTA,* January 3, 1940, pp. 2-3.

[16] "Hearings Scheduled on Alaska Refugee Bill; Ickes Backs Measure," *JTA,* May 9, 1940, p. 1.

[17] "New Frontiers in Alaska" (editorial), *JF,* May 1940, pp. 3-4.

[18] "Alaska Colonization Essential for National Defense, Ickes Tells Senate Group," *JTA,* May 14, 1940, pp. 1-2.

[19] Wise to Frankfurter, October 17, 1939; SSW-AJHS.

[20] "New Frontiers in Alaska," op. cit.

[21] "Another Alaska Bill" (editorial), *JF,* February 1941, pp. 5-7.

[22] *Congressional Record,* 77th Congress, 1st Session, vol. 87, part 1, p. 386.

[23] "New Bill Would Set Up International Quota for Alaska," *JTA,* January 30, 1941, p. 3.

[24] "Another Alaska Bill," op. cit.

[25] "New Bill Would Set Up International Quota for Alaska," op. cit.; "Interior Department Offers Own Alaska Bill to Replace Dickstein's," *JTA,* March 12, 1941, p. 3.

[26] This episode, reconstructed from taped interviews with Tamura, is found in Marvin Tokayer and Mary Swartz, *The Fugu Plan* (New York: Paddington Press, 1979), p. 72; notes of the conversations with Tamura are in the possession of Tokayer, according to a letter from Tokayer to the author, December 9, 1982.

[27] For a detailed examination of this period, see Edward S. Shapiro, "The Approach of War: Congressional Isolationism and Anti-Semitism, 1939-1941," *AJH,* September 1984, pp. 47-65.

[28] Cohen, op. cit. p. 183.

[29] "Washington Sees Similarity Between Lindbergh's and Berlin's Anti-Jewish Propaganda," *JTA,* September 14, 1941, p. 1.

[30] "Lindbergh's Anti-Jewish Speech Meets with Severe Criticism in American Press," *JTA,* September 15, 1941, p. 2.

[31] Justine Wise Polier and James Waterman Wise, eds., *The Personal*

Letters of Stephen Wise (Boston: Beacon Press, 1956), p. 235.

[32] Quoted in Yehuda Bauer, *American Jewry and the Holocaust: The American Jewish Joint Distribution Committee, 1939-1945* (Detroit: Wayne State University Press, 1981), p. 36.

[33] Richard C. Rothschild, "Are American Jews Falling Into the Nazi Trap?" *CJR*, January-February 1940, pp. 9-17.

[34] "American Jewish Committee and Jewish Labor Committee Reply to Lindbergh," *JTA*, September 19, 1941, p. 4.

[35] "Statement on Lindbergh Attack," *CW*, October 3, 1941, p. 15.

[36] "2,000 Jews Slain in Rumanian Terror; Eyewitness Tells of Brutalities," *JTA*, January 30, 1941, pp. 1-2.

[37] See "Thousands of Bukovina Jews Evacuated Into Soviet Interior," *JTA*, July 8, 1941, p. 1; "Thousands of Jews Killed by Nazi Bands in Zhitomir and Berditchev," *JTA*, July 9, 1941, p. 1; "Thousands of Jews Among Civilians Killed in Nazi-Soviet War; 500 Executed in Lublin," *JTA*, July 10, 1941, p. 1. Estimates of the total number of Jews killed by the Einstzgruppen range from 1 million to 2 million.

[38] See, for example, "Nazis Force Jews in Minsk District to Dig Their Own Graves," *JTA*, August 12, 1941, p. 1.

[39] "Tisha B'ab—1941" (editorial), *Op*, August 1941, p. 4.

[40] See *JTA*, October 2, 1941, p. 3.

[41] See *JTA*, October 23, 1941, p. 1.

[42] See *JTA*, November 16, 1941, p. 1.

[43] "Tragic Silence" (editorial), *CW*, October 31, 1941, p. 3.

[44] Baruch Braunstein, "Men and Events: 'Death-Space' for Jews Abroad," *Op*, December 1941, p. 22.

[45] Baruch Braunstein, "Men and Events: Jewish Suffering Not Recognized," *Op*, February 1942, p. 21.

[46] *Life*, February 23, 1942, pp. 26-27.

[47] "What Jews Must Remember" (editorial), *CW*, March 20, 1942, p. 3.

[48] "Our Support of Russia" (editorial), *CW*, May 1, 1942, p. 3.

[49] "Hungarian Troops in Occupied Yugoslavia Charged with Killing 100,000 Serbs, Jews," *JTA*, May 8, 1942, p. 1.

[50] "War Will Annihilate Three Million Jews in Europe, Dr. Goldmann Reports," *JTA*, May 11, 1942, p. 3.

[51] "Warsaw Ghetto is 'Hell on Earth' Says Eye-Witness Report," *JTA*, May 13, 1942, p. 2.

[52] "500 Delegates at Session," *CW*, May 15, 1942, p. 22.

[53] "Nazis Execute Thousands of Jews in Kaunas and Vilna Districts," *JTA*,

May 15, 1942, p. 1.

[54] Quoted in "Our Brother's Keeper," *CW,* May 29, 1942, p. 11.

[55] "Over 7,000 Greek Jews Die from Starvation: Jews Aid Guerrilla War Against the Nazis," *JTA,* May 15, 1942, p. 1.

[56] "Slovakia Deports 5,000 Jews to Hungary; Hundreds Die in Woods Escaping Raids," *JTA,* May 18, 1942, p. 1.

[57] "Accounts of Nazi Pogroms in Occupied White Russia Related at Moscow Jewish Rally," *JTA,* May 25, 1942, p. 3.

Chapter 5: The Right to Fight

[1] The phrase is that of an official of the Emergency Committee for Zionist Affairs. See Kahn to Earle, April 18, 1940; 1:4; PSGP.

[2] Joseph Schectman, *Fighter and Prophet: The Vladimir Jabotinsky Story —The Last Years* (New York: Thomas Yoseloff, 1961), p. 389.

[3] "Zionist Leaders Here Frown on Jabotinsky Army Plan," *JTA,* June 19, 1940, pp. 2-3.

[4] Ibid.

[5] Morris Waldman, Nor By Power (New York: International Universities Press, 1953), pp. 67-68.

[6] Robert Silverberg, *If I Forget Thee O Jerusalem: American Jews and the State of Israel* (New York: William Morrow, 1970), p. 183.

[7] Ibid, pp. 184-85.

[8] Meyer W. Weisgal, "Events and Trends in American Jewry," *CW,* September 11, 1942, pp. 18-20.

[9] "A Misleading Slogan," *NP,* June 21, 1940, p. 1.

[10] "Jews Fight for the Right to Fight" (advertisement), *NYT,* January 5, 1942, p. 13.

[11] Ibid.

[12] For example, Kahn to Earle, op. cit.

[13] "First Proposal Made by the Committee for a Jewish Army to the Emergency Committee on Zionist Affairs," December 3, 1941; 1:5, PSGP.

[14] Fineman to Bergson, January 8, 1943; 1:7, PSGP.

[15] Lourie to Wechsler, January 6, 1942; 1:6, PSGP.

[16] Lourie to Wechsler, January 26, 1942; 1:6, PSGP.

[17] Winograd to Wise, February 28, 1942; 102:7, SSW-AJHS.

[18] "Circular Letter to Division Directors of the Committee for a Jewish Army, #22, July 13, 1942"; File: Committee for a Jewish Army—New York—Circular Letters to Division Directors, 1942-1943; 3/2/6, MZ.

[19] Levand to Streslin, January 16, 1943; File: Emergency Committee to Save the Jewish People of Europe, Serial number 45—B'nai B'rith; 5/7/11, MZ.

[20] See File: Committee for a Jewish Army—New York, Zionist Opposition, 1941-1943; 3/3/24, MZ.

[21] Kaufman to the CJA, January 16, 1942; File: Committee for a Jewish Army—New York, Acceptances and Refusals 1941-1942; 3/1/2, MZ.

[22] "Nazi Punishment Seen by Roosevelt," NYT, July 22, 1942, p. 1.

[23] "Misguided Action," Zio, September 1, 1942, p. 8.

[24] "Revisionist Agitation for a Jewish Army," Rec, February 20, 1942, p. 5.

[25] Cited in "Circular Letter to Division Directors of the Committee for a Jewish Army, #71—September 10, 1942"; File: Committee for a Jewish Army—New York: Circular Letters to Division Directors, 1942-1943; 3/2/6, MZ.

[26] "Report of Activities of the American Friends of a Jewish Palestine for the Promotion of the Jewish Army Plan," p. 4; File: American Friends of a Jewish Palestine—Jewish Army Plan, 1941; 10/19, MZ.

[27] "Ranking American Zionists Condemn Own Policies," Zio, October 1, 1942, p. 4.

[28] "Senator Johnson's Post" (editorial), IJPS, March 5, 1943, p. 3-A.

[29] "A Proclamation of the Moral Rights of the Stateless and Palestinian Jews" (advertisement), NYT, December 7, 1942, pp. 14-15.

[30] "Hitler's Enemy No. 1 Must Be Our Ally No. 1" (advertisement), NYP, August 31, 1943, p. 11.

[31] "Action, Not Pity, Can Save Millions Now" (advertisement), NYT, February 8, 1943, p. 8.

[32] Ibid.

[33] Lourie to Cohen, December 11, 1942; 1:7, PSGP.

[34] Memo, S. A. Fineberg to Geo. J. Hexter, "Subject: The Jewish Army"; File: War and Peace: Jewish Army, 1940-1943; Box 15, AJCA.

[35] Quoted in Isaac Zaar, Rescue and Liberation: America's Part in the Birth of Israel (New York: Bloch, 1954), p. 36.

[36] Fineman to Bergson, op. cit.

Chapter 6: "The Awful Burden"

[1] Text quoted in Yehuda Bauer, "When Did They Know?," Mid, April 1968, pp. 57-58.

[2] Simon Segal, "Memorandum Re: Polish-Jewish Situation discussed at

Press Luncheon given by Bund,'' June 3, 1942; File: Poland, 1942; Box 11, AJCA.

³ Adler to Lehman, July 3, 1933, in Ira Robinson, ed., *Cyrus Adler: Selected Letters,* 2 vols. (Philadelphia. New York: Jewish Publication Society, 1985), p. 272.

⁴ Cohen, op. cit., p. 240.

⁵ Wise, "In Sorrow and Protest," *CW,* August 14, 1942.

⁶ Kubowitzki to Wise et al., August 21, 1942, quoted in Monty Noam Penkower, *The Jews Were Expendable: Free World Diplomacy and the Holocaust* (Chicago: University of Illinois Press, 1933), p. 76.

⁷ Quoted in Morse, op. cit., p. 13.

⁸ Ibid., p. 9; Stephen Wise, *Challenging Years* (New York: Putnam, 1949), p. 275.

⁹ Text in Joseph Friedenson and David Kranzler, *Heroine of Rescue* (New York: Mesorah Publications, 1984), pp. 87-88.

¹⁰ Memo, Z. Shuster to Waldman, September 8, 1942; File: Poland, 1942; Box 11, AJCA.

¹¹ Memo, David Rosenblum to Maurice Wertheim, "New Reports of Mass Murders in Poland," September 9, 1942; File: Poland, 1942; Box 11, AJCA.

¹² Mentioned in Shuster to Waldman, op. cit., p. 2.

¹³ Ibid.; also, Penkower, op. cit., pp. 68-69.

¹⁴ Rosenblum to Wertheim, op. cit., p. 2.

¹⁵ Voss, *Stephen S. Wise,* p. 250.

¹⁶ Quoted in *Review of the Yiddish Press,* week ending September 22, 1942, pp. 1-2.

¹⁷ *Review of the Yiddish Press,* week ending October 1, 1942, p. 4.

¹⁸ Wise to FDR, December 2, 1942; File: Correspondence Between FDR and Wise, 1929-1945; SSW-AJHS.

¹⁹ See *NYT,* December 9, 1942, p. 20.

²⁰ Wise to Niles, December 9, 1942; SSW-AJA.

²¹ "Fasting Is Not Enough" (editorial), *Rec,* December 25, 1942, p. 4.

Chapter 7: "The Paramount Consideration"

¹ "American Jewish Committee Adopts Program On Post-War Europe and Palestine," *JTA,* February 1, 1943, pp. 2-3.

² Quoted by Samuel Merlin in "Letters from Readers," *Com,* September 1983. Bergson mistakenly believed that his group's full-page advertisement in *NYT* on February 16, 1943, had provoked the Jewish establishment to

plan the Madison Square Garden rally. See "Circular Letter to Division Directors of the Committee for a Jewish Army #162, February 2, 1943"; File: Emergency Committee to Save the Jewish People of Europe— Political Circular Letters 1943-1944; 8/5/11; MZ.

3 Telegram, Hecht to Waldman; File: Mr. Proskauer, Emergency Committee 43-44; AJCA.

4 Memorandum, Frank Trager to David Rosenblum, February 1, 1943; File: Mr. Proskauer, Emergency Committee, 43-44; AJCA.

5 Merlin to Ziff, April 23, 1943; 1:8; PSGP.

6 Ben Hecht, *Child of the Century* (New York: Simon and Schuster, 1954), p. 564.

7 Merlin to Ziff, op. cit.; "Tuesday to be Day of Prayer for Jews," *NYT,* March 6, 1943, p.8.

8 Isaac Zaar, *Rescue and Liberation: America's Part in the Birth of Israel* (New York: Thomas Yoseloff, 1954), pp. 42-43.

9 Hecht, op. cit., pp. 575-76.

10 "The Garden Meeting" (editorial), *Op,* March 1943, p. 4.

11 "America's Continued Silence" (editorial), *CW,* February 19, 1943, p. 3.

12 "Dr. Wise Asks U.S. to Open Gates to Jews," *IJPS,* March 1, 1943, p. 5.

13 Quoted in "Declaration and Resolution," *CW,* March 5, 1943, p. 16.

14 Proskauer to Rabbi Norman Gerstenfeld, March 25, 1943; File: Joint Emergency Committee on European Jewish Affairs; Box 8, AJCA.

15 "Meeting of the Joint Emergency Committee on European Jewish Affairs, Held at the Harmonie Club, Monday, March 15, 1943, at 8:00 P.M."; File: Joint Emergency Committee on European Jewish Affairs, Box 8, AJCA.

16 "Unity in Crisis" (editorial), *Op,* April 1943, p. 7.

17 Richard E. Gutstadt to Maurice Bisgyer, March 23, 1943; File: War and Peace: Jewish Army, 1940-1943; Box 15, AJCA.

18 Samuel L. Schenieur to Charles Sherman, April 6, 1943; File: War and Peace: Jewish Army, 1940-1943; Box 15, AJCA.

19 "Report on Attempts to Stage *We Will Never Die* in Kingston, Rochester, Buffalo, Baltimore, Gary, and Pittsburgh"; 13:57; PSGP.

20 David Deutsch, "Heard in the Lobbies," *IJPS,* March 26, 1943, p. 1-E.

21 Hecht, op. cit., p. 565; referred to in Proskauer to Gerstenfeld, op. cit.

22 Office Memorandum, S. S. Alden to Mr. Ladd, "Hebrew Committee of National Liberation—Registration Act," March 24, 1945, #100-316012; FBI.

23 Baruch Braunstein, "Men and Events: What—Another Refugee Con-

ference?," *Op,* April 1943, p. 25.

[24] *IJPS,* March 12, 1943, p. 3-C.

[25] "Retribution Is Not Enough," *Rec,* March 5, 1943, pp. 19-21.

[26] "Save European Jewry Now!" (editorial), ibid., pp. 8, 24.

[27] "Letter to Under-Secretary of State Sumner Welles from the Joint Emergency Committee for European Jewish Affairs, April 14, 1943"; File: Joint Emergency Committee for European Jewish Affairs; ZA.

[28] "Meeting of the Joint Emergency Committee for European Jewish Affairs, Held at the Harmonie Club, Saturday, April 10, 1943, at 8:30 P.M.''; File: Joint Emergency Committee on European Jewish Affairs; Box 8, AJCA.

[29] "Meeting of the Joint Emergency Committee for European Jewish Affairs, Held at the Harmonie Club, April 18, at 5:00 P.M.''; File: Joint Emergency Committee on European Jewish Affairs; Box 8, AJCA.

[30] Proskauer to Gerstenfeld, op. cit.

[31] Israel, op. cit., p. 307.

[32] "Bermuda Conferees Agree to Another Conference," *IJPS,* April 30, 1943, p. 3; Israel Goldstein, "Bermuda Failure," *CW,* May 7, 1943, p. 8.

[33] Wise to Goldmann, April 22, 1943; Box 1001, SSW-AJA.

[34] Wise to Goldmann, April 23, 1943; Box 1001, SSW-AJA.

[35] "Chronicles: Review of Events, March-April," *CJR,* June 1943, pp. 276-300.

[36] "Down With Fascism Forever, Is Cry of 1943" (editorial), *NJM,* January 1943, p. 145.

[37] Chairman, Committee on Public Relations to Samuel G. Rosenthal, March 5, 1943; File: War and Peace: Jewish Army, 1940-1943; Box 15, AJCA.

[38] Letter to Gabriel Lowenstein, June 25, 1943; File: War and Peace: Jewish Army 1940-1943; Box 15, AJCA. The writer specifically states that he is writing in the name of Waldman.

[39] Waldman, *Nor By Power,* p. 213.

[40] "Meeting of the Joint Emergency Committee on European Jewish Affairs, May 24, 1943"; File: Joint Emergency Committee on European Jewish Affairs; Box 8, AJCA.

[41] *Congressional Record,* May 3, 1943, Appendix A2315.

[42] Bergson to Lucas, May 6, 1943; File: Emergency Committee to Save the Jewish People of Europe: The Bermuda Conference, May 1943; 1/11/11; MZ.

[43] *NYT,* May 17, 1943, p. 17.

[44] Ibid.

[45] Wise to FDR, April 28, 1943; Personal File, #3292—Stephen Wise; FDR; Edwin M. Watson to Wise, May 12, 1943; Personal File, #3292—Stephen Wise; FDR; Wise to Watson, July 13, 1943; Personal File, #3292—Stephen Wise; FDR; Watson to Wise, July 15, 1943; Personal File, #3292—Stephen Wise; FDR.

Chapter 8: "There May Be No Jews Left to Save"

[1] "National Assembly to Fix Jewish Attitude on War and Peace," *IJPS,* January 25, 1943, pp. 3-4.

[2] Ibid.

[3] "Call for the American Jewish Conference," *CW,* April 23, 1943, p. 24.

[4] "Platform of the Delegates of the American Jewish Congress to the American Jewish Conference," *CW,* June 4, 1943, p. 20.

[5] "Its Purpose and Significance," *CW,* June 18, 1943, pp. 3-12.

[6] Stephen S. Wise, "The American Jewish Conference: A Forecast," *Op,* August 1943, p. 5.

[7] Minutes of the Zionist Organization of America Executive Committee Meeting, February 20, 1943, p. 54; ZA.

[8] A. S. Lyrique, "Trust the Common Man," *CW,* June 18, 1943, p. 5.

[9] Rabbi Baruch Rabinowitz to Rabbi Jonah B. Wise, July 2, 1943; File: Emergency Committee to Save the Jewish People of Europe—1st Emergency Conference to Save the Jewish People in Europe, July 20-27, 1943; 2/1/11; MZ.

[10] "Meeting of the Joint Emergency Committee for European Jewish Affairs Held at Offices of American Jewish Congress, July 15, 1943"; File: Joint Emergency Committee for European Jewish Affairs"; Box 8, AJCA.

[11] Ibid.

[12] Ibid.

[13] "Joint Emergency Committee for European Jewish Affairs, Meeting held Tuesday, August 10, 1943, at 3:00 P.M., at the Congress Offices"; File: Joint Emergency Committee for European Jewish Affairs; Box 8, AJCA.

[14] Ibid.

[15] "In the Spirit of Dedication" (editorial), *CW,* August 20, 1943, p. 4.

[16] Stephen S. Wise, "The American Jewish Conference," *Op,* October 1943, p. 11.

[17] Ibid.

[18] "American Jewish Conference Divided on Palestine Question," *JTA*, August 31, 1943, p. 1.

[19] Alexander S. Kohanski, ed. *The American Jewish Conference: Organization and Proceedings of the First Session: August 29 to September 2, 1943, New York* (New York: American Jewish Conference, 1944), p. 79.

[20] Alexander S. Kohanski, ed. *The American Jewish Conference: Proceedings of the Second Session, December 3-5, 1944, Pittsburgh, Pa.* (New York: American Jewish Conference, 1945), p. 217. This observation was made by Rabbi Max J. Wohlgelernter, a member of the AJConference's Committee on the Rescue of European Jewry.

[21] Kohanski, *Proceedings of the First Session*, p. 1 – 6.

[22] See "American Jewish Conference Concludes with Resolutions on Numerous Jewish Problems," *JTA*, September 3, 1943, p. 1.

[23] "After the Conference" (editorial), *CW*, September 24, 1943, p. 6.

[24] Marie Syrkin, "Was the Conference 'Historic'?," *CW*, September 24, 1943, pp. 6-7.

[25] "After the Conference" (editorial), *Op*, October 1943, p. 6.

[26] "Washington March of 500 Rabbis" (editorial), *EF*, quoted in *TA*, November 1943, p. 6.

[27] "House Gets Refugee Plan," *NYT*, September 15, 1943, p. 7; "Moves for Admission of 100,000 Refugees," *NYT*, October 15, 1943, p. 21; "Asylum in America" (editorial), *JF*, November 1943, p. 4.

[28] "Asylum in America" (editorial), *CW*, September 23, 1943, p. 2.

[29] "Congress Should Act" (editorial), *CW*, October 8, 1943, p. 4.

[30] Waldman, *Nor By Power*, p. 137.

[31] "The Dickstein Joint Resolution," Memo to Mr. Waldman and Mr. Gottschalk, September 28, 1943; File: Immigration: Refugees, Rescue of (1942-1948); Box 7, AJCA.

[32] Letter to Fred Lazarus, Jr., December 14, 1943; File: Immigration, 1940-1944; Box 6, AJCA.

[33] See "Circular Letter to Division Directors of the Committee for a Jewish Army #210—September 14, 1943"; File: Committee for a Jewish Army—New York: Circular Letters to Division Directors 1942-1943; 3/2/6; MZ.

[34] "Revival of Conscience" (editorial), *JF*, November 1943, p. 4.

Chapter 9: "The Dignity of a People"

[1] "Political Letter: Volume II—Number 1," in File: Emergency Committee to Save the Jewish People of Europe—1st Emergency Conference to Save the Jewish People of Europe, July 20-27, 1943; 2/1/11; MZ.

[2] Ibid.

[3] The conference was originally scheduled to begin July 6. See "Circular Letter to Division Directors of the Committee for a Jewish Army #193"—July 1, 1943; File: Committee for a Jewish Army—New York: Circular Letters to Division Directors 1942-1943; 3/2/6; MZ.

[4] "Plight of Jews in Europe Laid Partly to U.S.," *DT*, August 10, 1943, p. 5.

[5] Hillel Seidman, "Moynihan at the Start of His Career and Not the End," *Hatzofeh*, February 13, 1976, p. 6.

[6] William D. Hassett, *Off The Record with FDR, 1942-1945* (New Brunswick, N.J.: Rutgers University Press, 1958), p. 209.

[7] Seidman, op. cit.

[8] Penkower, op. cit., p. 294.

[9] Zaar, op. cit., p. 64.

[10] "Propaganda By Stunts" (editorial), *Op,* November 1943, p. 4.

[11] Quoted in "Circular Letter #213—October 14, 1943—The Press on the Rabbinical Demonstration"; File: Emergency Committee to Save the Jewish People of Europe, Serial #90—The March of the 500 Rabbis—October 1943; 11/11/2; MZ.

[12] See *NYT,* November 24, 1943, p. 13; *NYT,* August 12, 1943, p. 12.

[13] Sarah E. Peck, "The Campaign for an American Response to the Nazi Holocaust, 1943-1945," *JCH,* April 1980, p. 397, n. 39.

[14] For text of the resolutions, see House of Representatives Committee on International Relations, *Problems of World War II and Its Aftermath, Part 2* (Washington, D.C.: U.S. Government Printing Office, 1976), pp. 15-16.

[15] Gillette to Selden, August 1, 1944; 1:12; PSGP.

[16] As it was referred to in a full-page Bergson group ad in *NYT,* May 4, 1943, p. 17.

[17] *Problems of World War II,* op. cit., p. 35.

[18] Ibid., p. 3.

[19] Ibid., pp. 82-83.

[20] Ibid., p. 96.

[21] Ibid., p. 101.

[22] Ibid., p. 213.

[23] "The Story of a Resolution: While Jews in Nazi Europe Wait—and Are Taken Away," *TA*, January 1944, p. 10.

[24] *Problems of World War II*, op. cit., pp. 218-19.

[25] "A Year in the Service of Humanity: A Survey of the Activities of the Emergency Committee to Save the Jewish People of Europe, July 1943-August 1944"; 5:22; PSGP.

[26] *Problems of World War II*, op. cit., pp. 218-19.

[27] Ibid., pp. 222-23.

[28] Ibid., p. 231.

[29] Ibid., p. 232.

[30] Ibid., p. 233.

[31] Ibid., pp. 235-36.

[32] "Meeting of the Joint Emergency Committee on European Jewish Affairs Held at the Offices of the American Jewish Congress, Friday, November 5, 1943, at 2:30 P.M."; File: Joint Emergency Committee on European Jewish Affairs; Box 8, AJCA. Also, American Jewish Conference, *Report of the Interim Committee and the Commission on Rescue* (New York: American Jewish Conference, November 1, 1944).

[33] F. Hodel, "Memorandum for the Files," January 4, 1944; File: American Jewish Conference; Box 2, WRB.

[34] "Memorandum—Issued by the Interim Committee of the American Jewish Conference," December 29, 1943, 8 pp; ZA.

[35] Text in File: Emergency Committee to Save the Jewish People of Europe —American Jewish Congress 1943-1944; MZ.

[36] *NYP*, January 3, 1944, p. 24.

[37] Cited in *TA*, August 29, 1944, p. 5.

[38] Quoted in "Circular Letter to Division Directors of the Committee for a Jewish Army #278"—January 17, 1944; File: Committee for a Jewish Army—New York: Circular Letters to Division Directors 1942. 1943, 3/2/6; MZ.

[39] "The American Jewish Conference and the Emergency Committee" (editorial), *Rec*, January 21, 1944, p. 4.

[40] Quoted in *TA*, January 1944, p. 9.

[41] "On the Question of Rescue" (editorial), *CW*, December 10, 1943, p. 3.

[42] "A Harmful Organization" (editorial), *CW*, December 24, 1943, p. 5.

[43] Wise to Tobin, February 5, 1945; 102:7; SSW-AJHS.

[44] See *CW*, December 24, 1943, and "Statement by the Commission on

Rescue of the American Jewish Conference," December 27, 1943; 7:1; AZEC.

[45] "'Sabotage' Is Seen in Rescue of Jews," *NYT,* January 3, 1944, p. 9.

[46] Morgenthau Diaries, p. 197, Book 694; FDR.

[47] Morgenthau Diaries, p. 195, Book 694; FDR.

[48] Morgenthau Diaries, p. 202, Book 694; FDR.

[49] "Roosevelt Establishes Refugee Rescue Board; Jewish Leaders Hail Measure," *JTA,* January 24, 1944, pp. 1-2.

[50] "Sen. Gillette Withdraws His Rescue Resolution; Says Roosevelt's Board Covers It," *JTA,* January 25, 1944, p. 1.

[51] "U.S. Is Asked to Use Pressure on Axis Satellite Governments to Help Jews," *JTA,* February 13, 1944, p. 3.

[52] "'Show of Shows' Nets $80,000 for War Fund," *NYT.* March 14, 1944, p. 15.

[53] "Success of War Refugee Board Depends on Palestine Immigration, Dr. Silver Says," *JTA,* January 28, 1944, p. 2.

[54] "American Jewish Committee Adopts Program for Post-War Solution of Jewish Problems," *JTA,* January 31, 1944, pp. 1-3.

[55] Morgenthau Diaries, p. 219, Book 707; FDR.

[56] Morgenthau Diaries, pp. 220-21, Book 707; FDR.

[57] "Roosevelt Urges People in Nazi Lands to Save Jews; Cites Tragedy of European Jewry," *JTA,* March 26, 1944, pp. 1-2.

[58] "American Jewish Conference Welcomes Roosevelt Warning to Nazis," *JTA,* March 27, 1944, p. 4.

[59] "Judge Proskauer Thanks Roosevelt for His Appeal for Rescue of Jews from Hungary," *JTA,* March 31, 1944, p. 3.

[60] "Government Funds Necessary" (editorial), *CW,* March 10, 1944, p. 4; "Roosevelt Urges People in Nazi Lands to Save Jews; Cites Tragedy of Hungarian Jewry," *JTA,* March 26, 1944, p. 1.

[61] Morgenthau Diaries, p. 181, Book 721; FDR.

[62] "Procession to City Hall, Work Stoppage Marks Anniversary of Warsaw Ghetto Battle," *JTA,* April 20, 1944, p. 2.

[63] "A Realistic Proposal" (editorial), *CW,* April 28, 1944, pp. 3-4.

[64] "Free Ports for Refugees" (editorial), *NYT,* May 4, 1944, p. 18.

[65] "Roosevelt Receives First Report on Activities of War Refugee Board in Rescuing Jews," *JTA,* May 12, 1944, p. 1.

[66] "Episcopal Convention in Washington Urges Government to Find Havens for Refugees," *JTA,* May 16, 1944, p. 3.

[67] "Congressional or Executive Action on 'Free Port' Plan Is Expected in

Washington,"*JTA,* May 15, 1944, p. 3.

[68] Ibid.

[69] "Action on 'Free Port' Plan Will Need Backing of Congressional Leaders,"*JTA,* May 17, 1944, p. 4.

[70] "Back War Refugees Here," *NYT,* May 30, 1944, p. 8; "Senate Resolution Asks Use of Ellis Island As 'Free Port' for Refugees,"*JTA,* May 31, 1944, p. 3; "Heads Group to Aid Jews," *NYT,* June 2, 1944, p. 15.

[71] "Roosevelt's Statement on 'Free Ports' Pleases Congressional Leaders in Washington,"*JTA,* June 1, 1944, p. 3; "Roosevelt Backs Refugee 'Ports'," *NYT,* May 31, 1944, p. 4.

[72] "U.S. Will Establish 'Free Ports' in Abandoned Army Camps, Roosevelt Announces," *JTA,* June 4, 1944, p. 1 (the JTA was jumping the gun by wording its headline in this fashion); "May Use Army Camps As Refugee Haven," *NYT,* June 3, 1944, p. 15.

[73] "Plan for Establishing 'Free Port' in Military Camps Proceeding Rapidly, Pehle Discloses,"*JTA,* June 6, 1944, p. 2.

[74] "Immediate Admission to U.S. of 1,000 Refugees from Europe Announced by Roosevelt,"*JTA,* June 11, 1944, p. 1-3.

[75] "American Jewish Conference Hails Roosevelt's Order Admitting 1,000 Refugees,"*JTA,* June 12, 1944, p. 3.

[76] "Symbols and Their Uses" (editorial), *CW,* June 23, 1944, p. 3-4.

[77] Marie Syrkin, "Free Port," *JF,* July 1944, pp. 6-8.

[78] Quoted in "Admission of 1,000 Refugees to United States Is Not Enough, House Is Told,"*JTA,* June 12, 1944, p. 2.

[79] Ibid.

[80] "Congress Postpones Hearings on Bills to Establish 'Free Ports' in the United States,"*JTA,* June 23, 1944, p. 3.

[81] "New Havens Urged for Stricken Jews," *NYT,* August 8, 1944, p. 19.

[82] Minutes of the American Zionist Emergency Council Executive Committee, August 31, 1944, and September 11, 1944; LX:4—"AZEC Minutes, Executive Committee, 9/28/43-12/11/43"; ZA.

Chapter 10: "Our Government Will Do What It Can"

[1] "Jewish Organizations Acclaim Roosevelt's Establishment of a Refugee Board,"*JTA,* January 24, 1944, p. 3.

[2] "American Jewish Committee Wires Thanks to President Roosevelt," *JTA,* January 15, 1944, p. 1.

[3] "The Task of Rescue" (editorial), *CW,* February 11, 1944, pp. 3-4.

[4] "Government Funds Necessary" (editorial), *CW,* March 10, 1944, p. 4.

[5] Cited in *JTA,* March 21, 1944, p. 2.

[6] Waldman to Proskauer, March 21, 1944; File: U.S. Gov't: State Department; Box 14, AJCA.

[7] Quoted in "Saving the Last Million" (editorial), *CW,* May 19, 1944, pp. 3-4.

[8] Cited in Martin Gilbert, *Auschwitz and the Allies* (New York: Holt, Rinehart and Winston, 1982), p. 210.

[9] "Hungary's Jews" (editorial), *Op,* May 1944, p. 4.

[10] "American Jewish Conference Welcomes Roosevelt Warning to Nazis," *JTA,* March 27, 1944, p. 4.

[11] "Saving the Last Million" (editorial), *CW,* May 19, 1944, pp. 3-4.

[12] Ibid.

[13] Warren to Smertenko, July 19, 1944, cited in File: Emergency Committee to Save the Jewish People of Europe—Hungary 1943-44; 2/4/11; MZ.

[14] Memorandum, M. Jung to M. Gottschalk, June 20, 1944; File: Hungary 1944, 1949-50; Box 6, AJCA.

[15] Quoted in David S. Wyman, "Why Auschwitz Was Never Bombed," *Com,* May 1978, pp. 38-39.

[16] Quoted in Kubowitzki to Pehle, August 29, 1944; File: World Jewish Congress—1; Box 29, WRB.

[17] *MJ,* June 27, 1944, p. 1.

[18] "Deportation of Jews from Hungary 'Within Twenty Days' Ordered by Minister of Interior," *JTA,* July 2, 1944, p. 1.

[19] "Railwaymen in Hungary and Poland Urged to Save Jews by Sabotaging Transportation," *JTA,* July 14, 1944, p. 2.

[20] "Germans Reported Willing to Exchange Hungarian Jews for Supplies," *JTA,* July 2, 1944, p. 1.

[21] "Agudas Israel Opens Fifth Annual Convention at Ferndale, New York," *JTA,* June 23, 1944, p. 4; "Agudas Israel Convention Calls for Jewish Unity in Rescue Activities," *JTA,* June 25, 1944, p. 4.

[22] "Convention of Central Conference of American Rabbis Opposes Houston Congregation," *JTA,* June 25, 1944, p. 4.

[23] "American Jewish Conference Urged to Include American Scene in its Program," *JTA,* June 26, 1944, p. 3.

[24] "Agudas Israel Convention Protests Against White Paper; Urges Cooperation with Arabs," *JTA,* June 27, 1944, p. 4.

[25] "Central Conference of American Rabbis Votes to Retain Neutrality on Zionism," *JTA,* June 27, 1944, p. 3.

[26] "Rabbinical Assembly of America Opens Four Day Session on Spiritual Reconstruction," *JTA*, June 27, 1944, p. 4.

[27] "Rabbinical Assembly Endorses Jewish Commonwealth and Free Ports," *JTA*, July 2, 1944, p. 3.

[28] "Rabbinical Council of America Opens Fifth Annual Convention in New York," *JTA*, July 11, 1944, p. 2.

[29] Gottschalk to Hexter, August 16, 1944; File: Immigration: Refugees, Rescue of (1942-1948); Box 7, AJCA.

[30] "Meeting of the Joint Emergency Committee for European Jewish Affairs Held at the Office of the American Jewish Congress, September 24, 1943, at 1:00 P.M."; File: Joint Emergency Committee for European Jewish Affairs; Box 8, AJCA.

[31] "American Jewish Conference Reports on Rescue Measures to Save Hungarian Jews," *JTA*, July 12, 1944, p. 13.

[32] "Steps Taken by the American Jewish Committee in Behalf of the Jews of Hungary," July 17, 1944; File: Hungary 1944, 1949-50; Box 8, AJCA.

[33] Gottschalk to Hexter, August 6, 1944. Cited in Edward David Pinsky, "Cooperation Among American Jewish Organizations in Their Efforts to Rescue European Jewry During the Holocaust, 1939-1943," Ph.D. dissertation, New York University, 1980, p. 101.

[34] Department of State—Division of Near Eastern Affairs, Memorandum of Conversation, January 10, 1944; PSGP 3:67.

[35] Memorandum of Conversaton with Nahum Goldmann, May 19, 1944; 867 N.01/2347 PS/LC; NA.

[36] Office Memorandum—United States Government, D. M. Ladd to E. A. Tann, May 23, 1944; Subject: Hillel Kook, alias Peter Bergson; Hebrew Committee of National Liberation; FBI.

[37] Somers and Rogers to Local Board #31, March 18, 1944; File: Committee for a Jewish Army—New York: Selective Service System, U.S.A., 1942-1943; 24/3/3; MZ.

[38] Office Memorandum—United States Government, D. M. Ladd to E. A. Tamm, May 23, 1944, p. 3; Subject: Hillel Kook, alias Peter Bergson; Hebrew Committee of National Liberation; Document #310922-3; FBI.

[39] AZEC Minutes for April 17, 1944; File: AZEC Minutes—Executive Committee, 9/28/43-12/11/43; LX:4; AZEC.

[40] AZEC Minutes for May 1, 1944; File: AZEC Minutes—Executive Committee, 9/28/43-12/11/43; LX:4; AZEC.

[41] AZEC Minutes for May 15, 1944; File: AZEC Minutes—Executive Committee, 9/28/43-12/11/43; LX:4; AZEC.

[42] Ibid.

[43] "40,000 Here Seek Way to Save Jews," *NYT,* August 1, 1944, P. 17.

[44] Wyman, op. cit., p. 40.

[45] I. L. Kenen, "Report of Meeting with John W. Pehle, Executive Director and Messrs. Lesser and Friedman of the War Refugee Board, August 16, 1944," and Memo, Eugene Hevesi to Dr. Slawson, August 17, 1944; both in File: Hungary 1944, 1949-50; Box 6, AJCA.

[46] I. L. Kenen, "Memorandum of Measures of Relief and Rescue of Jews Surviving in and Deported from Hungary," August 23, 1944; File: Hungary 1944, 1949-50; Box 6, AJCA.

[47] Gilbert, op. cit., p. 321.

[48] "Holocaust survivor: Allies could have bombed crematoria," *JW,* March 29, 1981, p. 28; Gilbert, op. cit.

[49] See *CW,* November 24, 1944, p. 16.

[50] Stephen S. Wise, "Justice to the Jew," *CW,* December 1, 1944, pp. 10-11.

[51] Dr. Nahum Goldmann, "Building for a Jewish Furure," ibid., pp. 12-13.

[52] "Proceedings of World Conference," *CW,* December 1, 1944, pp. 15-16.

[53] Ibid.

[54] "All Budapest Jews Reported Deported to Germany; Marched from City in 'Death Columns,'" *JTA,* November 28, 1944, p. 3.

[55] "War Reparations Asked by World Jewish Conference; Funds to be Spent in Palestine," *JTA,* November 30, 1944, p. 2.

[56] *Conference Record,* July, 1945, pp. 1-2.

[57] Joshua Trachtenberg, "Conference or Assembly? An Analysis and a Challenge," *CW,* November 3, 1944, pp. 6-7.

[58] Mark Migdal, "Review and Preview: Fourteen Months of American Jewish Conference," *CW,* December 1, 1944, pp. 6-7.

[59] "Two Great Conferences" (editorial), *Op,* December 1944, p. 7.

[60] Kohanski, *Proceedings of the Second Session,* op. cit., p. 210.

[61] Ibid., p. 219.

[62] Ibid.

[63] "American Jewish Conference Rejects Proposals to Widen the Scope of Its Activities," *JTA,* December 6, 1944, pp. 1-2.

[64] Nahum Goldmann, "Jewish Heroism in Siege," *ID,* Winter 1963-1964, p. 7.

Chapter 11: "Somebody Has Failed Us"

[1] Jervis Anderson, *A. Philip Randolph: A Biographical Portrait* (New York: Harcourt, 1973).

[2] Herbert Garfinkel, *When Negroes March: The March on Washington Movement in the Organizational Politics for FEPC* (Gleacoe, Ill: Free Press, 1959), p. 37.

[3] Ibid., p. 39.

[4] Anderson, op. cit., p. 251.

[5] Ibid., p. 252; Daniel S. Davis, *Mr. Black Labor: The Story of A. Philip Randolph, Father of the Civil Rights Movement* (New York: Dutton, 1972), p. 107.

[6] Anderson, op. cit., p. 257.

[7] Garfinkel, op. cit., p. 54.

[8] Anderson, op. cit., p. 258.

[9] Garfinkel, op. cit., p. 61.

[10] Leon Friedman, "Election of 1944," in Arthur M. Schlesinger, Jr., ed., *History of American Presidential Elections, 1784-1968, vol. 4, 1940-1968* (New York: McGraw Hill, 1971), p. 3023.

[11] Ibid., p. 3037.

[12] Ibid.

[13] Ibid.

[14] Robert E. Sherwood, *Roosevelt and Hopkins: An Intimate History* (New York: Harper and Brothers, 1950), p. 822.

[15] Francis L. Loewenheim, Harold D. Langley, and Manfred Jones, eds., *Roosevelt and Churchill: Their Secret Wartime Correspondence* (New York: Dutton, 1975), p. 406.

[16] Memo, Cox to Hopkins, February 7, 1944; File: Growing Crisis in Poland; Box 337, HH.

[17] Memo, Daniels to the President, June 2, 1944; File: Poland, 1944, Jan-July; Box 66-PSF, FDR.

[18] John Morton Blum, ed., *The Price of Vision: The Diary of Henry Wallace, 1942-1946* (Boston: Houghton Mifflin, 1973), pp. 301-2

[19] Quoted in "Polish Pressure Campaign Takes Form," *Foreign Nationality Groups in the United States—Memorandum by the Foreign Nationalities Branch to the Director of Strategic Services,* No. 179 (April 1, 1944), p. 6; File: Poland 1944, Jan-July; Box 66-PSF, FDR.

[20] Ibid.

21 Ibid., p. 1.

22 Memorandum, David K. Niles to Grace Tully, June 6, 1944, and untitled reports dated May 25, 1944, and May 28, 1944; File: Poland 1944, January-July; Box 66—PSF, FDR.

23 Blum, op. cit., p. 324.

24 Memo, Hull to FDR, March 28, 1944; File: Poland 1944, Jan-July; Box 66-PSF, FDR.

25 Ibid.

26 See *NYT,* June 8, and June 11, 1944.

27 Israel, op. cit., p. 354.

28 Report by Dasher in John G. Winant to Harry L. Hopkins, September 1, 1944; File: Growing Crisis in Poland; Box 337, HH.

29 Winant to Hopkins, September 1, 1944; File: Growing Crisis in Poland; Box 337, HH.

30 See *NYHT,* August 18, 1944, p. 16.

31 "Enter Dulles, Willkie," *Newsweek,* August 28, 1944, p. 38.

32 "Dewey Demands 'Light' on Poland; Wagner Defends Roosevelt Policy," *NYT,* October 19, 1944, p. 1.

33 "Dewey Denounces 'Secret Diplomacy'; States His Policy," *NYT,* October 19, 1944, p. 1.

34 "Roosevelt Backs Restored Poland," *NYT,* October 12, 1944, p. 1.

35 Hopkins to Winant, September 4, 1944; File: Growing Crisis in Poland; Box 337, HH; Loewenheim et al., op. cit., p. 592.

36 Stephen S. Wise, "As I See It: 'The Jewish Vote,'" *Op,* November 1932, p. 15.

37 Wise to Mack, October 20, 1933; quoted in Voss, *Stephen S. Wise,* p. 196.

38 Wise to Hoover, September 9, 1936; quoted in Voss, *Stephen S. Wise,* p. 213.

39 "Rabbi Stephen S. Wise Sees No 'Jewish Vote,'" *NYT,* November 2, 1936, p. 12.

40 "No Jewish Issue" (editorial), *Op,* September 1937, p. 9.

41 "Joint Emergency Committee for European Jewish Affairs, Meeting held Tuesday, August 10, 1943, at 3:00 P.M., at the Congress Office," p. 8; File: Joint Emergency Committee for European Jewish Affairs; Box 8, AJCA.

42 Wise to Rosenman, August 24, 1943; File: Wise, Stephen S.; Box 4, SR. For details of the intended statement, see Monty N. Penkower, "The 1943 Joint Anglo-American Statement on Palestine," *The Herzl Year Book,* vol. 8 (New York: Herzl Press, 1978).

[43] See *WT,* October 7, 1943.

[44] M. J. Nirenberger in *MJ,* October 7, 1943, cited in File: Emergency Committee to Save the Jewish People of Europe, Serial 90—"The March of the 500 Rabbis—October '43''; 11/11/2, MZ.

[45] S. Dingol in *ID,* October 16, 1943, cited in File: Emergency Committee to Save the Jewish People of Europe, Serial 90—"The March of the 500 Rabbis—October '43''; 11/11/2, MZ.

[46] Shlomo Grodzensky in *YK,* October 15, 1943, cited in File: Emergency Committee to Save the Jewish People of Europe, Serial 90—"The March of the 500 Rabbis—October '43''; 11/11/2, MZ.

[47] Samuel Margoshes in *ID,* October 10, 1943, cited in File: Emergency Committee to Save the Jewish People of Europe, Serial 90—"The March of the 500 Rabbis—October '43''; 11/11/2, MZ.

[48] Zivyon in *DF,* October 16, 1943, cited in File: Emergency Committee to Save the Jewish People of Europe, Serial 90—"The March of the 500 Rabbis—October '43''; 11/11/2, MZ.

[49] Eri Jabotinsky to J. Mirelman, L. Altman, J. Helpern, Schaffer, October 12, 1943; File: Emergency Committee to Save the Jewish People of Europe, Serial 87—Jabotinsky, Eri, 1943-1945; 8/10/11, MZ.

[50] Ibid.

[51] *WN,* November 3, 1943, cited in File: Correspondence with State Leaders: New York and North Carolina, 1940-1948; New York Lieutenant Governor Election, 1943; Box 1134, DNC.

[52] Ibid.

[53] Blum, op. cit., p. 265, p. 1.

[54] Letter, Eri Jabotinsky, December 9, 1943; File: Emergency Committee to Save the Jewish People of Europe, Serial 87—Jabotinsky, Eri, 1943-1945; 8/10/11, MZ.

[55] Gilbert, op. cit., p. 171.

[56] Ibid., p. 173.

[57] Ibid.

[58] Nahum Goldmann, "Memo: War Refugee Board," March 23, 1944; File: World Jewish Congress—1; Box 29, WRB.

[59] Israel, op. cit., pp. 336-37.

[60] Quoted in *Zio,* July 1944, p. 6.

[61] Wise to the President, June 28, 1944; File: Correspondence Between FDR and Wise, 1927-1945; SSW-AJHS.

[62] "The Voice of America," *Zio,* July 1944, p. 8.

[63] Telegram, Wise to the President, July 7, 1944; Personal File 3292—

Stephen Wise; FDR.

[64] Wise to the President, September 16, 1944; File: Correspondence Between FDR and Wise, 1927-1945; SSW-AJHS.

[65] Wise to Rosenman, September 26, 1944; File: Wise, Stephen S.; Box 4, SR.

[66] Memo, Rosenman to FDR, September 16, 1944; File: Palestine; Box 13, SR.

[67] Memo, FDR to Rosenman, September 16, 1944; File: Palestine, Box 13, SR.

[68] Memorandum by the Secretary of State to President Roosevelt, July 26, 1944; reprinted in *Foreign Relations of the United States, 1944,* vol. 5, p. 606.

[69] Undated, untitled memorandum; Official File 300: Democratic National Committee, 28—New York State 1933, 1945, T-Z; DNC.

[70] Memorandum, S. A. Gordon to Early, June 2, 1944; Official File 300: Democratic National Committee; 26—F-H; DNC.

[71] Memorandum, Robert Glenn to Niles, October 2, 1944; Official File 300: Democratic National Committee; 26—F-H; DNC.

[72] James A. Farley, *Jim Farley's Story: The Roosevelt Years* (New York: McGraw-Hill, 1948), p. 369.

[73] Quoted in Schechtman, *The United States and the Jewish State Movement* (New York: Thomas Yoseloff, 1966), p. 4.

[74] "Chronicles of Events," *CW,* May 19, 1944, p. 2.

[75] Ibid.

[76] "Fighting With Ballots" (editorial), *CW,* June 23, 1944, p. 5-6.

Bibliography

Theodore Abel. *The Nazi Movement: Why Hitler Came To Power.* New York, 1966.

Irving Abella and Harold Troper. *None Is Too Many: Canada and the Jews of Europe, 1933-1948.* Toronto, 1982.

Cyrus Adler and Aaron M. Margolith. *With Firmness in the Right: American Diplomatic Action Affecting Jews, 1840-1945.* New York, 1946.

Selig Adler. *The Isolationist Impulse.* London, 1957.

————. *The Uncertain Giant, 1921-1941: American Foreign Policy Between The Wars.* New York, 1965.

Herbert Agar. *The Saving Remnant: An Account of Jewish Survival.* New York, 1960.

Norman Angell. *You and The Refugee: The Morals and Economics of The Problem.* Harmondsworth, England, 1939.

Jacob Apenszlak, ed. *The Black Book of Polish Jewry: An Account of The Martyrdom of Polish Jewry Under The Nazi Occupation.* New York, 1943.

Hannah Arendt. *Eichmann In Jerusalem: A Report on The Banality of Evil.* New York, 1965.

Ehud Avriel. *Open The Gates.* New York, 1975.

Thomas A. Bailey. *The Man In The Street: The Impact of American Public Opinion in Foreign Policy.* Gloucester, Mass., 1964.

Yehuda Bauer. *A History of The Holocaust.* New York, 1982.

————. *The Jewish Emergence From Powerlessness.* Toronto, 1979.

————. *American Jewry and The Holocaust: The American Jewish Joint Distribution Committee, 1939-1945.* Detroit, 1981.

————. *My Brother's Keeper: A History of The American Jewish Joint Distribution Committee, 1929-1939.* Philadelphia, 1974.

————. *The Holocaust in Historical Perspective.* Seattle, 1978.

————. *From Diplomacy To Resistance: A History of Jewish Palestine, 1939-1945.* Philadelphia, 1970.

————. *Bricha: The Organized Escape of The Jewish Survivors of Eastern Europe, 1944-1948.* New York, 1970.

Bernard Bellush. *Franklin D. Roosevelt As Governor of New York.* New York, 1955.

Yitshaq Ben-Ami. *Years of Wrath, Days of Glory.* New York, 1982.

Marion T. Bennett. *American Immigration Policies: A History.* Washington, D.C., 1967.

Norman Bentwich. *They Found Refuge.* London, 1956.

William S. Bernard. *American Immigration Policy.* New York, 1950.

Bruno Bettelheim. *The Informed Heart: Autonomy In A Mass Age.* New York, 1960.

Maurice Bisgeyer. *Challenge And Encounter: Behind The Scenes In The Struggle For Jewish Survival.* New York, 1967.

Andre Biss. *A Million Jews To Save.* Cranbury, 1975.

Edwin Black. *The Transfer Agreement.* New York, 1984.

Sol Bloom. *The Autobiography of Sol Bloom.* New York, 1948.

Eric H. Boehm. *We Survived.* New Haven, 1949.

Willi A. Boelcke, ed. *The Secret Conferences of Dr. Goebbels: The Nazi Propaganda War, 1939-1943.* New York, 1970.

Randolph L. Braham. *The Politics of Genocide: The Holocaust In Hungary.* New York, 1981.

———, ed. *Jewish Leadership During The Nazi Era: Patterns of Behavior In The Free World.* New York, 1985.

———. *Eichmann And The Destruction of Hungarian Jewry,* 2 vols. New York, 1961.

———. *The Destruction of Hungarian Jewry: A Documentary Account,* 2 vols. New York, 1963.

Gordon Brook-Shephard. *The Anschluss.* Philadelphia, 1963.

Christopher Browning. *The Final Solution and The German Foreign Office.* New York and London, 1978.

Alan Bullock. *Hitler: A Study In Tyranny.* New York, 1961.

James MacGregor Burns. *Roosevelt: The Lion and The Fox.* New York, 1956.

———. *Roosevelt: The Soldier of Freedom, 1940-1945.* New York, 1970.

Hadley Cantril and Milder Strank, eds. *Public Opinion, 1935-1946.* Princeton, N.J., 1951.

Sam Caumi. *Jonah Bondi Wise.* New York, 1967.

Emanuel Celler. *You Never Leave Brooklyn.* New York, 1952.

Winston Churchill. *The Second World War.* Boston, 1948-1953 (6 vols.)

———. *The Gathering Storm.* New York, 1948.

Naomi Cohen. *Not Free To Desist. The American Jewish Committee, 1906-1966.* Philadelphia, 1972.

Norman Cohn. *Warrant For Genocide: The Myth of The Jewish World-Conspiracy and The Protocols of The Elders of Zion.* New York, 1967.

Katherine Elizabeth Crane. *Mr. Carr of State: Forty-Seven Years In The Department Of State.* New York, 1960.

Richard Crossman. *Palestine Mission.* New York, 1947.

Bartley C. Crum. *Behind The Silken Curtain.* New York, 1947.

Merle Curti. *American Philanthropy Abroad.* New Brunswick, N.J., 1963.

Robert Dalek. *Franklin D. Roosevelt and American Foreign Policy, 1932-1945.* New York, 1979.

Maurice R. Davie. *Refugees In America: Report of The Committee for The Study of Recent Immigration From Europe.* New York, 1947.

Lucy S. Dawidowicz. *The War Against The Jews, 1933-1945.* New York, 1975.

————. *The Holocaust and The Historians.* Cambridge, 1981.

————, ed. *A Holocaust Reader.* New York, 1976.

Martin Dies. *Martin Dies' Story.* New York, 1963.

Robert A. Divine. *American Immigration Policy, 1924-1952.* New Haven, 1957.

Michael N. Dobkowski. *The Politics of Indifference: A Documentary History of Holocaust Victims In America.* Washington, D.C., 1982.

————. *The Tarnished Dream: The Basis of American Anti-Semitism.* Westport, Conn., 1979.

William Dodd, Jr., and Martha Dodd, eds. *Ambassador Dodd's Diary, 1933-1938.* New York, 1941.

Alexander Donat. *The Holocaust Kingdom.* New York, 1965.

Herbert Druks. *The Failure To Rescue.* New York, 1977.

Josiah E. DuBois, Jr. *The Devil's Chemists.* Boston, 1952.

Marek Edelman. *The Ghetto Fights.* New York, 1946.

James A. Farley. *Jim Farley's Story: The Roosevelt Years.* New York, 1948.

Helen Fein. *Accounting For Genocide: National Responses and Jewish Victimization During The Holocaust.* New York, 1979.

Henry L. Feingold. *The Politics of Rescue: The Roosevelt Administration and The Holocaust, 1938-1945.* New Brunswick, N.J., 1970.

Laura Fermi. *Illustrious Immigrants: The Intellectual Migration From Europe, 1930-1941.* Chicago, 1968.

Harold Fields. *The Refugee in The United States.* New York, 1938.

Harold Flender. *Rescue in Denmark.* New York, 1963.

Arnold Forster. *A Measure of Freedom.* Garden City, N.Y., 1950.

Lloyd Free and Hadley Cantril. *The Political Beliefs of Americans.* New Brunswick, N.J., 1967.

Max Freedman, an. *Roosevelt and Frankfurter: Their Correspondence, 1928-1945.* Boston, 1967.

Frank Freidel. *Franklin D. Roosevelt.* Boston, 1952-1973 (4 vols.).

Philip Friedman. *Martyrs and Fighters: The Epic of The Warsaw Ghetto.* New York, 1954.

————. *Their Brothers' Keepers.* New York, 1957.

Saul Friedman. *No Haven For The Oppressed: United States Policy Toward Jewish Refugees, 1938-1945.* Detroit, 1973.

Morris Frommer. The American Jewish Congress: A History, 1914-1950.

William A. Gamson. *Power and Discontent.* Homewood, Ill., 1968.

Peter Gay. *Weimar Culture: The Outsider As Insider.* New York, 1968.

Louis L. Gerson. *The Hyphenate in Recent American Politics and Diplomacy.* Lawrence, Kans., 1964.

Martin Gilbert. *Auschwitz and The Allies.* New York, 1981.

————. *Exile and Return: The Struggle For A Jewish Homeland.* Philadelphia, 1978.

————. *Final Journey: The Fate of The Jews in Nazi Europe.* New York, 1979.

Nahum Goldmann. *The Autobiography of Nahum Goldmann: Sixty Years of Jewish Life.* New York, 1969.

Walter Goodman. *The Committee: The Extraordinary Career of The House Committee on Un-American Activities.* New York, 1968.

Moshe R. Gottlieb. *American Anti-Nazi Resistance, 1933-1941: An Historical Analysis.* New York, 1982.

Madison Grant. *The Passing of The Great Race.* New York, 1916.

Edward E. Grusad. *B'nai B'rith: The Story of The Covenant.* New York, 1966.

Hans Habe. *The Mission.* New York, 1966.

Arthur Hadley. *The Empty Polling Booth.* Englewood Cliffs, N.J., 1978.

Samuel Halperin. *The Political World of American Zionism.* Detroit, 1981.

Ben Halpern. *The Idea of The Jewish State.* Cambridge, Mass., 1961.

Oscar and Mary F. Handlin. *A Century of Jewish Immigration to The United States.* New York, 1949.

M. L. Hansen. *The Immigrant in American History.* Cambridge, Mass., 1940.

William D. Hassett. *Off The Record With FDR, 1942-1945.* New Brunswick, N.J., 1958.

Alfred A. Hassler. *The Lifeboat Is Full.* New York, 1969.

Ben Hecht. *A Guide for The Bedevilled.* New York, 1945.

————. *Perfidy.* New York, 1961.

————. *A Child of The Century.* New York, 1954.

Arthur Hertzberg, ed. *The Zionist Idea: A Historical Analysis and Reader.* New York, 1959.

John Higham. *Strangers In The Land: Patterns of American Nativism, 1860-1925.* New York, 1966.

Raul Hilberg. *The Destruction of The European Jews.* Chicago, 1961.

————. *Documents of Destruction: Germany and Jewry, 1933-1945.* Chicago, 1971.

E. E. Hirschler. *Jews From Germany in The United States.* New York, 1955.

Ira Hirschmann. *Life Line To A Promised Land.* New York, 1946.

————. *Caution To The Winds.* New York, 1962.

————. *The Embers Still Burn.* New York, 1949.

Adolf Hitler. *Mein Kampf.* (Trans. by Ralph Manheim.) Boston, 1943.

Rolf Hochhuth. *The Deputy.* New York, 1964.

Rudolf Hoess. *Commandant of Auschwitz: The Autobiography of Rudolf Hoess.* London, 1954.

Heinz Hohne. *The Order of The Deaths Head: The Story of Hitler's SS.* London, 1969.

House of Representatives Committee on International Relations. *Problems of World War II and Its Aftermath.* Washington, D.C., 1976.

Cordell Hull. *The Memoirs of Cordell Hull* (2 vols.). New York, 1948.

Harold L. Ickes. *The Secret Diary of Harold L. Ickes, Volume Two: The Inside Struggle* and *Volume Three: The Lowering Clouds.* New York, 1954.

Fred L. Israel, ed. *The War Diary of Breckinridge Long.* Lincoln, Neb., 1966.

Stephen Isaacs. *Jews and American Politics.* New York, 1974.

Charles E. Jacob. *Leadership in The New Deal: The Administrative Challenge.* Englewood Cliffs, N.J., 1967.

Elizabeth Janeway. *Powers of The Weak.* New York, 1980.

Manfred Jonas. *Isolationism in America, 1935-1941.* Ithaca, N.Y., 1966.

S. Shepard Jones and Denys P. Myers, eds. *Documents on American Foreign Relations, January 1938-June 1939.* Boston, 1939.

Francis Kalnay and R. Collins. *The New America.* New York, 1941.

Chaim A. Kaplan. *Scroll of Agony.* New York, 1964.

Jan Karski. *Story of A Secret State.* Boston, 1943.

Donald P. Kent. *The Refugee Intellectual: The Americanization of Immigrants, 1933-1941.* New York, 1953.

Felix Kersten. *The Kersten Memoirs, 1940-1945.* New York, 1957.

Ruth Kluger and Peggy Mann. *The Last Escape.* New York, 1973.

Lionel Kochan. *Pogrom: 10 November 1938.* London, 1957.

Alexander Kohanski, ed. *The American Jewish Conference: Its Organization and Proceedings, Aug. 29-Sept. 2, 1943.* New York, 1944.

Gabriel Kolko. *The Politics of War: The World and United States Foreign Policy, 1943-1945.* New York, 1968.

David Kranzler. *Heroine of Rescue: The Incredible Story of Recha Sternbuch Who Saved Thousands from The Holocaust.* New York, 1984.

————. *Japanese, Nazis and Jews: The Jewish Refugee Community of Shanghai, 1938-1945.* New York, 1976.

————. *Solomon Schonfeld: His Page In History.* New York, 1981.

Ota Kraus and Erich Kulka. *The Death Factory: Documents on Auschwitz.* London, 1966.

Eugene M. Kulischer. Europe On The Move. New York, 1948.

Fiorello H. LaGuardia. *The Making of An Insurgent: An Autobiography, 1882-1919.* New York, 1961.

Walter Langer. *The Mind of Adolf Hitler: The Secret Wartime Report.* New York, 1972.

William E. Langer and Everett Gleason. *The Challenge to Isolation, 1937-1940.* New York, 1952.

Walter Lacqueur. *The Terrible Secret.* Boston, 1980.

————. *Russia and Germany: A Century of Conflict.* Boston, 1967.

————. *A History of Zionism.* New York, 1972.

Harold Lasswell and Abraham Kaplan. *Power and Society.* New Haven, Conn., 1950.

Moses Leavitt. *The JDC Story, 1914-1952.* New York, 1953.

Alfred M. Lee and Elizabeth B. Lee, eds. *The Fine Art of Propaganda: A Study of Father Coughlin's Speeches.* New York, 1939.

Allen Lesser. *Jewish Immigration, 1654-1880, 1881-1924.* New York, 1939.

William E. Leuchtenberg. *Franklin D. Roosevelt and The New Deal, 1932-1940.* New York, 1963.

Nora Levin. *The Holocaust: The Destruction of European Jewry, 1933-1945.* New York, 1968.

Ralph Levering. *The Public and American Foreign Policy, 1918-1978.* New York, 1978.

Mark Levy and Michael Kramer. *The Ethnic Factor: How America's Minorities Decide Elections.* New York, 1972.

Deborah E. Lipstadt. *Beyond Belief: The American Press and The Coming of The Holocaust, 1933-1945.* New York, 1986.

Louis P. Lochner, ed. *The Goebbels Diaries, 1942-1943.* Garden City, New York, 1948.

Haskel Lookstein. *Were We Our Brothers' Keepers?* Bridgeport, Conn., 1986.

Leo Lowenthal and Norbert Guterman. *Prophets of Deceit: A Study of The Techniques of The American Agitator.* New York, 1949.

John Lukacs. *The Last European War.* Garden City, New York, 1976.

Arthur Morse. *While Six Million Died: A Chronicle of American Apathy.* New York, 1967.

Gustavus Myers. *History of Bigotry in The United States.* New York, 1960.

Emanuel Neumann. *In The Arena.* New York, 1976.

Sheldon M. Neuringer. *American Jewry and United States Immigration Policy, 1881-1953.* New York, 1980.

Albert Nirenstein. *A Tower From The Enemy: Contributions To A History of Jewish Resistance in Poland.* New York, 1959.

Arnold A. Offner. *American Appeasement: United States Foreign Policy and Germany, 1933-1938.* Cambridge, Mass., 1969.

Michael Parenti. *Power and The Powerless.* New York, 1978.

Emanuel Pat. *In The Struggle: Jacob Pat and His Generation.* New York, 1971.

James T. Patterson. *Congressional Conservatism and The New Deal: The Growth of The Conservative Coalition in Congress, 1933-1939.* Lexington, Ky., 1967.

Monty Noam Penkower. *The Jews Were Expendable: Free World Diplomacy and The Holocaust.* Urbana, Ill., 1983.

Frances Perkins. *The Roosevelt I Knew.* New York, 1946.

William Perl. *The Four-Front War: From The Holocaust to The Promised Land.* New York, 1979.

Leon Poliakov. *Harvest of Hate: The Nazi Program for The Destruction of The Jews of Europe.* Syracuse, N.Y., 1954.

Justine Wise Polier and James Waterman Wise, eds. *The Personal Letters of Stephen Wise.* Boston, 1956.

Joseph M. Proskauer. *A Segment of My Times.* New York, 1950.

Malcolm J. Proudfoot. *European Refugees, 1939-1952; A Study in Forced Population Movement.* Evanston, Ill., 1956.

Peter Pulzer. *The Rise of Political Anti-Semitism in Germany and Austria.* New York, 1964.

Aaron Rakeffet-Rothkoff. *The Silver Era: Rabbi Eliezer Silver and His Generation.* New York, 1981.

Basil Rauch. *Roosevelt From Munich To Pearl Harbor: A Study in The Creation of A Foreign Policy.* New York, 1950.

Herman Rauschning. *The Voice of Destruction.* New York, 1940.

Gerald Reitlinger. *The Final Solution: The Attempt To Exterminate The Jews of Europe.* New York, 1961.

Emanuel Ringelbaum. *Notes From The Warsaw Ghetto.* New York, 1958.

E. M. Robertson. *Hitler's Pre-War Policy and Military Plans, 1933-1939.* New York, 1967.

Ira Robinson, ed. *Cyrus Adler: Selected Letters, 1863-1940.* (2 vols.). New York, 1985.

Jacob Robinson. *And The Crooked Shall Be Made Straight.* New York, 1965.

Sophia Robinson. *Refugees At Work.* New York, 1942.

John Roche. *The Quest For The Dream*. New York, 1963.

Eleanor Roosevelt. *This I Remember*. New York, 1949.

Elliot Roosevelt, ed. *F.D.R.: His Personal Letters, 1928-1945*. New York, 1950.

Elmo Roper. *You and Your Leaders: Their Actions and Your Reactions, 1936-1956*. New York, 1957.

N. A. Rose, ed. *Baffy: The Diaries of Blanche Dugdale, 1936-1947*. London, 1973.

Samuel Rosenman, ed. *The Public Papers and Addresses of Franklin D. Roosevelt*. (13 vols.). New York, 1938-1941.

————. *Working With Roosevelt*. New York, 1952.

Robert Ross. *So It Was True: The American Protestant Press and The Nazi Persecution of The Jews*. Minneapolis, 1980.

Ralph Lord Roy. *Apostles of Discord: A Study of Organized Bigotry and Discrimination on The Fringes of Protestantism*. Boston, 1953.

Howard M. Sachar. *The Course of Modern Jewish History*. New York, 1958.

Frederick A. Sanborn. *Design For War: A Study of Secret Power Politics, 1937-1941*. New York, 1951.

Joseph B. Schechtman. *The United States and The Jewish State Movement*. New York, 1966.

————. *Fighter and Prophet: The Last Years*. New York, 1961.

Arthur M. Schlesinger, Jr. *The Age of Roosevelt: The Crisis of The Old Order, 1919-1933*. Cambridge, Mass., 1957.

————. *The Age of Roosevelt: The Politics of Upheaval*. Cambridge, Mass., 1957.

Simon Segal. *The New Order in Poland*. New York, 1942.

Andrew Sharf. *The British Press and The Jews Under Nazi Rule*. London, 1964.

Whitney H. Shepardson and William O. Scroggs. *The United States in World Affairs, 1938*. New York, 1939.

A. J. Sherman. *Island Refuge: Britain and Refugees from The Third Reich, 1933-1938*. Los Angeles, 1974.

Robert Sherwood. *Roosevelt and Hopkins*. New York, 1948.

William L. Shirer. *The Rise and Fall of The Third Reich*. New York, 1960.

Abba Hillel Silver. *Vision and Victory: A Collection of Addresses*. New York, 1949.

Marshall Sklare, ed. *The Jews: Social Patterns of An American Group*. New York, 1958.

Jacob Sloan, ed. *Notes From The Warsaw Ghetto: The Journal of Emanuel Ringelbaum*. New York, 1958.

Charles Herbert Stemer. *Jews in The Mind of America*. New York, 1966.

Fritz Stern. *The Politics of Cultural Despair: A Study in The Rise of The Germanic Ideology*. Berkeley, Calif., 1961.

Judith Stiehm. *Non-Violent Power: Active and Passive Resistance in America*. Lexington, Mass., 1972.

Lothrop Stoddard. *The Rising Tide of Color*. New York, 1920.

———. *The Revolt Against Civilization*. New York, 1922.

———. *Racial Realities in Europe*. New York, 1924.

Donald S. Strong. *Organized Anti-Semitism in America: The Rise of Group Prejudice During The Decade 1930-1940*. Washington, D.C., 1941.

Graham H. Stuart. *The Department of State: A History of Its Organization, Procedure and Personnel*. New York, 1949.

Yuri Suhl. *They Fought Back*. New York, 1965.

Arieh Tartakower and Kurt Grossman. *The Jewish Refugee*. New York, 1944.

Dorothy Thompson. *Refugees: Anarchy or Organization*. New York, 1938.

H. R. Trevor-Roper. *The Last Days of Hitler*. London, 1947.

Isaiah Trunk. *Jewish Responses to Nazi Persecution: Collective and Individual Behavior in Extremis*. New York, 1982.

Charles Tull. *Father Coughlin and The New Deal*. Syracuse, N.Y., 1965.

Unity in Dispersion: A History of the World Jewish Congress. New York, 1948.

Melvin I. Urofsky. *A Voice That Spoke For Justice: The Life and Times of Stephen S. Wise*. Albany, N.Y., 1982.

———. *We Are One: American Jewry and Israel*. Garden City, N.Y., 1978.

———. *American Zionism from Israel to The Holocaust*. Garden City. N.Y., 1976.

Carl Hermann Voss. *Rabbi and Minister: The Friendship of Stephen S. Wise and John Haynes Holmes*. Cleveland, 1964.

———. *Stephen Wise: Servant of The People*. Philadelphia, 1969.

Rudolf Vrba and Alan Bestic. *I Cannot Forgive*. New York, 1964.

Morris D. Waldman. *Nor By Power*. New York, 1953.

Bernard Wasserstein. *Britain and The Jews of Europe, 1939-1945*. London, 1979.

Meyer Weisgal. *Meyer Weisgal. . . So Far: An Autobiography*. New York, 1971.

Alex Weissberg and Joel Brand. *Desperate Mission*. New York, 1958.

Michoel Dov Weissmandl. *Min Hametzar*. New York, 1960.

Sumner Welles. *Time For Decision*. New York, 1941.

Nathaniel Weyl. *The Battle Against Disloyalty*. New York, 1951.

William A. Williams, ed. *The Shaping of American Diplomacy*. Chicago, 1963.

Mark Wischnitzer. *To Dwell in Safety.* Philadelphia, 1949.

———. *Visas to Freedom: The History of H.I.A.S.* Cleveland, 1956.

Stephen S. Wise. *As I See It.* New York, 1944.

———. *Challenging Years: The Autobiography of Stephen Wise.* New York, 1949.

David S. Wyman. *Paper Walls: America and The Refugee Crisis, 1938-1941.* Boston, 1968.

———. *The Abandonment of The Jews.* New York, 1984.

James Yaffee. *The American Jews: Portrait of A Split Personality.* New York, 1968.

Leni Yahil. *The Rescue of Danish Jewry.* Philadelphia, 1969.

Roland Young. *Congressional Politics in The Second World War.* New York, 1956.

Isaac Zaar. *Rescue and Liberation: America's Part in The Birth of Israel.* New York, 1954.

Index